George Orwell and Religion

ALSO AVAILABLE FROM BLOOMSBURY

George Orwell the Essayist, Peter Marks
Orwell, Politics, and Power, Craig L. Carr

George Orwell and Religion

Michael G. Brennan

Bloomsbury Academic
An imprint of Bloomsbury Publishing Plc

B L O O M S B U R Y
LONDON · OXFORD · NEW YORK · NEW DELHI · SYDNEY

Bloomsbury Academic
An imprint of Bloomsbury Publishing Plc

50 Bedford Square	1385 Broadway
London	New York
WC1B 3DP	NY 10018
UK	USA

www.bloomsbury.com

BLOOMSBURY and the Diana logo are trademarks of Bloomsbury Publishing Plc

First published 2017

© Michael G. Brennan, 2017

British Library Cataloguing in Publication Data
A catalogue record for this book is available from the British Library.

ISBN: HB: 978-1-4725-3194-0
PB: 978-1-4725-3073-8
ePDF: 978-1-4725-2360-0
ePub: 978-1-4725-3308-1

Library of Congress Cataloging-in-Publication Data
A catalog record for this book is available from the Library of Congress.

Cover design: Eleanor Rose
Cover image © Getty Images

Typeset by Fakenham Prepress Solutions, Fakenham, Norfolk NR21 8NN
Printed and bound in India

For Geraldine, Christina and Alice

CONTENTS

ACKNOWLEDGEMENTS

While writing this book I have received much helpful advice from Bernadette Barnett, Mark Bland, Geraldine Brennan, Robert Jones, Matthew Lord, Francis O'Gorman, Martin Stannard, Alexander Waugh and Charles Whittaker. I also remain especially indebted to the work of previous biographers and critics of Orwell whose works are listed in the bibliography. I am grateful to the staff of the British Library, London, the Brotherton Library, University of Leeds, and the Special Collections of University College, London (especially Dan Mitchell), for their always generous responses to my enquiries and requests for materials. The School of English and Faculty of Arts, University of Leeds, have also productively supported this research project. Finally, I offer special thanks to David Avital (Publisher, Literary Studies at Bloomsbury), with whom I first discussed this project. His always helpful advice has been greatly appreciated, as has invaluable support from other members of the Bloomsbury team, including Luke Neima (Editorial Intern), Mark Richardson (Editorial), Jennifer Laing (Copyeditor) and Kim Storry (Fakenham Prepress Solutions).

PREFACE: RELIGION AND 'SAINT GEORGE'[1]

Eric Arthur Blair (1903–50), also known after November 1932 as George Orwell, has usually been viewed as an agnostic socialist or atheist humanist who held little regard for organized religion, especially the Christian traditions of his two ancestral families: his father's English Blairs and his mother's French Limouzins.[2] He presented himself throughout his literary career as 'an atheist [who] yet retained a highly religious sense of morality' and insistently sought for a 'morality suitable for a post-Christian age'.[3] In a letter of 11 April 1940, discussing an intended socialist publication 'The Manifesto of the Common Man', he asserted that it was invariably wise 'never to mention religion' (XII.139) in public debate if it could possibly be avoided. Nevertheless, he insisted in March 1943 that a writer's 'political and religious' beliefs (XIV.285) would always be coloured by his aesthetic and literary achievements and that it was essential for commentators to trace such connections.

Although a self-professed atheist, Orwell retained a sentimental and aesthetic affection for the buildings, ceremonies and liturgies of the Anglican Church. His first marriage took place in June 1936 at the rural parish church of St Mary's in Wallington, Hertfordshire; and his second marriage (on his deathbed) was held in October 1948 in a private room at University College Hospital. Both services were conducted according to the Anglican marriage rites. He was also insistent that his adopted son should be baptized into the Anglican Church. Similarly, his will stated – to the surprise of his closest friends – that he wished to be buried according to the rites of the Church of England (not cremated), despite having been from his adult years a resolute non-worshipper. His unexpectedly conventional wish was fulfilled through the privileged influence of two friends, the Anglo-American aristocrat David Astor and the Old Etonian writer Anthony Powell. They, along with the journalist Malcolm Muggeridge, arranged for his funeral service to be conducted in London at the Powell family's regular place of worship, Christ Church (now St George's Cathedral), Albany Street. The service, Muggeridge noted, was attended almost entirely by non-believers and a selection of Orwell's Jewish friends and publishing associates.[4] It was followed by his interment in the country churchyard of All Saints, Sutton Courtenay, Oxfordshire, near the Astor family's ancient country seat (purchased by Astor in 1945). Blair's small, plain headstone – bearing only his name and dates – stands alongside the monumental box-tomb of Herbert Asquith, 1st Earl of Oxford and Asquith, the prime minister of England (1908–16) during much of Eric's childhood.

Even this brief outline of key moments in Orwell's personal contacts with Anglicanism, via his marriages, his son's christening and his own death, hints that a detailed interrogation of his personal attitudes towards religion may prove interesting. Furthermore, his comment that it is best never to mention religion if it can possibly be avoided seems both inaccurate and ironic when matched against the evidence of his voluminous literary output. It is no exaggeration to say that Orwell simply could not leave religion alone, not only in his private correspondence and notebooks but also in his published fiction, journalism and reviews. His writings are rich in sustained and incidental commentaries on Catholicism, the Church of England, nonconformist British sects, Hinduism, Burmese Christian sects and Islam, as well as the threats to personal spirituality and social structures posed by the rampant hostility of twentieth-century Communism, Fascism and Nazism towards organized religions. The centrality of a sense of the spiritual to the human condition, coupled with the contemporary inter-action of sociological and political issues with religious affairs, mattered greatly to Orwell and, as this study proposes, came to occupy a funda-mental role in his creative thought processes and literary concerns.

From a religious perspective, Blair's mother, Ida Mabel Limouzin, possessed an interesting Anglo-French family background in England and Burma but her dominating influence over his early years has tended to receive only passing attention from his biographers. She was born in Penge, Surrey, but was then raised in Moulmein, Burma, before taking up residence in Oxfordshire and London for most of her married life. The sustained influence of the Limouzins over the transition of Eric Blair into George Orwell will form a key element in first chapter of this study, and his mother also provides an intriguing link between Anglicanism and Catholicism during her son's childhood. It has only been recently estab-lished that Eric's formal education between the ages of five and eight began at her behest – unusually for a Anglo-Indian colonial child – at a Catholic (and not, as previously assumed, an Anglican) convent school in Henley-on-Thames.[5] This period of primary study was followed by his boarding at two Anglican institutions, St Cyprian's in Eastbourne and Eton College in Berkshire. However, the impact of the strict Catholic educational principles on his earliest school days should not be underestimated, especially in relation to his notorious (and still unexplained) hostility towards Roman Catholicism in later life.

This study also needs to address the powerful but sometimes confusing impact of how the archly secular writer George Orwell has been posthum-ously endowed with a quasi-mythic reputation as 'St George', initially as a tribute to his assumed intellectual integrity, socialist idealism and stylistic purity but also, increasingly, as a reverential gesture often tinged with implicitly religious – indeed hagiographical – elements. Such a process seems ironic in that Orwell himself insisted on the importance of observing the distinctions between criticism and 'hagiography' (XVIII.101) when assessing the reputation of the Jesuit priest and poet Gerard Manley Hopkins.[6] Orwell's friend and admirer V. S. Pritchett, the agnostic son of a Christian Scientist family and one-time foreign correspondent for the *Christian Science Monitor*, played a major role in promulgating this process of secular canonization soon after his death at the age of forty-six on 21 January 1950. In a tribute published seven days later, Pritchett described him as 'a kind of saint' and 'the wintry conscience of a generation'. He reaffirmed these terminologies three years later by christening him a 'difficult saint' and 'the comfortless saint of the Left and its only religious figure', for whom politics offered an 'opportunity for redemption, salvation and martyrdom'.[7] His long-time friend Christopher Hollis noted with admiration his 'unique courage' in expressing in his writings both his own and modern humanity's 'spiritual loneliness' and proposed that many of Orwell's moral perspectives could be 'explained by the acute sense of sin by which he was haunted'. Another close friend, Anthony Powell, felt that Orwell 'was in his way a sort of saint, even if not one in sparkling raiment bright'.[8]

Such terminologies recall Orwell's own light-hearted admonition in February 1946 over tendencies towards literary idolatry which he suspected were often inherent within the minds of authors. In a review of Colm Brogan's *The Democrat at the Supper Table* he claimed that narcissism was a natural instinct among novelists and it was unusual not to find somewhere in their works a lightly disguised self-portrait as a 'hero, saint, or martyr'. In a more sternly delivered essay (January 1949) on Mahatma Gandhi, whose asceticism he found deeply suspect, Orwell warned that self-conscious 'sainthood' was a status always to be avoided by living men and women (XX.7). Yet, despite such reservations, Orwell himself seemingly underwent a rapid posthumous apotheosis and transfiguration. In 1954, the critic John Atkins deemed him a social 'saint' with the identity of a secularized populist hero, while in 2003, the historian Piers Brendon regarded him as a commendable 'saint of common decency'.[9] Likewise, one of his most recent biographers, D. J. Taylor, describes him as 'above all, a moral force, a light glinting in the darkness, a way through the murk', echoing the poet Robert Conquest's description of him as a 'moral genius'.[10] The academic L. F. Rushbrook-Williams, who was Orwell's boss at the BBC during the early 1940s, felt that he was someone who in bygone days would have 'been either canonised – or burnt at the stake'; and in 2011, *Spectator* journalist Robert Gray described him with deliberate paradox as a 'very Christian atheist'.[11] His friend and later joint literary executor Sir Richard Rees was even more sceptical when classifying him as early as 1951 as 'one of those self-mortifying saints who kissed the sores of lepers', as well as being 'a religious or "pious" atheist' and a 'strenuous and self-martyrising man'.[12] Rees also remarked in 1961 that Orwell 'seldom spoke of religion because he considered the word to have been fouled by centuries of hypocrisy'. In view of such contradictory perspectives, Scott Lucas understandably titled the conclusion to his study of Orwell: 'Escaping St George'.[13]

Christopher Hitchens asserted that, while Orwell was 'by no means the "saint" mentioned by V. S. Pritchett and Anthony Powell', it seemed feasible, even for atheist admirers, to recognize that 'he took some of the supposedly Christian virtues and showed how they could be "lived" without piety or religious belief'.[14] Hitchens's comments are particularly relevant to Orwell's own attitudes towards religion since he draws a clear distinction between an 'atheist', who might still wish that there was evidence to support a belief in God, and an 'antitheist', who is confident that there was, and never would be, any evidence to support God's existence. Like Orwell, Hitchens regarded the concept of an all-prevailing God as an essentially totalitarian one and antithetical to personal freedom of thought and expression as proposed in his anti-religious polemic, *God Is Not Great: How Religion Poisons Everything* (2007). This is not to say, however, that traditional religious sentiments lacked any value to Orwell. Richard Hoggart highlighted how Christopher Hollis – the son of the Anglican Bishop of Taunton and a fellow Etonian who later converted to Catholicism – insisted only six years after Orwell's death that he had been a 'deeply religious man who, for reasons both temperamental and cultural, could not accept any religion ... a believer without a religion, a man full of convictions, full not only of a moral sense but of metaphysical assumptions'. Lionel Trilling concluded that, 'although Orwell admired some of the effects and attitudes of religion, he seems to have had no religious tendency in his nature, or none that went beyond what used to be called natural piety'.[15]

Given the insistent presence of such highly charged concepts in Orwell criticism, this study seeks to explore exactly what levels of creative stimulation the private Eric Blair and the public George Orwell drew from his considerations of religious customs, beliefs and institutions. It should be emphasized, however, that a distinct division between his real and fictive identities is rarely clear-cut, sustainable or even meaningful in terms of Blair–Orwell's ideas and observations about religion in his fictions, essays, journalism, private correspondence, diaries and working notes. Stephen Ingle rightly suggests that Eric Blair 'possessed a deeply ingrained religiosity that hardly fitted with [the] vaunted atheism' of George Orwell.[16] While there is certainly truth in this observation, it is important not to slide over the essential inconsistencies between the historical individual and his fictive persona. Both may and should be regarded as potentially unreliable narrators in relation to their respective commentaries on religious matters. Hence, although in this study distinctions will sometimes be drawn between the personal observations of Eric Blair and the public writings (both fictional and factual) of George Orwell after November 1932, such a clear demarcation between these two identities often remains slippery and elusive.

During his literary career Orwell presented himself as neither conformist nor attracted to any established religious faith and, as a natural dissenter, he was unwavering in his rejection of the concept of a spiritual afterlife. Yet there are grounds to suggest that he frequently sought to live by a personal moral code that shared elements with Judeo-Christian beliefs. Christopher Hollis suggested in 1956 that Orwell 'half-understood' humanity's need for God and that many of his views 'only made sense on the assumption of an implicit acceptance of a future life'.[17] Even so, this study does not seek to speculate over what may have been Eric Blair's subjective religious perspectives and private beliefs at various stages of his life. Instead, it focuses upon the extent of his documented spiritual experiences and knowledge of religious affairs and institutions specifically in relation to how these engagements impinged upon or inspired his diverse published output of almost two million words during only two decades of publications.

The various public identities of George Orwell as a writer since the 1940s are in themselves works of considerable imaginative creativity and diversity, partly prompted by the writer himself but, more often, fashioned by his contemporary and later readers and, most notably, posthumously. In his seminal study *The Politics of Literary Reputation: The Making and Claiming of 'St. George' Orwell* (1989), John Rodden traces how literary reputations tend to come into being 'in different ways at different times under different conditions', noting in Orwell's case his distinct but interconnected identities as 'The Rebel', 'The Common Man', 'The Prophet' and 'The Saint'. He also counsels how flexible and unstable literary reputations tend to be in creating images of a writer who, unusually and idiosyncratically, became a 'symbolic figure from virtually the moment of his death':

> They are radically contingent – partly make-believe and always makeshift and made over – being variously created, fashioned, built, manufactured, suppressed, and distorted – in a constant interaction of images and information in and through social relations. Ordinary usage, which characterized reputations as 'monuments', disguises this sociohistorical process as an inherited product, thereby veiling the fact that reputations emerge over time and leading us to project a single aspect for the diverse whole.[18]

In a chapter subheading subtitled '"St. George", The Halfway Saint' Rodden details how V. S. Pritchett and Richard Rees were chiefly responsible for Orwell's rapidly promulgated posthumous reputation as a 'saint' through which intangible qualities often attributed to his life and writings, such as 'authenticity', 'decency', 'honesty' and 'compassion', were treated metaphorically and metonymically. Rodden explains that, when a man who happens to be a writer is denoted as a 'saint', the figural and metaphorical dimension of his reputation becomes 'especially pronounced' and that 'the more completely the literal is collapsed into the metaphorical – the man Orwell into the metaphor "saint" and ultimately the figure "St George" – the greater the power of the image and the stronger the identification invited between perceiver and perceived'.[19] Orwell has even been appropriated by Catholic intellectuals who favourably compare him and his writings with G. K. Chesterton, Hilaire Belloc, Graham Greene, Evelyn Waugh, Charles Péguy, Leon Bloy and Jacques Maritain.[20] The dangers of such an approach were encapsulated by the writer and critic Angus Calder who in 1968 noted 'the reputation for utter integrity, for sheer goodness, that has prompted Orwell's canonization'. But the prevalence of such eulogistic terms jars resonantly against Orwell's crass dismissal of the writer and journalist D. B. Wyndham Lewis, the 'Beachcomber' columnist of the *Daily Express* and a Catholic convert, as a 'stinking RC' (X.268) and an incidental character in *Down and Out in Paris and London* as a 'horrible old Jew' (I.34) whose red beard reminded him of Judas Iscariot.[21] After Orwell's death even his close friend Malcolm Muggeridge admitted that 'he was inclined at times to be vaguely anti-Semitic'.[22] Was, then, Orwell's publicly acclaimed 'integrity' and 'goodness' at times implicitly combined with an anti-Catholicism and anti-Semitism verging upon, as Gordon Bowker remarks, a 'veritable Jansenist tendency to damn whole categories of people'?[23]

It should be noted at this point, however, that a significant difference developed during the 1940s between anti-Catholic and anti-Semitic elements in his writings. While the former was sustained throughout his literary career the latter was promulgated in his writings only prior to the Second World War and then rapidly eradicated from his publications once intelligence about the horrors of Nazi persecution of the Jews began to circulate in England. Indeed, from 1945, Orwell offered a strident public voice in the denunciation of anti-Semitism even though during the same period – the last five years of his life – he showed no inclination to temper or adjust his apparently pathological hatred of the Catholic hierarchy. The danger inherent in memorializing Orwell's supposed 'utter integrity' and 'sheer goodness' touches upon the obvious risks of secular hagiography. Posthumously, such idealized concepts may create powerfully lingering impressions of an author's life and writing practices. But, in reality, they serve only to distort and disguise how he had originally sought to utilize some of his source materials and to exploit his own public reputation, along with misrepresenting the intended moral, social and religious perspectives of his publications.

Consequently, this study will pose a series of key questions in relation to the development of Orwell's career as a writer. How did his family background, notably that of the Limouzins (whom Eric irreverently nicknamed 'The Lemonskins' or 'The Automobiles'), impact upon his childhood and youthful views of religion, especially Roman Catholicism?[24] What textual evidence of his personal observations on religious matters has survived in the form of diaries, letters, working notes or other miscellaneous private documents? How may this kind of material be related to his published fictional writings and journalism? What views did he express, both publicly and privately, not only about the Church of England and Catholicism but also about British non-conformists such as Methodists and Baptists, the Jewish faith and other religions, especially Buddhism and Hinduism, which he encountered abroad as a colonial officer? Did these views change or develop during his lifetime since, although he only published for twenty years, his literary career encompassed, as Peter Davison notes, 'the twilight of Imperialism, the Depression, the Thirties, the Spanish Civil War, the Second World War, and the post-war Labour Government'? Christopher Hitchens observed that the 'three great subjects of the twentieth century were imperialism, fascism and Stalinism' – all of which became central to Orwell's literary output.[25]

Specifically, it also needs to be asked whether there are religious issues over which Orwell may be deemed to have been inaccurate, misinformed or even determinedly bigoted. Why was his use of incidental religious references so often laced with comedy, sarcasm or cynicism? Why was he so resolutely hostile towards Roman Catholicism? Was this specific hostility rooted in his inherent suspicion of all forms of orthodoxies, including not only Catholicism but also Marxism and Communism? Does Orwell ultimately belong within the long-established English literary tradition of anti-Catholicism, dating from post-Reformation denunciations of the wealth and potency of the Catholic Church and incorporating the often salacious depiction of Catholic priests and nuns in the Gothic fiction of Matthew Lewis's *The Monk* (1796) and Anne Radcliffe's *The Italian* (1797), and the anti-Catholicism of Charles Dickens's *Barnaby Rudge* (1841) and Charlotte Brontë's *Villette* (1853)? Or did Orwell's intense hostility develop from more specific personal factors during his early life? It even needs to be asked whether Orwell's anti-Catholicism was merely a casual projection of his personal religious prejudice or whether he deliberately utilized it as a mode of discourse through which he implicitly sought to highlight or interrogate a range of other secular and sociological concerns.

Even more problematic is the question of how a modern reader should respond to Orwell's sometimes demeaning and apparently anti-Semitic depictions of Jewish figures in his pre-war writings? 'He often spoke without verifying his facts', the anarchist Nicolas Walter once noted (not without a touch of admiration); 'often he was grossly unfair'.[26] Is this statement also true of Orwell's depiction of religious individuals and institutions? John Rodden proposes:

Close attention to the pattern of Orwell's remarks linking Judaism, anti-Semitism, Catholicism, Anglicanism, and Communism shows how curiously anti-nomial his thinking was and how schematized and blinkered by politics his religious thought could be. He frequently compared and contrasted these 'isms' according to criteria like political power, popularity among intellectuals, and the role of doctrinal orthodoxy … It is startling to see, piecing together scattered journalistic references, how often the lines of Orwell's thought on Catholicism, Communism, and anti-Semitism ran on parallel tracks. So preoccupied was Orwell with questions pertaining to Catholics and Jews in the light of English political conditions that he saw these two religious groups in diametrically opposed terms, never giving attention to anything like a Judeo-Christian tradition.[27]

The key issue here seems to lie in Orwell's habitual treatment in his writings of pre-war Jews and pre- and post-war Catholics from predominantly external and hostile perspectives. He studiously avoided more personalized considerations of how numerous individuals, families and communities who had loyally belonged to these faiths and social communities for generations – often through extreme hardship, deprivation and persecution – viewed the spiritual and social significance of their religious institutions and customs. His compassionate and egalitarian attempts to share at first hand the experiences and perspectives of tramps and derelicts in *Down and Out in Paris and London*, miners in *The Road to Wigan Pier*, civil war combatants in *Homage to Catalonia* and other marginalized, exploited or dissident figures still seem admirably humane to most readers. But Orwell's often dismissively partisan comments on Catholics and pre-war Jews, in contrast to his far more objective accounts of Buddhism and Hinduism in Burma, seem to have been focused primarily upon the behaviour and utterances of a minority of vocal intellectual Catholics and working-class or poverty-stricken Jews. Ironically, he roundly condemned in *The Road to Wigan Pier* those intellectually blinkered 'book-trained socialists' (V.196) who pretended that Marxist intellectuals were the true representatives of the working class, even though a small group of elitist metropolitan Catholics seemed in his writings to stand metonymically for all English Catholics.

Furthermore, Orwell's comments on both Catholics and pre-war Jews were almost entirely focused only upon perceived *male* behaviour, despite both religions being strongly matriarchal and female in their traditional practices. Daphne Patai notes that in *The Road to Wigan Pier* 'Orwell's contacts with women are limited to viewing them at some distance. He does not speak to them, does not explore their lives or possibilities, as he does men's.' She goes on to explain that this 'limited visibility of women' is regrettable because, by his own account, there were some 36,000 insured workers in Wigan, 10,000 of whom were female.[28] In similar fashion, by generally ignoring in his writings the many thousands of middle-class and working-class Catholic women in England, Orwell was able to concentrate his anti-Church ire upon an unrepresentative metropolitan male elite of (often convert) Roman Catholics whose writings and public utterances so irritated him. This calculated disparity tends to dominate much of his writings because, as Christopher Hitchens notes: 'it's hardly an exaggeration to say that Orwell wrote for a male audience'.[29]

While Orwell's hostility towards Catholicism remained unabated until his death in 1950, momentous external factors, centred upon the rise of Nazi Fascism and the Holocaust, ensured that he radically adjusted his perspectives on Jews from the early 1940s, culminating in the publication for the *Contemporary Jewish Record* of his influential essay, 'Antisemitism in Britain' (April 1945). John Newsinger remarked that it is 'important to recognise that Orwell's political thinking was never static, but changed and developed over the years'.[30] While this is also true of his responses to anti-Semitism, the same cannot be said of his attitude towards Roman Catholicism, which remained unwaveringly hostile. Orwell was no Marxist but he did sometimes share what has been denoted as a Marxist habit of thought – especially in his treatment of all things Roman Catholic – by revealing a 'tendency to develop a universal theory and then to adjust objective reality to fit it, rather than the other way around'.[31] This study will also illustrate how his references to Catholicism were habitually rooted in a distinctive stylistic tendency towards polemical pamphleteering and factional political debate, resulting in a highly partisan form of writing.[32] This mode of writing, simultaneously both engaging and controversial, became intrinsic to the potency and lasting appeal of Orwell's major works, as John Wain explained:

> The 'kind' to which Orwell's work belongs is the polemic. All of it, in whatever form – novels, essays, descriptive sketches, volumes of autobiography – has the same object: to implant in the reader's mind a point of view, often about some definite, limited topic … but in any case about an issue over which he felt it was wrong not to take sides. A writer of polemic is always a man who, having himself chosen what side to take, uses his work as an instrument for strengthening the support for that side.[33]

While Orwell's published political analyses were often subtly complex, multi-layered and memorably penetrating, in private conversation he took personal delight in asserting partisan and provocatively illogical views. Malcolm Muggeridge recalled that over lunch one day Orwell suddenly declared that 'All tobacconists are Fascists', and then doggedly elaborated upon this proposition as though it were a self-evident truth.[34] Daphne Patai has also demonstrated how:

> One of Orwell's favorite rhetorical stratagems is the blanket generalization, often blatantly biased. I offer a few examples only: 'No real

revolutionary has ever been an internationalist' ... 'All left-wing parties in the highly industrialized countries are at bottom a sham ... A humanitarian is always a hypocrite' ... 'I have never met a genuine working man who accepted Marxism' ... His writings are littered with such sweeping assertions, a rhetorical technique that brushes aside reservations and challenges by the sheer force and confidence with which these declarations are made.[35]

Similarly, in Orwell's eyes, the elitist and totalitarian tendencies of Roman Catholicism remained beyond any factually informed or nuanced arguments. It is also important to note here how his reactionary views on Catholicism have been broadly accepted by later generations of writers. As recently as 2002 Christopher Hitchens observed that Orwell readily recognized, like many of his contemporaries, that Fascism was the 'distillation of everything that was most hateful and false' in Western European society, 'a kind of satanic summa of military arrogance, racist solipsism, schoolyard bullying and capitalist greed'. But he continued: 'His one especial insight was to notice the frequent collusion of the Roman Catholic Church and of Catholic intellectuals with this saturnalia of wickedness and stupidity; he alludes to it again and again.' He also noted that Orwell 'had a rooted dislike for supernatural propaganda, especially in its Roman Catholic form'.[36]

In view of such comments still circulating in twenty-first-century criticism, journalism and the media, Orwell's pronouncements on the place of religion in society remain of paramount importance to a meaningful understanding of his writings and their continued relevance for a modern-day readership. As D. J. Taylor explains:

> Broadly speaking he realised – and he did so a great deal earlier than most commentators of either Right or Left – that the single most important crisis of the twentieth century was the decline in mass religious belief and, its corollary, in personal immortality. God was dead and yet the secular substitutes put in His place, whether totalitarian or western consumer capitalism, merely travestied human ideals and aspirations. The task facing modern man, as Orwell saw it, was to take control of that immense reservoir of essentially spiritual feeling – all that moral sensibility looking for a home – and use it to irrigate millions of ordinary and finite lives.[37]

This study, therefore, will systematically analyse what kinds of religious and spiritual issues and experiences attracted Orwell's critical attention and how his views on such matters changed and developed during his literary career. Throughout, one central question will remain at the fore of this investigation: how should Orwell's perspectives on religion and spirituality impact upon twenty-first-century readings of his fictions, journalism and correspondence?

1

Educating Eric Blair and *Burmese Days*

Family religious influences and Sunnylands Catholic Convent School (1903–11)

Sir Richard Rees, one of the writer's earliest supporters and closest friends, insisted in May 1967 that 'if you want to understand Orwell, you have to understand Blair'.[1] As a child of the British Empire, Blair's parentage combined contacts with Anglo-French, Anglo-Indian and Franco-Burmese social and religious cultures. He was born on 25 June 1903 in Motihari, Bihar, in British India near the Nepal border where his father Richard Walmesley Blair (1857–1939) was working in the Opium Department of the Indian Civil Service. Richard, then aged thirty-nine, had married his Anglo-French wife, Ida Mabel Limouzin (1875–1943), on 15 June 1897 at the neo-Gothic Anglican mission church of St John in the Wilderness in Naini Tal (Nainital), a hill station between Rampur and Srinagar in the north-west province of India. Soon afterwards, he was posted to the sweltering, disease-ridden Gaya region, eighty miles south of Patna, at the centre of the Bengal opium trade. He later moved to the higher-level and generally healthier Motihari where, when he was aged forty-six, his only son Eric was born. The child was baptized on 30 October 1903 in the town's Protestant mission, known as the 'Regions Beyond Missionary Union', which had opened there in 1900.[2] In retrospect, Orwell admitted that as a child he had 'believed in God, and believed that the accounts of him were true' (XIX.379), although after that date – towards the end of the First World War – he consistently denied holding any kind of religious faith. He later told Christopher Hollis that he had merely accepted 'mechanically the Christian religion without having any sort of affection for it'.[3]

Orwell himself once remarked that it was impossible to compile a 'really revealing history of a man's life without saying something about his parents and probably his grandparents'.[4] Since he rarely saw his father, the young Eric's religious influences prior to his schooling would have been primarily maternal and dominantly female in character. Although his mother, Ida Mabel, has long been recognized by Orwell biographers as a bohemian spirit, hardly any attention has been paid to the potential significance of her family's religious background to her son's later often hostile and dismissive views of institutional religion, especially Roman Catholicism. Ida Mabel's father was Francis Matthew Limouzin (1835–1915), whose family originated from the strongly Catholic region of Limoges, France.[5] Francis may have been born in either France or Burma and it seems possible that his immediate family, and certainly his ancestors, would have been practising Catholics. His second wife was Theresa (also known as Thérèse and Teresa) Catherine Halliley (1843–1925), whose combination of names also suggests a Catholic heritage. He married her by special licence in Moulmein on 24 August 1865, only six months after the death of his first wife and two of their children.[6] Francis already had three children by his first wife, Eliza Emma Fallon (1842–65): Arthur Frank (b. 9 July 1862), Emily (b. c. 1863) and Alice May (b. 30 August 1864). But the deaths, soon after Alice's birth and in rapid succession, of Emily (d. 16 November 1864), Eliza (d. 18 January 1865) and then Arthur (d. 31 January 1865), suggest that the Limouzin family had been hit by some kind of lethal illness, perhaps typhoid which was then common in Burma.[7]

Almost ten years later Frank and Theresa Limouzin were staying on vacation with her Halliley relatives in Penge, Surrey, when Ida was born on 18 May 1875.[8] Ida's parents already had five children, Norah Grace (1866–1945), Charles William (1868–1947), Frank Edmond (1869–1908), Hélène Kate, also known as Nellie and Ellen (1870–1950) and Blanche Evelyn (b. 1872), but they may have deliberately returned from Burma earlier in 1875 so that their sixth child could be born and baptized in England. The Limouzins had two more children, Mina Eliza (bapt. 5 April 1880) and George Alfred (bapt. 8 February 1882). Two of Ida's siblings, Charles and Hélène Kate, were to play important roles in Eric Blair's childhood and early years as an aspiring writer. Although it has not previously been noted by Orwell's biographers, it is clear that the Limouzins were keen to sustain their personal contacts with the Hallileys and English life since the 1881 National Census records three of Frank's children, Alice May (the only surviving child of his first wife), Norah Grace and Ellen Kate as then studying at 'Parkfields' on Westcroft Road, a boarding school in Carshalton, Surrey, along with a member of the Halliley family.[9]

Ida grew up in the port of Moulmein, Burma, at the mouth of the Salween River, where the Limouzins had traded in timber, shipbuilding and other import and export goods since the 1820s when the British first began to assume control over the region. In 1852, the East India Company had annexed the ancient kingdom of Pegu and those of Ava and Rangoon were also later taken by the British. Hence, Ida's family remained in close contact with British imperialism in Burma and also, through her mother's Halliley family, with England and Ceylon – the latter connection echoed in *Coming*

Up For Air in which Hilda Bowling's brother Harold works in some 'official job' (VII.139) in Ceylon. Ida retained her French passport until her marriage in June 1897 and through her French nationality would have known the small but thriving Catholic community in Moulmein, belonging to the Southern Burma vicariate then under the charge of the French Missions Etrangères from Paris. During the first decade of the twentieth century, about 1,400 Catholics lived at Moulmein and the southern vicariate had over 230 churches and chapels with schools and missions run by members of the Catholic Christian Brothers, the Sisters of the Good Shepherd and St Joseph of the Apparition.[10] Hence, the Limouzins resided in a region of Burma in which the French Roman Catholic community was thriving and where Ida would have grown up within a Catholic and French-speaking colonial environment, even if her parents and immediate family were no longer practising Catholics.

During the early 1890s, Ida's elder sister Hélène Kate taught at the Anglican Diocesan School for Girls at Rangoon, but Ida travelled farther afield to work in the girls' department of a boys' school at Naini Tal, Bengal, where she was to meet Richard Blair.[11] This institution is most likely to have been St Joseph's College, opened in 1892 as a school by four Irish Catholic Christian Brothers in the buildings of a former Italian Capuchin seminary. If this was the case, then Ida Limouzin's personal contacts with Catholicism would have been either sustained or renewed there. Their eldest child, Marjorie Frances Blair, was born on 21 April 1898 in Gaya, Bengal, where she was baptized on the following 25 June. By the early 1900s, Hélène Kate had come to England (where she was known as Nellie) and rented a flat in Ladbroke Grove, Notting Hill.[12] It has not previously been noted that Ida also then visited England with her infant daughter, Marjorie, since she is recorded in the 1901 National Census as then resident with her mother-in-law, Frances Catherine Blair (c. 1820–1908), née Hare, at 4 Brunswick Place, Bath, where her husband Richard had been privately tutored until he was eighteen.[13]

In contrast to the Limouzins, the Blairs possessed a traditional Anglican English background stretching back several generations. Orwell's great-great-grandfather, Charles Blair (1743–1802), of Down House, Dorset, was a wealthy country gentleman and absentee landlord of sugar planta-tions in Jamaica who in 1765 had married Lady Mary Fane, the second daughter of Thomas Fane, eighth Earl of Westmorland.[14] Their ancestry was recorded in an eighteenth-century Blair family Bible, which the widower of Orwell's sister Marjorie had retained.[15] This Charles had a son also called Charles (1776–1854) who was born in Whitchurch, Dorset, and by 1851 was a retired captain of the Fourth Dragoon Guards, living at 15 Pulteney Street, Bath. His son, Thomas Richard Arthur Blair (1802–67) – George Orwell's grandfather – was ordained in 1839 as a deacon of the Church of England by the Bishop of Calcutta and as a priest in 1843 by the Bishop of Tasmania. In 1854, he returned to England and on the way married a fifteen-year-old girl, Fanny, at the Cape of Good Hope, by whom he had ten children, the youngest being Eric's father, Richard. He served as vicar of Milborne St Andrew, Dorset, the reputed model for Thomas Hardy's Millpond St Jude's in *Far From the Madding Crowd*. Orwell wryly acknowledged this family heritage in a light-hearted poem, 'A happy vicar I might have been / Two hundred years ago' (X.524), first published in *The Adelphi* (December 1936).[16]

Thomas Blair erected, at considerable expense to the parish, a new vicarage in 1856, and the idyllic surrounding landscapes of his church at Milborne St Andrew, founded in the eleventh century, typified Orwell's lingering affection for the physical externalities and landscapes of English country churches. As Piers Brendon notes, Orwell came to be regarded as a 'a radical socialist with a conservative nostalgia for the shabby-genteel England of his Edwardian childhood', especially the reassuring centrality of church life to intimate local communities.[17] Similarly, the philosopher A. J. Ayer remarked: 'Though he held no religious belief, there was something of a religious element in George's socialism. It owed nothing to Marxist theory and much to the tradition of English Nonconformity.'[18] There is even some truth in Cyril Connolly's affectionate jibe that Orwell was a 'rebel in love with 1910'.[19] But the comfortable religious traditions of earlier generations were rapidly lost to the war-ravaged and socially dislocated professional classes of the early twentieth century and strident reactions against conventional religious assumptions and traditions became an insistent undercurrent in the youthful writings of Eric Blair.

After an outbreak of the plague in the Motihari region and Richard Blair's imminent transfer to a new post at Monghyr on the Ganges, Ida Blair took her two children in 1904 permanently to England for what Orwell later described in *The Road to Wigan Pier* as a typical 'lower-upper-middle class' (V.113) childhood.[20] Apart from one brief visit home on leave in 1907, when Eric's younger sister Avril was conceived, Ida did not see her husband again until 1912.[21] Ida, Marjorie and Eric settled at Henley-on-Thames in various rented properties. In September 1904, they moved to 52 Vicarage Road which Ida called 'Ermadale' by combining the first two letters of Eric's and Marjorie's names. In April 1905, they rented another property, 'The Nutshell', at 22 Western Road from where in the 1911 Census Ida described herself as a 'Certified Midwife'. They later moved to a larger four-bedroom house, 'Roselawn', on Station Road, in the village of Shiplake, a few miles south of Henley. In 1915, to economize, they returned to Henley to a smaller semi-detached three-storeyed house, 36 St Mark's Road. This residential itinerary is significant because throughout their time in Oxfordshire the Blairs lived in Henley close to the thirteenth-century Mary the Virgin church and in Shiplake near the twelfth-century St Peter and St Paul church where Alfred Lord Tennyson had been married in 1850. Like his grandfather's living at Milborne St Andrew, these churches were picturesque Anglo-Norman foundations and they undoubtedly fostered

Orwell's life-long emotional attachment to the architectural fabric and pastoral landscapes of English Anglicanism.[22]

In addition to Ida's sister Nellie, her brother Charles was also then resident in England since in 1904 he married a Charlotte Cozens in London.[23] Ida and Nellie, and sometimes their eldest sister Norah who had also returned to England, attended Suffragette meetings, concerts and theatres in London. They moved within Fabian circles, mixing with H. G. Wells, G. K. Chesterton and E. E. Nesbit, the author of *The Ballads and Lyrics of Socialism* as well as *The Railway Children*. The radical Christian socialist Conrad le Despenser Roden Noel, the 'Red Vicar' of Thaxted, was at that time curate of Nellie's local parish in Paddington. He controversially displayed in his church the red flag and that of Sinn Féin Irish republicans alongside the flag of Saint George. He was a pioneer of socialism, working in the poor lodging houses among the destitute of London. Given Eric Blair's later involvements in such activities, as recorded in *Down and Out in Paris and London*, it seems likely that his mother's and aunts' radical socialist leanings during his childhood exercised a significant formative influence over his later activities as a documentary writer exposing the living conditions of the poorest members of the English and Parisian working-classes.

The Reverend Conrad Noel and Eric Blair, although committed socialists and unmaterialistic in lifestyle, also had much in common in terms of their privileged family backgrounds and political leanings. They both had aristocratic forbears (Noel's grandfather was the first Earl of Gainsborough and Blair's great-great-great-grandfather was the Earl of Westmorland), both were educated at public schools (Noel at Wellington and Cheltenham College and Blair, for one term at Wellington and then Eton) and both emphatically rejected the upper-middle-class circles into which they had been born. (Noel's father had been a Groom of the Privy Chamber to Queen Victoria.) Both men were stern critics of the ruling classes and the stark disparities in wealth and poverty within British society during the first decades of the twentieth century. Noel was a keen supporter of the Soviet Union and the Marxist British Socialist Party (from 1920 the Communist Party of Great Britain), although his idealistic blending of socialism and Christian compassion ultimately owed more to William Morris than Karl Marx. He founded the Catholic Crusade, a group of Anglican socialists, and some of its members were later founder members of British Trotskyism. Echoes of his idealistic politics may perhaps be traced in Blair's later responses to Trotsky and Russian totalitarianism in *Animal Farm*. Noel's tombstone in Thaxted Church bears a simple motto with a distinctly Orwellian resonance: 'He loved justice and hated oppression.' Most significantly, for the early formulation of Eric Blair's religious views, Noel was strongly anti-Roman Catholic, 'regarding the Roman Church as decadent in ceremonial, and fascistic in its politics. He was opposed to those Anglo-Catholics who copied Rome, and preferred to call himself a "Catholic Socialist".' It seems likely, therefore, that Noel's anti-Roman Catholic views – as filtered to the young Eric Blair via his mother and aunt Nellie – played a formative role in the development of George Orwell's lifelong hostility towards the Catholic Church and papal authority.[24]

Eric Blair's personal contacts with Roman Catholicism began when he was only five years old, although this point was long obscured by a significant biographical error perpetuated by most of Orwell's biographers and critics until 2003. His childhood friend Jacintha Buddicom may have been the original source of this confusion when she stated in 1974 that Eric and her brother Prosper 'must have been together in the baby class in the Anglican Convent School in Henley'. In the same year, Peter Stansky and William Abrahams followed her lead, writing in *The Unknown Orwell*: 'At five he was ready for school, and Mrs Blair enrolled him at a day school nearby, Sunnylands, run by Anglican nuns, where Marjorie was already a pupil.' Similarly, Bernard Crick wrote in his authorized 1980 *George Orwell. A Life*: 'At the age of 5 he was sent, like his sister Marjorie before and sister Avril after him, to a small Anglican convent school in Henley.' Michael Shelden side-stepped this issue in 1991 by describing Sunnylands merely as 'a small day school', but D. J. Taylor in 2003 again stated that it was 'staffed by Anglican nuns'. Even Peter Davison's definitive edition of *The Complete Works of George Orwell, Volume Ten, A Kind of Compulsion, 1903-1936*, stated in 1998: 'The children were first educated at an Anglican convent school'; and that Eric 'had attended a small Anglican convent school for three years'.[25]

The problem with these statements lies in the misattribution of 'Anglican'. As established by the local historian Charles Whittaker and first stated in print by Gordon Bowker in *Inside George Orwell: A Biography* (2003) the institution attended by Marjorie, Eric (from 1908 until 1911) and Avril Blair in Henley-on-Thames was opened not by Anglican but by Catholic nuns – a crucial difference in view of Orwell's still unexplained antipathy towards Roman Catholicism.[26] Ida Blair's diary for 1905 records her visiting the convent to discuss the admission of Marjorie, and this contact suggests that she bore no personal prejudice against Catholics if they could provide her eldest daughter with a sound primary education. Bowker explains that the young Eric was sent 'as a day-boy to the convent which Marjorie attended – not an Anglican convent, as has been thought (no such convent existed in Henley), but a Catholic convent run by French Ursulines exiled from France after religious education was banned there in 1903'.[27] The French Ursulines were a Catholic order of nuns, exiled because of their faith and loyal affiliation to the papal authority of Pope Pius X (d. 1914) and his predecessor Pope Leo XIII (d. 1903), who in 1900 had instigated the union of Ursuline convents worldwide. Described as the 'feminine teaching congregation *par excellence*', the Ursulines sought to adapt their strict monastic lifestyle to the demands of their professional work as teachers but still maintained a highly disciplined and ascetic regime in their institutions.[28]

In 1903, restrictive laws were passed preventing the work of Christian education anywhere in France. Four Ursuline nuns left Le Havre and arrived in Henley on 6 September 1904 where they met up with two other Ursulines who had already taken up residence in the town. Another group of Ursulines fled Boulogne-sur-Mer at the same time and founded in 1904 an Ursuline school at Westgate-on-Sea, Kent, specializing in the education of the children of colonial or forces parents.[29] Two years later, four other nuns who had originally gone to Wimbledon came to the Henley community and other Ursuline nuns from France, including their Mother Superior Madame Marie du Sacré Coeur, also joined them. Their small school at 23 Station Road (just around the corner from Henley's Catholic Church of the Sacred Heart) was for both boarders and day pupils and they also taught in the local parish school and gave private French lessons to adult members of the Henley community.[30] Eventually, all three of Ida Blair's children attended this school. The Ursulines left Henley on 26 August 1913 and returned to Paris, taking with them some English girls, including Eric's eldest sister Marjorie, to complete their education.[31]

Orwell is not known to have left any personal records about his time at Sunnylands, other than a whimsical statement in a posthumously published memoir of his schooldays, 'Such, Such Were the Joys', noting that he had held a brief childish infatuation for a girl called Elsie at his local 'convent school' (XIX.373).[32] His only other references to nuns occur in *A Clergyman's Daughter* when he mocks nuns in their convents 'scrubbing floors and singing Ave Marias, secretly unbelieving' (III.294); and a nasty vignette in a letter written, probably in July 1931, to Brenda Salkeld, a Southwold school teacher who was the daughter of a vicar and one of his closest youthful friends. His letter recalled a childhood story about the death of Robin Hood and how his men had 'raped & murdered the nuns' and then burnt their convent. He noted that there seemed no evidence in the traditional ballads about these events and so he assumed that his childhood group had simply made up this narrative, sarcastically concluding that this was because of their desire for a 'happy ending' (X.206). As late as 1946 he commended in the *Manchester Evening News* (3 January) Antonia White's novel *Frost in May* (1933) as an 'acid' but 'essentially truthful' description of daily life in a typical Catholic convent school, noting how her nuns combined 'shrewdness' with 'narrow-mindedness'. Their teaching methods in White's novel, perhaps recalling his own days with the Ursulines, offered a remarkable blend of 'intense intellectuality' and 'refined spiritual bullying' (XVIII.9). Jacintha Buddicom noted that the Ursuline nuns at Henley were very strict and unsympathetic towards boys. From the experiences of her brother Prosper, who had probably been in the same class as Eric, she concluded that the 'nuns were not very enthusiastic about little boys, and would only admit them young enough for the baby class', recalling that Prosper used to refer to them later as '*damn devils*'.[33]

There is no proof that Eric's time with the Ursulines was necessarily unhappy but this intimate contact with Catholicism at such an impressionable age (between five and eight years) should certainly be taken into account when assessing his long sustained adult suspicion of all things Roman Catholic. The question remains as to why Ida Blair chose to send all three of her children to this Catholic convent school and whether any other boys, apart from Eric, attended it. Was it simply because the nuns were Frenchwomen, and, having recently arrived in Henley, were willing to accept children of all Christian denominations? Or was it because Ida (descended from Anglo-French Catholic lines) retained from her Burmese days a lingering admiration for the educational standards of Catholic missionary schools? Whatever the case, Gordon Bowker suggests that this convent school may have provided the mature George Orwell with the catalyst for 'two important and enduring aspects of his complex personality – his unremitting hostility towards Roman Catholicism and an acute sense of guilt'.[34]

St Cyprian's, Eastbourne, and Eton College, Windsor (1911–21)

From late September 1911 until December 1916, Blair boarded at a private Anglican preparatory school, St Cyprian's at Eastbourne, East Sussex, founded in 1899 and so named after an early Christian martyr who had been decapitated for heresy. It had been chosen for him by his mother, primarily at the recommendation of her brother Charles Limouzin who knew its headmaster, Lewis Chitty Vaughan Wilkes, through their local golf club. Bernard Crick states that the young Eric was also 'strongly recommended by his local convent school', although he supplies no source for this information.[35] As detailed in 'Such, Such Were the Joys', Blair hated his time there but its moral ethos of muscular Christianity and regular attendance at its 'raw-looking pinewood chapel' (XIX.369), referred to in his letters home ('nearly time for Chapel', 1 October 1911, X.6, and time to 'get ready for Chapel', 12 May 1912, X.16), exerted a strong influence over his developing views on social and religious issues as well laying the foundations for an intimate knowledge of Biblical language.

Cicely Wilkes, the forceful wife of the headmaster, taught English Literature and insisted upon the Authorized Version of the Bible as a model for good writing. She would take selected passages and then revise them into less fluent and elegant versions. This exercise in 'bad oratory or journalese', as Michael Shelden describes it, clearly demonstrated the innate qualities of the original versions – an exercise later advocated by Orwell in his essay on literary style, 'Politics and the English Language'. This essay cites an eloquent passage from *Ecclesiastes* ('I returned, and saw under the sun, that the race is not to the swift') to demonstrate how it might be translated into modern, jargonized English of the 'worst sort' (XVII.425). On Sundays the boys were also expected to memorize at least one chapter from the Old or New Testament.[36] This process fostered Orwell's impressive knowledge of the Bible (commenting to his mother in a letter of 4 February 1912: 'about time I learnt my Scrip[t]ure', X.11), which was reinforced by his attendance at morning chapel prayers and his enduring pleasure in biblical readings, especially from the Apocrypha. Blair's friendship at St Cyprian's with Cyril Connolly was also to play an important role in the later dissemination of his writings via the journal *Horizon*, which Connolly edited. Connolly's own religious doubts expressed in his 1945 *The Unquiet Grave* ('Those of us who were brought up as Christians and who have lost our faith have retained the Christian sense of sin without the saving belief in redemption. This poisons our thought and so paralyzes us in action'), echo Blair's growing religious scepticism as an adolescent, despite his retention of a 'weak and wavering affection for Anglicanism'.[37]

'Such, Such Were the Joys' delineates how St Cyprian's sowed the seeds of many of the social and religious discontents which pervaded Blair's later life. As he explains in this painfully bitter essay, the intellectual, religious and moral codes piously inculcated at the school ultimately seemed contradictory in that they were rooted in a strict nineteenth-century asceticism while, simultaneously, trying to cater for the 'luxury and snobbery of the pre-1914 age'. St Cyprian's stood for a relentless work ethic motivated by an all-pervading fear of poverty and destitution in later life and a high respect for academic excellence, coupled with the usual grim sexual puritanism and self-castigation typical of 'low-church Bible Christianity'. But, contrary to this ethos, the working class, intelligence and foreigners were held in contempt while money and social privilege were highly esteemed, especially if the wealth was inherited rather than merely earned. St Cyprian's wanted its students to be both good Christians and socially successful which, the mature Orwell felt, was impossible (XIX.375).

This period of his schooldays inculcated into the youthful Blair an unquestioning belief that the status quo and prevailing moral standards of early twentieth-century English society simply could not be challenged. It was assumed that the powerful, the rich, the strong and the elegant were always right and entirely merited their exalted positions in society. Nevertheless, even as a young schoolboy, Blair was aware that he was incapable of '*subjective* conformity' in religious matters. The assumption that God existed and must be loved stood beyond question. Until he was about fourteen, he did not think to ponder or query this dogma. But, even then, he implicitly knew that he could not love this remote and authoritarian Biblical God and instead hated him, 'just as I hated Jesus and the Hebrew patriarchs'. From the Old Testament he felt far more sympathy with such flawed individuals as Cain, Jezebel and Haman and in the New Testament he was attracted by the likes of Ananias, Judas and Pontius Pilate. The intensely religious ethos of St Cyprian's ultimately confused the young Blair and merely taught him that religion seemed constantly to challenge its hopeful followers with 'psychological impossibilities' (XIX.379). When he read the Prayer Book, he learned that he must love and fear God but nowhere could he find an explanation of how it was possible to love someone whom you also feared.

While resident between 1912 and 1915 at Shiplake, the young Eric befriended a local girl, Jacintha Buddicom, who further stimulated his questioning of Christian practices by precociously regarding herself as a teenage pantheist.[38] Her views exerted a strong influence over the younger and impressionable Eric, as illustrated by his 1918 poem 'The Pagan' which defined their gods as ranging spirits 'Above the earth, beneath the sky', allowing their 'Naked souls' to be 'alive and free' (X.50–1). His religious doubts and scruples were also tempered by their shared enthusiasm for H. G. Wells's *A Modern Utopia* (1905) which dismissed traditional denominational church institutions and instead treated religion as a natural and personal necessity, as crucial to the individual as other human appetites. Wells's reputation as a social prophet and radical free thinker would have already been familiar to Eric from his mother's and aunt Nellie Limouzin's involvements in London Fabian circles. Wells's Utopians rejected the concept of prelapsarianism and avoided organized religion in favour of a yearly pilgrimage of spiritual solitude to commune with a God who was seen as a mystical entity rather than as a personified higher power. These ideas strongly appealed to Jacintha and Eric – they read together from her father's copy of the work – and he told her that he hoped one day to write 'that kind of book' (X.45).[39] Even so, it is misguided to view the dystopian perspectives of *Nineteen Eighty-Four* as the ultimate product of this boyish ambition since Wells's social and political ideas, tinged with elitism, natural selection and eugenics, were alien to Orwell's liberal instincts. Wells advocated a World State governed by a benign dictatorship of technocrats and scientists who were generally indifferent to art, culture and the humane ideals of democracy. Consequently, the two most influential dystopias of the first half of the twentieth century, Aldous Huxley's *Brave New World* (1932) and Orwell's *Nineteen Eighty-Four* (1949), were, as Krishan Kumar notes, 'both directed, in part at least, at what Huxley called "the horror of the Wellsian Utopia"'.[40]

Nevertheless, it is worth pausing to consider how *A Modern Utopia*'s radical ideas about the socio-psychological potency of religious belief and practice may have impacted on the impressionable Eric Blair. Wells's metatextual musings in this work engaged in a constant dialogue not only with his own concept of 'New Republicanism' in *Mankind in the Making* (1903) and his attempt at social prophecy in *Anticipations* (1901) but also ultimately with the central concepts of Plato's *Republic*. He was also strongly influenced by the agnostic Darwinian insistence of T. H. Huxley (the grandfather of Aldous Huxley, who briefly taught Eric at Eton), that the reorganization of societies upon a new and purely scientific basis was not only practicable but the 'only political object much worth fighting for'.[41]

With Homer regarded as the equivalent of the Bible for Plato's Athens, the Book of the Samurai in *A Modern Utopia* seems very much in accord with Orwell's lifelong literary attachment to biblical language as inculcated by Mrs Wilkes at St Cyprian's. Wells writes:

> Our Founders made a collection of several volumes, which they called, collectively, the Book of the Samurai, a compilation of articles and extracts, poems and prose pieces, which were supposed to embody the idea of the order. It was to play the part for the *samurai* that the Bible did for the ancient Hebrews. To tell you the truth, the stuff was of very unequal merit; there was a lot of very second-rate rhetoric, and some nearly namby-pamby verse. There was also included some very obscure verse and prose that had the trick of seeming wise. But for all such defects, much of the Book, from the very beginning, was splendid and inspiring matter. From that time to this, the Book of the Samurai had been under revision, much has been added, much rejected, and some deliberately rewritten. Now, there is hardly anything in it that is not beautiful and perfect in form. The whole range of noble emotions finds expression there, and all the guiding ideas of our Modern State. (167)

The Samurai are required to read aloud extracts from the Book of the Samurai for at least ten minutes every day and also to read every month at least one book published during the previous five years. Literature is endowed in *A Modern Utopia* with a mission of assessing and enhancing society, very much in accord with Orwell's own motivations as later expressed in 'Why I Write' in the short-lived literary magazine, *Gangrel* (Summer 1946).

Marriage in Wells's utopian state is organized along strictly secular lines and remains entirely independent of any formal religious ceremonials that might be chosen by the participants since the State does not concern itself with private religious practices. His utopian religion also repudiates the Christian Doctrine of Original Sin, insisting as a cardinal belief that 'man, on the whole, is good'. For the Samurai, the existence of religion is a natural phenomenon and 'something inseparably in the mysterious rhythms of life' (176), although it can be readily corrupted by human veniality and excess. In terms which would have directly appealed to the schoolboy Blair, it repudiates the traditional ceremonials of Catholicism and High Church Anglicanism. Wells insists that the Samurai eschew the religiosity of 'dramatically lit altars, organ music, and incense', just as they are 'forbidden the love of painted women, or the consolations of brandy' (177). Similarly, the Samurai are taught to be suspicious of any alternative religions, philosophies or intellectual pretensions that seek to comprehend and define the nature of individual spirituality. The God of the Samurai is viewed as a 'transcendental and mystical God' who escapes the 'delusive unification of every species under its specific definition that has dominated earthly reasoning' and which 'vitiates all terrestrial theology'. Ultimately, religion for Wells's Samurai becomes a quintessentially unique relationship between each person and his God rather than one between man and other men and 'a man may no more reach God through a priest than love his wife through a priest' (177–8). Wells then explicitly condemns – in terms which would have appealed to the young Eric Blair and remained permanently with the mature George Orwell – the authoritarian, even totalitarian, instincts of medieval Christendom and Roman Catholicism:

> In Western Europe true national ideas only emerged to their present hectic vigour after the shock of the Reformation had liberated men from the great tradition of a Latin-speaking Christendom, a tradition the Roman Catholic Church has sustained as its modification of the old Latin-speaking Imperialism in the rule of the *pontifex maximus*. There was, and there remains to this day, a profound disregard of local dialect and race in the Roman Catholic tradition, which has made that Church a persistently disintegrating influence in national life. (192)

Blair's transition in early 1917 from St Cyprian's to Wellington for one term and then in May to Eton marked the culminating academic moments of his school career.[42] He entered Eton as one of its elite King's Scholars where he was taught the subjects for which he had most aptitude – Latin, Greek and French – by the eminent classical scholar, Andrew Sydenham Farrar Gow, later fellow of Trinity College, Cambridge. Some of his classes were also taken by a recent Oxford graduate and alumnus of the school, Aldous Huxley, who was (ineffectively) teaching French during Orwell's first year at Eton to pay off his student debts. But, to the intense disappointment of both his parents and the staff of St Cyprian's, Eric systematically disconnected from his formerly diligent academic pursuits – a marked change of attitude, which, significantly, coincided with an equally precipitous disengagement from the school's traditional devotional practices and his own family's religious heritage. A sceptical antinomian inertia descended upon his responses to all forms of organized Christian religion, which rarely went beyond passive attendance at school chapel or Latin Founder's Prayers.[43] Whatever the psychological reasons for these two dramatic shifts in attitude – perhaps the onset of adolescence, an unease in finding himself surrounded by other exceptionally able King's Scholars or a sense of familial displacement after being at boarding schools since the age of twelve – it seems likely that Blair's loss of interest in both his academic work and Christian religious practices was closely interlinked. This stark transition from being a scholarly religious conformist (even if an immature and unquestioning one) to a dilatory and agnostic student effectively limited the future trajectory of his professional life but, in retrospect, probably enhanced significant elements of his later literary career.

Blair considered himself to have grown into a disillusioned religious sceptic at Eton, embracing the outward identity of an 'aloof cynic and Socratic disputer of all things sacred'.[44] Suggesting that he had been overwhelmed by the relentless conformity of the school's devotional practices, he later commented that there were at least six masters there 'making a very good living out of the Crucifixion'.[45] Although his detailed knowledge of the Bible and appreciation of the Authorized Version's language inculcated at St Cyprian's remained permanently with him, he rejected the basic theological contexts of Christianity. Even John Milton's *Paradise Lost*, asserting 'eternal providence' and justifying 'the ways of God to men' (I.25–6), alienated him and he noted in his Everyman copy of Milton's *Poems* (X.52) that he was a poet for whom he had no love but had merely been compelled to study.[46] Nevertheless, the great spiritual themes of *Paradise Lost* and *Paradise Regained* were, as Gordon Bowker notes, 'echoed in every work of imagination he later produced, although, pessimistically, he reversed the sequence.[47] He also later admitted that through reading *Paradise Lost* he suddenly realized the 'joy of mere words' in their 'sounds and associations' (XVIII.317).

Blair was also fascinated by the radical reinterpretation of the gospels and representation of alternative forms of religious devotion and martyrdom found in George Bernard Shaw's preface to his play *Androcles and the Lion* (1912), retelling the fable of the Christian slave saved from sacrifice in the Colosseum by his former kindness to a savage lion which is meant to kill him. Christopher Hollis records Cyril Connolly's statement that Blair was '"immersed in ... the atheistic arguments of *Androcles and the Lion*" at the age of fifteen'.[48] Its preface, 'On the Prospects of Christianity', substantially longer than the play itself, interrogates the Gospels and casts Jesus as an inspiring spiritual leader. But it also proposes that his teachings were lost with the Crucifixion and that later Christian churches were based upon the teachings of either St Paul or the prisoner Barabbas who was freed by Pilate at the Passover rather than Jesus. In a determinedly subversive section of his argument, 'Was Jesus a Coward?', Shaw argues:

Setting aside the huge mass of inculcated Christ-worship which has no real significance because it has no intelligence, there is, among people who are really free to think for themselves on the subject, a great deal of hearty dislike of Jesus and of contempt for his failure to save himself and overcome his enemies by personal bravery and cunning as Mahomet did. I have heard this feeling expressed far more impatiently by persons brought up in England as Christians than by Mahometans, who are, like their prophet, very civil to Jesus, and allow him a place in their esteem and veneration at least as high as we accord to John the Baptist.

The young Orwell was just such an iconoclastic individual since he increasingly felt that he could still believe in a God but disliked the persona of Jesus and considered it impossible to reconcile Christianity with normal 'social success' (XIX.376). As a disenchanted King's Scholar who harboured ambitions of becoming a writer, Orwell would have also been interested by some of Shaw's more provocative asides, such as his view that 'the Bible is so little read that the language of the Authorized Version is rapidly becoming obsolete'; and his mischievous assertion that modern Christian commentators had no more 'right to regard Annas and Caiaphas as worse men than the Archbishop of Canterbury and the Head Master of Eton'. As a colonial child and later disillusioned colonial officer, Orwell would have also appreciated Shaw's responses to the intractable problems in holding together millions of believers in so many diverse religions within the crudely imperialist framework of British and French colonialism:

> I suggest that the causes which have produced this sudden clearing of the air include the transformation of many modern States, notably the old self-contained French Republic and the tight little Island of Britain, into empires which overflow the frontiers of all the Churches. In India, for example, there are less than four million Christians out of a population of three hundred and sixteen and a half millions. The King of England is the defender of the faith; but what faith is now THE faith? The inhabitants of this island would, within the memory of persons still living, have claimed that their faith is surely the faith of God, and that all others are heathen. But we islanders are only forty-five millions; and if we count ourselves all as Christians, there are still seventy-seven and a quarter million Mahometans in the Empire. Add to these the Hindoos and Buddhists, Sikhs and Jains ... and you have a total of over three hundred and forty-two and a quarter million heretics to swamp our forty-five million Britons, of whom, by the way, only six thousand call themselves distinctively 'disciples of Christ', the rest being members of the Church of England and other denominations whose discipleship is less emphatically affirmed.

Shaw's preface also contains comments of prescient relevance to Orwell's later activities as a documenter of the conditions of the poor and disenfranchized. It notes just how difficult it is for modern-day Christians (especially privileged Etonians) to match Jesus's rejection of materialism and Mammon: 'If we ask our stockbroker to act simply as Jesus advised his disciples to act, he will reply, very justly, "You are advising me to become a tramp".' Insisting upon the pressing need for the redistribution of wealth in contemporary society, Shaw's preface – absorbed by Orwell a decade prior to the beginning of his career as a published writer – serves as an influential precursor to the exposés of extreme social inequalities in *Down and Out in Paris and London* and *The Road to Wigan Pier*:

> Now it needs no Christ to convince anybody today that our system of distribution is wildly and monstrously wrong. We have million-dollar

babies side by side with paupers worn out by a long life of unremitted drudgery. One person in every five dies in a workhouse, a public hospital, or a madhouse. In cities like London the proportion is very nearly one in two ... The need for a drastic redistribution of income in all civilized countries is now as obvious and as generally admitted as the need for sanitation.

At Eton, Blair involved himself in the production of a handwritten school magazine, *The Election Times*, with five issues produced by members of the 1916 Election, including contributions by Blair, who served as the magazine's business manager. Authorial attributions cannot always be definitively made for these often unsigned articles, but Blair was certainly editorially involved in, and perhaps the author of, an imaginative Wellsian fantasy, 'A Peep into the Future' (1918), in which prayers to Science temporarily replace those to God in a secularized school chapel. The traditional Grace before meals is replaced by the incantation, 'Science bless us', and at the end of the meal, 'Blessings of Science', prompting a required communal response 'Bless her' (X.48–9). In later life, as Leroy Spiller notes, he tended to regard 'all religions as remnants of a prescientific epoch'.[49] He is also a likely author of a spoof essay, 'Is There Any Truth in Spiritualism?', for Eton's *College Days* written by 'the Bishop of Borstall', concluding with the Shakespearean epithet: 'There are more things in heaven and earth, Horatio ...' (X.70).[50] At about this time (c. 1916–18), Blair drafted a play, *The Man and the Maid*, bearing on its first page in his hand the self-mocking marginal note 'master piece ii', and suggestive of a recent reading of Shakespeare's *The Tempest*.[51] In this drama Lucius, the son of the sorcerer Miraldo, cries out in its first scene, 'I can feel God calling me', when he wishes to escape from the island. But Lucius receives from his father a stern (if contradictory) warning: 'Heaven forbid ... For what is god but nature.' He goes on to suggest that the allure of Nature is no more than another route to debauchery (X.32). From this point onwards in this juvenile and probably incomplete play, references to religion and pantheism peter out, except for a concluding description of the lady whom Lucius seeks (but never meets) as a 'religious person' (X.43).

At Eton, Robert Gray notes, Blair became a 'thoroughgoing sceptic, albeit one especially well versed in the Bible and the Book of Common Prayer'. He was known, according to Cyril Connolly, as 'the Election atheist' who was occasionally beaten for being late for prayers.[52] Peter Davison suggests that he might have taken his personal moral code at this age from the sixth chapter of St Paul's epistle to the Romans, which he would have heard at the beginning of every Lent term at Eton: 'Abhor that which is evil, cleave to that which is good ... [be] not slothful [but] fervent in spirit ... Mind not high things, but condescend to men of low estate'. Nevertheless, he was duly prepared for confirmation in the Church of England by the King's Scholars' Master in College, the traditionally devout John Crace.

This was despite Blair's subversive attitude towards the potency of the Holy Ghost (whom he referred to as 'Old Man Ghost') and mischievous gift to the headmaster, Cyril Argentine Alington, a strict Anglican priest and royal chaplain, of a neo-Shavian essay which irreverently questioned the authority of God, thereby earning Blair the punishment of a 'Georgic' (the copying out of four to five hundred lines of Latin verse). The most famous anecdote of Blair's anti-Christian stance at Eton was recorded by Christopher Hollis, who described how he approached a new boy, Noel Blakiston, on the cricket field. Blair told him that he was collecting data on the religious affiliations of new boys, asking him whether he was 'Cyrenaic, Sceptic, Epicurean, Cynic, Neoplatonist, Confucian or Zoroastrian?' When the puzzled Blakiston answered that he was a Christian, Blair enigmatically responded: 'Oh, we haven't had that before.' Despite such casual adolescent jesting over religious matters, in late November 1918 (with his mother in attendance) Blair was duly confirmed in the college chapel by the distinguished Anglican theologian, Charles Gore, Bishop of Oxford.[53] But in a 1946 review of Winwood Reade's *The Martydom of Man*, Orwell brushed aside the religious education of his youth, stating that the version of Jesus 'thrust' upon him by his teachers 'outraged common sense'. Instead, he sympathized with Reade's depiction of Christ not as a 'Great Moral Teacher' but merely as a fallible 'human being' and a typical Jewish religious fanatic (XVIII.152).

Despite this mask of schoolboy cynicism, Blair must have been affected by the regular roll call of the fallen in the school chapel. Of the 5,687 Etonians who saw active service during the war, 1,160 were killed and 1,467 were wounded, with 13 Victoria Crosses, 548 DSOs and 744 MCs awarded to his near-contemporaries at school.[54] Like many of those born between 1903 and 1906 – such as Evelyn Waugh (b. 1903), John Wyndham (b. 1903), Malcolm Muggeridge (b. 1903), Graham Greene (b. 1904), Anthony Powell (b. 1905) and Samuel Beckett (b. 1906) – Blair harboured a lingering sense of guilt at being one of the fortuitous survivors from a generation of young men decimated by this global conflict. He wrote frankly in 'My Country Right or Left' (1940) that his contemporaries who had been just too youthful to participate grew uneasily aware of the 'vastness' of their missed experience and how he personally felt a 'little less than a man' through missing it (XII.270).[55] He told his friend Sir Richard Rees that 'his generation must be marked for ever by the humiliation of not having taken part' in the war, a comment which Rees regarded as a characteristic example of his 'exaggerated sense of honour carried to the point of Promethean arrogance'. Even his father, at the age of sixty, had joined the Henley Territorials and was commissioned – reputedly as the oldest subaltern in the British Army – as a Temporary Second Lieutenant. He was posted from November 1917 until May 1918 to the Western Front with the 51st (Ranchi) Indian Labour Company looking after horses in an allied depot and then to Marseilles with the Royal Artillery until he was demobilized in December 1919. Eric's mother, and his sister Marjorie, had also moved to London, renting a flat at 23 Mall Chambers, Kensington, and joined the war effort: the former working in the Ministry of Pensions and the latter as a motorcycle dispatch rider for the Women's Legion. Coupling this sense of inadequacy with his loss at Eton of any kind of religious faith, the schoolboy Blair became like a 'self-flagellating anchorite', Gray concludes, 'consumed by guilt at having been cast among the fortunate in a singularly unfortunate world'.[56]

Burma (1922–7) and *Burmese Days* (1934)

Following mediocre academic results, Eric Blair left Eton in December 1921 and in the New Year began studying for the Imperial Police. He attended a crammer, 'Craighurst', on the Suffolk coast since his parents had recently retired to nearby Southwold. On 23 November 1922, he was listed as seventh out of twenty-nine successful candidates in the academic examinations, although he only just passed the riding test, coming twenty-first out of twenty-three. In view of some of his mother's relatives still being at Moulmein, he applied to Burma for his first posting, listing the United Provinces as his second choice because his father had served there. His maternal grandmother, Theresa Catherine Limouzin, then aged about seventy-nine, still lived at Moulmein and was noted for her preference for native dress although she had never mastered the native language.[57] His aunt Norah was also a well-known figure within the local community, since, after attending her Carshalton boarding school, she had returned to Burma and married in June 1884 Henry Branson Ward, now Deputy Conservator of the Forestry Department. Prefiguring Flory's relationship with Ma Hla May and the unfortunate Eurasian Mr Francis in *Burmese Days*, his uncle Frank also still lived in Moulmein with his Burmese mistress Mah Hlim and their Eurasian child Kathleen, who was four years older than Eric.[58]

Blair sailed from Liverpool on 27 October 1922 aboard the Bibby Line SS *Herefordshire* via the Suez Canal, Ceylon and Rangoon. Ceylon would have been of passing interest to him because the father of his Moulmein grandmother had been William Halliley (1820–86), a senior civil servant in the Customs Department at Trincomalee, Ceylon. Blair arrived in Burma on 27 November 1922 and began his induction at the Police Training School at Mandalay where he rapidly learnt Burmese and Hindustani (and opted to study a third, the Shaw-Karen tongue, belonging to the Karen ethnic group). He had a natural aptitude for languages and a fellow trainee, Roger Beadon, recalled: 'he was able to go into a Hpongyi Kyaung, which is one of these Burmese temples, and converse in a very high-flown Burmese with the Hpongyis, or priests, and you've got to be able to speak Burmese very well to be able to do that'. These contacts, primarily aimed at enhancing Blair's linguistic skills, enabled him to learn more about the religion, culture and social issues of the region. He also mingled with some sad outcasts from the Anglo-Indian society, including Captain H. R. Robinson, a former Indian Army officer seconded to the Burma police service who had 'gone native' and become, variously, a Buddhist priest, opium addict, businessman and later author of *A Modern De Quincey* about his experiences which Orwell later reviewed.[59]

After one month during late 1923, at Burma's principal hill station at Maymyo, Blair was posted in early 1924 to the frontier outpost station of Myaungmya in the Irrawaddy Delta. During this period, he became an increasingly critical observer of colonial society in both Moulmein and the cosmopolitan seaport of Rangoon as he experienced at first hand the country's fraught political and religious tensions. Although Burma was still technically part of India, it had been excluded from the Montagu-Chelmsford Report of 1918, initiating constitutional reforms in India. This fomented widespread sedition, led by the nationalist movement of the Young Men's Buddhist Association (originally modelled on the British YMCA), effectively leaving the country under martial law. A boycott of British goods was instigated, with young Buddhist monks carrying small canes to beat anyone found breaking the boycott. Despite his pleasure in discussing local matters with temple priests, he grew to detest the aggressive political militancy of younger Buddhist monks. When Christopher Hollis, two years his senior at Eton, met up with him on his way back to England after a debating tour, he noted with distaste that he had developed 'an especial hatred ... for the Buddhist priests, against whom he thought violence especially desirable – and that not for any theological reason but because of their sniggering insolence'. Blair himself wrote in 'Shooting an Elephant' (*New Writing*, Autumn 1936) that the young Buddhist priests, of which there were several thousand in the town, were the worst protestors since all they did was hang around on street corners jeering at Europeans. With an ironic echoing of Biblical Latin, he encapsulated his own uneasy position as an agent of colonial oppression, viewing the British Raj as an intolerable but unbending tyranny forced 'in saecula saeculorum [King James Bible: 'world without end'], upon the will of prostrate peoples'. Yet, in the same paragraph, he ruefully admitted that it would be highly pleasurable to 'drive a bayonet into a Buddhist priest's guts' (X.501–22).[60]

These intense feelings apparently enhanced Blair's personal fascination with Burmese religious institutions and their officials. During the second half of 1924, he was posted to Twante and began to attend there the local churches of the Karen tribe, many of whom had been converted to Christianity by American Baptist Missions but still conducted services in their own language. Population estimates suggest that by the mid-1920s there were some 175,000 Christian Karens in Burma.[61] Characteristically, he later emphasized that these contacts were not engendered through any religious sentiments on his part but were due to their priests' conversation being far more interesting than that of his fellow British colonials. Nevertheless, these unusual encounters (at least for a junior colonial officer) demonstrate Blair's recognition, regardless of his own professed lack of spiritual beliefs, that established religious institutions and their practitioners formed a central element in understanding another country's cultures and social structures.

Blair's grandmother Theresa Catherine died at Moulmein in 1925. He only moved to the town as an Assistant Superintendent in April 1926 and so would have missed the funeral. He does not seem to have made any mention of this family bereavement in his written records. Nor is there any known record of her death in local official registers, and Gordon Bowker speculates that she may have 'died something of an outcast, at least from the Anglican communion'.[62] However, it has not previously been noted by Orwell's biographers that probate documents back in England record that Theresa Catherine died on 3 August 1925 and left the considerable sum of £2,731 11s 2d. Their share of this money greatly assisted the Blair family's uncertain financial position at Southwold since, with post-war inflation, Richard's modest and increasingly inadequate pension was steadily drawing the family towards the edge of genteel poverty.[63] After years of renting properties in Southwold, the Blairs finally purchased their own home, Montague House, 36 High Street, using their legacy from Theresa Catherine.

Another transfer in September 1925, this time to Insein in the Yangon Division, probably led to one of Eric Blair's most famous early essays, 'A Hanging' (1931), although hangings were also common in Moulmein. They were carried out in the town's notorious prison, the second largest in Burma. He may have been inspired to draft this account by Somerset Maugham's short story, 'The Vice-Consul', about an execution by the British of a native in Shanghai. Both narratives create a disturbing contrast between the callous indifference of colonials and the sheer helplessness of oppressed natives. But Blair's account is also characterized by its pointed conjunction of deeply felt native religious utterances and the empty blasphemies of colonial secular language. The prison superintendent, an army doctor dutifully performing this unpleasant administrative duty, encapsulates the crass brutality of British colonialism by unconsciously framing his utterances with the name of God Himself. Attempting to hasten the process, he cries out: 'For God's sake ... The man ought to have been dead by this time'; and when the hanging is finished he casually mutters: '"Well, that's all for this morning, thank God".' In contrast, it is the terrified dignity and final religious devotions of the condemned Hindu native – his crime is unspecified – that provides Blair with an essentially spiritual insight into the sanctity of all human life. As he watches the man alter his stride to avoid a puddle, he suddenly realizes the 'mystery, the unspeakable wrongness, of cutting a life short'. As the noose is put around the condemned man's neck, he makes a high, repetitious cry of 'Ram! Ram! Ram! Ram!', which

Blair notes was neither fearful nor an anxious cry but rather 'steady, rhythmical, almost like the tolling of a bell' (X.207–9). This meaning of this phrase is not explained in the essay for his British readers but Blair would have certainly known that 'Ram' was a Hindu mantra expressing absolute devotion to Rama, the seventh avatar of Vishnu. Chanting 'Ram' three times was deemed the equivalent of reciting the thousands of other names for God and a potent means of bringing the individual into an intimate and eternal proximity with God. In other words, while the colonial superintendent invokes his Christian God merely as thoughtless oaths, the last words of the hanged native express the purity of his unwavering devotion to his Hindu God – a level of spirituality which implicitly puts his colonial executioners to shame.

Most of Blair's other written records compiled during his five years in Burma are frustratingly fragmentary. At some time between 1922 and 1927 he composed a seventeen-line poem, 'Dear Friend: allow me for a little while', which concludes with a despairing secular lament: 'I care not if God dies' since 'This life, this earth, this time will see me out' (X.89). Another poem written during this period, 'The Lesser Evil', adopts the persona of a well-intentioned Anglican missionary in Burma working a 'parson's week' – the period from Monday to Saturday in the following week (i.e. thirteen days) when he takes the intervening Sunday as a holiday. It sets up an opposition between his cosy spiritual world, represented by the Christians singing hymns with church bells ringing in the background, and the fallen secular world of the 'house of sin' or brothel which tempts him. Eventually, however, the missionary resists the temptations of the whores and turns again towards the 'house of God' (X.92–3). This poem clearly echoes Somerset Maugham's story, 'Rain', in which a missionary attempts to save a prostitute but ends up corrupted by her, and perhaps also gossip relating to colonials with Burmese mistresses, including Blair's uncle Frank Limouzin. Finally, some short drafts of an untitled play about a heavily indebted Francis Stone have survived, written on Government of Burma paper. One scene finds Stone imprisoned with a Christian, a bearded old man and a poet, apparently all political prisoners during a revolutionary movement which has abolished Christianity. The poet explores the insoluble dilemma of a spiritual man, anxious over the eternal life of his own soul, caught within a ruthlessly materialistic world. He quotes from the Bible to the Christian, 'For what shall it profit a man if he gain the whole world and lose his own soul' (Mark 8.36), and concludes that humanity faces the problem of how to 'serve God and Mammon, & cheat them both' (X.109). Although clearly pertinent to Blair's discussions of the tensions between Christianity and capitalism in *Down and Out in Paris and London*, the surviving sheets provide no indication of how he intended to draw this material into the overall dramatic action of his play.

Just before Christmas 1926 Blair was transferred to Katha, west of Mandalay, where he caught dengue fever and was granted six months' leave from 1 July 1927. He arrived back in England in August and stayed with his parents and younger sister at Southwold, where his uncle Charles Limouzin was also now retired. Once home, he decided to resign from the Indian Imperial Police as from 1 January 1928, hoping to become a full-time writer.[64] His Burmese experiences continued to be of considerable literary use to him and on 4 May 1929 the French journal, *Le Progrès Civique*, published his hostile article, 'How a Nation is Exploited: The British Empire in Burma'. In an introductory note, the journal's editor, Raoul Nicole, speculated that the ongoing turmoil in British India was likely to spread to 'English Indo-China' and how Blair's 'interesting article' highlighted 'the methods the British Empire uses to milk dry her Asian colonies' (X.142). Although offering a thorough economic, political and geographical survey of the country in terms of its exploitation by British colonials, Blair mentions little of its rich religious cultures, noting only that the Burmese were 'Buddhists' and their 'tribesmen worship various pagan gods' (X.143). He concludes that Anglo–Burmese relations are essentially those of a 'slave and master' (X.147) which, inevitably, vetoes any form of spiritual or religious bonding between the British colonialists and the native population.

Either towards the end of his time in Burma (perhaps at Katha) or soon after he was back in England at Southwold, Blair began to write rough drafts of a novel about 'John Flory', who became the central character of *Burmese Days* (1934). Only five separate fragments now survive and in the first, a short poem with a six-line prose introduction titled 'John Flory: My Epitaph', he imagines a native funeral for his disillusioned, alcoholic anti-hero, enriched by gambling and music which seem to him far preferable to traditional Anglican 'beastly mummeries' (X.95). These musings perhaps recall what he had learned of his grandmother's funeral in 1925 in Moulmein since, as noted, she had 'gone native' in her final years. The fourth fragment, 'An Incident in Rangoon', offers an intriguing glimpse into Blair's intended exploration of Flory's moral and physical decline in Burma and his failure to uphold the code of the 'pukka sahib' in terms which could be equally applied to most of his later anti-heroes, including Gordon Comstock in *Keep the Aspidistra Flying* and Winston Smith in *Nineteen Eighty-Four*. Significantly, he notes that all experiences in a man's life should ultimately be viewed as related to the 'greater life which goes on in his mind & spirit' (X.99), implying that an exclusively secular focus upon human activities will inevitably prove both unsatisfactory and self-deluding.

This fragment also reveals Blair's keen anthropological interest in Burmese religious practices when he refers to the attendance by a staid senior government clerk at the renowned Shwe Dagon pagoda, one of the oldest and holiest of Buddhist shrines in Rangoon. But in his novel *Burmese Days* (begun autumn 1931; published 1934) Blair (henceforth Orwell) endows native religious practices with a more satirical twist, in that they are often utilized to reveal the self-seeking hypocrisy of the prosperous Burmese.

The novel opens with the corrupt and vicious U Po Kyin who acknowledges that, according to Buddhist beliefs, those who have led immoral lives will be reincarnated as rats, frogs or some other base animal. But, as a 'good Buddhist' – here meaning cunning and calculating – he intends to dedicate his final years to 'good works' (II.4) which, hopefully, will accumulate enough merit to compensate for his real behaviour. He plans to erect a series of pagodas, seeking advice from local priests as to exactly how many would be needed to bring him the requisite eternal benefits, and he will ensure that each has an array of small bells that tinkle in the wind since every tinkle equates to another prayer added to his spiritual account. He is habitually addressed by his unctuous servant Ba Taik as 'Most holy god' and never passes over a chance of cynically adding to his mounting account of merit. This accumulation of good deeds is regarded as no more than an ever-growing bank deposit with each separate gift to a priest bringing him closer to 'Nirvana' (II.13). Even when his wife Ma Kin warns him from the Pali scriptures of hell as a place of infinite torment where 'two red-hot spears will meet in your heart' (II.145), U Po Kyin feels assured that his mercenary balance of good deeds will save him from such a fate. Ultimately, U Po Kyin becomes his own devil, confessor and god, rapaciously sinning and then gratuitously granting himself absolution from his own greed and callousness.

Having dealt with the mercenary aspirations of the avaricious Burmese, Orwell then casts his satiric eye over the British colonial community. The novel begins its treatment of imperial Christianity innocently enough, describing a typical English cemetery set within white walls and next to a pathetic 'tin-roofed church' (II.14). But when the reader encounters the racist timber merchant Ellis the tone malevolently darkens. He openly expresses his admiration for the notorious massacre in the Sikh holy city of Amritsar in 1919 when British soldiers fired upon non-violent protestors and pilgrims near its Golden Temple, killing several hundred of them. His perverted praise of imperial brutality merely elicits from fellow colonial club members a non-verbal response similar to the nostalgic 'sigh' from Roman Catholics 'at the mention of Bloody Mary' (II.30) – one of Orwell's earliest and most pungent anti-Catholic asides. *Burmese Days* steadily develops a sustained interdenominational distaste for all organized religions. When Flory visits the home of his friend the pious Hindu Dr Veraswami, he casually remarks that coming to his house makes him feel like a shady Nonconformist minister surreptitiously bringing a 'tart' back home (II.35). The local European church turns out to depend for its maintenance upon its live-in Hindu *durwan* or doorkeeper. Old Mattu, a pathetic fever-ridden peasant, is forced to live alongside it in a primitive hut fabricated out of crushed kerosene cans, as yet another symbol of thoughtless colonial oppression.

Orwell's subversively satiric perspectives on religious matters in *Burmese Days* fostered his lasting fascination with various modes of totalitarian authority and repression, culminating in the dystopian world of *Nineteen Eighty-Four*. Flory's casual recollections of his crammer (recalling St Cyprian's) generate echoes of the grim repressions of the Roman Catholic Church's Tribunal of the Holy Office of the Inquisition, regarded by Blair as the historical encapsulation of the bigotry of popish doctrinal absolutism. On Saturday nights older boys systematically hold secret mock-Spanish Inquisitions, in which they wantonly torment younger boys in tortures prefiguring O'Brien's sadistic treatment of Winston Smith. Flory then progresses to a third-rate public school, which apes the major public schools with their traditional 'High Anglicanism' and a dire school song, 'The Scrum of Life', in which God is endowed with the role of the 'Great Referee' (II.64). Stirred by the potency of these perverted quasi-religious metaphors, Orwell damns another entire regime of totalitarian authority, this time the British Indian Civil Service. He despises it as a stultifying world in which, like in *Nineteen Eighty-Four*, free speech is inconceivable and every thought and word is rigorously controlled and censored by the repressive codes of the 'pukka sahib'. In a concluding spurt of disillusioned iconoclasm, Orwell yokes together the hapless trinity of colonial officer, religious cleric and barbarian, each trapped within an 'unbreakable system of taboos' (II.69–70).

Colonial religious practices in *Burmese Days* are consistently depicted as either meaningless or demeaning. Flory's servant Ko S'la dislikes his master attending the English church or, as he calls it, the 'English pagoda', even though Flory rarely bothers to visit it except for colonial funerals. Ko S'la cynically remarks that when a white man starts attending the English pagoda it is the 'beginning of the end' (II.117–18). Fleeting reminiscences of Flory's (and Orwell's) schoolboy biblical study result only in a crude parody of the Beatitudes when he tries to explain to Elizabeth his existential loneliness in Burma: 'Blessed are they who are stricken only with classifiable diseases! Blessed are the poor, the sick, the crossed in love' (II.185), because others can at least understand what is wrong with them. Similarly, when Elizabeth finally learns of his Burmese mistress, Flory's recollections of reading Shakespeare's *King Lear* produces an echoing parody of Edgar's tragic lament after he has mortally wounded his bastard brother Edmund: 'The gods are just and of our pleasant vices (pleasant, indeed!) make instruments to plague us', confirming that Flory has soiled himself 'beyond redemption' (II.203). For Flory, the concept of a Divinity serves only to heighten his awareness of his sinfulness and remoteness from the spiritual comforts supplied by traditional religious adherences.

The novel also raises – pointedly within a specifically religious context – the thorny issue of the numerous illegitimate Eurasian children produced by colonial officers. The pathetic character Mr Francis is the childlike adult son of a colonial clergyman and a South Indian woman. He laments that his father never became a bishop since he achieved only four converts in twenty-eight years of his ministry even though he did succeed, his son proudly notes, in having his book on another kind of vice, *The Scourge of Alcohol*, published by the 'Baptist Press' of Rangoon (II.123). It is noted of another two worshippers at the English church that they are the children of 'clergymen in holy orders' (II.127). The culminating church service of the novel, at which Flory's relationship with Ma Hla May is brutally exposed to the colonial community, is set up in tones which shift steadily from farce and pathos to pure tragedy. At six o'clock in the evening Old Mattu begins to toll the tiny bell in the 'six-foot tin steeple', a grim precursor to Flory's impending demise. The European Christian community of the local Kyauktada village, amounting to only fifteen in number, dutifully assembles at the church door for the evening service, a major social event in their lives since its itinerant minister can only visit every six weeks. The rest of the congregation comprises 'four pink-cheeked Karen Christians' who speak no English, and a mysterious dark-skinned Indian who always attends, probably, the rest of the worshippers assume, because he had been forcibly baptized as child by missionaries even though the majority of converted Indians usually lapse as adults. As Ellis mutters casual 'blasphemies behind his hymn-book', Flory, with an Orwellian sense of nostalgia, recalls his family's Anglican parish church back home in England and how he used to sit on winter Sundays in his pew, watching the yellow leaves fluttering against heavy, leaden skies. Such thoughts prompt him to wonder momentarily whether he might even still start a new life and shake off the 'grimy years' of his time in Burma (II.280–3).

The impossibility of such redemption renders Flory's suicide a fitting end to his life within Burma's nihilistic colonial landscapes. Orwell describes the former royal capital of Mandalay (captured by the British in 1885) as a deeply unattractive town, characterized by its five main products: 'pagodas, pariahs, pigs, priests and prostitutes' (II.296). Burma ultimately becomes for Orwell a dominating psychological concept, both literal and metaphorical, that shrouds the trajectory of his entire literary career. As he lay dying of pulmonary tuberculosis in a Cotswold sanatorium, he began to plan a novella, entitled 'A Smoking Room Story', which would have taken him back to Burma and the formative influences of his youth. Three pages of roughly drafted notes indicate that it focused upon the irrevocable changes wrought upon an innocent young man through his brutalizing experiences of colonialism in Burma. More recently, the totalitarian political repression of the Burmese people by its military rulers between 1962 and 2011 – leading to the renaming of the country as Myanmar – created a chilling, soulless dystopia comparable to that of Winston Smith's world. As Emma Larkin notes: 'In Burma there is a joke that Orwell wrote not just one novel about the country, but three: a trilogy comprised of *Burmese Days*, *Animal Farm* and *Nineteen Eighty-Four*'.[65]

2

Paris and London

Eric Blair as a social and religious commentator (1927–32)

Blair's interests in the poor and dispossessed peasants of Burma and the political unrest generated by the exploitative colonial regime of their authoritarian British masters fed naturally into his sympathy for the English and French working classes and the gross inequalities of European class systems of the 1930s. However, his first contact with the destitute and the cruelties enacted on them by society would have come through his childhood knowledge of workhouses. At Henley, Thomas Burns Dakin, a family friend of the Blairs whose son Humphrey married Eric's sister Marjorie, was medical officer to the local workhouse. He would also have been well aware of the proximity of his Eastbourne school, St Cyprian's, to the town's Union Workhouse, housed in an old Napoleonic barracks. It was situated only half a mile north of the school and the young Eric Blair would have regularly seen its ever-shifting population of vagrants and social outcasts.[1] Their grim social conditions and hopeless lives, largely bereft of spiritual meaning but heavily dependent upon the charitable activities of religious organizations in the absence of state support, now became the central focus of his creative energies as a writer.

In early autumn 1927, Blair moved from Southwold to London in the hopes of furthering his literary career. His aunt, Nellie Limouzin, was still living at Ladbroke Grove, probably with the French ex-anarchist and Esperantist Eugène Adam, also known after 1921 as Eugène Lanti ('L'anti', 'one against'), and she was able to introduce Eric to her current literary contacts. Like Nellie, Adam was a staunch socialist and he became in 1921 a founder member of the French Communist Party. Significantly for this study, he was also an outspoken opponent of Stalinism and his and Nellie's views were among the earliest to prompt Blair's later denunciation of Stalinist totalitarianism in *Animal Farm*. Blair's concern to document the experiences of the poor and destitute was also prompted by Jack London's exposé of the London slums in *The People of the Abyss* (1903) – a book he first read at Eton and praised in *The Road to Wigan Pier* (V.131) – and by his admiration for the urban reportage of the novels of George Gissing, *The Autobiography of a Super Tramp* (1908) by the Welsh hobo poet W. H. Davies and *Sinister Street* (1914) by Compton Mackenzie.

Following his first experiences in the Oxfordshire countryside and East End of London as an amateur tramp, Blair moved in spring 1928 to Paris, probably at the prompting of his aunt Nellie who had recently taken up residence there with Adam, whom she married in 1933. She had vacated her London flat on 1 April and so it seems likely that her nephew went to Paris almost as soon as she had arrived there. They may even have crossed the Channel together and he probably stayed in her twelfth-arrondissement apartment, 14 ave. Corbéra, before finding suitably drab rented accommodation in a cheap hotel at 6 rue du Pot de Fer in the fifth arrondissement, a strongly working-class district. Gordon Bowker notes that 'Eugène Adam and Nellie Limouzin, in an informal way, became his political tutors.' It can be argued that at this period they were the two most influential figures in encouraging the scope and direction of Blair's literary ambitions.[2] Adam became a crucial figure in the development of Blair's hostility towards Stalinism, designated by Adam as 'Red Fascism' (X.355), since he had enthusiastically travelled to Russia in 1922 but was forced to leave in 1926 in the face of a Stalinist move to take over the Communist Party at Moscow. Blair dressed as a tramp in Paris and stayed in cheap doss-houses, as described in 'The Spike' (1931) and the second half of *Down and Out in Paris and London* (published 9 January 1933). These two works served to establish his distinctive fictional identity as a secular missionary-reporter from urban wastelands and they formed a key stage in his authorial transition from Eric Blair, the public school-educated colonial officer, into George Orwell, the unmaterialistic humanitarian documenter of the alienated and dispossessed of 1930s society.

While in Paris Blair attempted to write either one or two novels, including an early version of *Burmese Days*, but none of this material has survived.[3] The rise of Western European communism now impinged on his increasingly radical views (still fostered by Nellie Limouzin and Eugène Adam) of the inequalities of French and British societies and the declining influence of organized religion within the daily life of the poor and working classes. Blair's first piece of published journalism, 'La Censure en Angleterre', appeared under the name 'E.–A. Blair' in the left-wing journal *Monde* (6 October 1928), edited by the communist novelist Henri Barbusse, whose mother was English and to whom Blair had been introduced by Nellie and Adam. Barbusse's influence on the development of Blair's literary career is underexplored but it seems likely that he provided him with an important early model for his later political and religious perspectives as a writer. Barbusse was then best known for his harrowing account of his service in the French army during the First World War, *Le Feu* (translated as *Under Fire*, 1916) – an important war-narrative precursor to *Homage to Catalonia*. In 1918, he had moved to Moscow and joined the Bolshevik Party and, strongly influenced by the Russian Revolution, in 1923 joined the French Communist Party through which he met Adam and Nellie. His *Light from the Abyss* (1919) and an incendiary collection of articles, *Words of a Fighting Man* (1920), advocated the overthrow of capitalism. His *The Knife Between My Teeth* (1921) confirmed his support for Bolshevism, and the October Revolution and his *Chains* (1925) demonstrated the unbroken chain of suffering of ordinary people through history and the impossibility of their struggle for freedom and justice.

Barbusse was attempting to establish a form of 'proletarian literature', akin to *Proletkult*, the experimental Soviet artistic institution closely allied to the 1917 Revolution, and the Russian Socialist Realism artistic movement which rapidly spread to other countries. The relevance, therefore, of his publications during the 1920s to Blair's *Down and Out in Paris and London* remains obvious. But, more subversively, his apparently committed but intrinsically pliant and self-interested perspectives on the Russian Revolution may later have been fed into the duplicity of the lethal power struggle between the authoritarian pigs, Napoleon (Stalin) and Snowball (Trotsky), in *Animal Farm*. In 1936, he published a flattering biographical study, *Stalin. A New World Seen Through the Man*, but his former colleague, the Russian Bolshevik writer Victor Serge, who became an outspoken critic of Stalin's regime of terror (and, incidentally, like Adam, died in Mexico City in 1947), noted that Barbusse had previously dedicated a book to Leon Trotsky before Joseph Stalin definitively won his power struggle against him. As soon as Barbusse recognized Stalin's absolute ascendancy in Russia, he roundly denounced Trotsky as a traitor to the ideals of the Revolution.

Returning to Barbusse's *Under Fire*, one of its most powerful scenes questions the relevance of religion to the ordinary combatants trapped in the apocalyptic chaos of warfare. It focuses on a French field refuge point, roughly fashioned from a cave, a mud-soaked hell in which the 'tepid stinks of acetylene and bleeding men' (279) fill the atmosphere. He meets a seriously injured aviator, half of whose body and face is burned, muttering to himself, '"Gott mit uns!" and "God is with us!"' (280). This airman recalls how, flying between Allied and enemy lines, he witnessed from above 'two religious services being held under my eyes', one French and one German, with each being 'a reflection of the other' and their prayers combining into a 'single chant that passed by me on its way to heaven' (282). This probably dying aviator grows 'fierce to pursue the answer to the gigantic conundrum, "what is this God thinking of to let everybody believe like that, that He's with them? Why does He let us all – all of us – shout out side by side, like idiots and brutes, "God is with us!" – "No, not at all, you're wrong; God is with us"?' Another 'pain-racked voice' in the refuge concludes:

I don't believe in God ... I know He doesn't exist – because of the suffering there is. They can tell us all the clap-trap they like, and trim up all the words they can find and all they can make up, but to say that all this innocent suffering could come from a perfect God, it's damned skull-stuffing. (283–4)

Barbusse's interchanges in this scene encapsulate the central religious dilemma focused upon by Orwell's own writings during the 1930s: how can a beneficent God allow the sufferings of the world to be experienced so cruelly by the poor, oppressed and destitute of supposedly civilized societies? From his time in Paris, Eric Blair formulated literary perspectives which took on secular, socialist and communist tones, implicitly questioning the relevance to ordinary people, especially in times of duress and hardship, of traditional religious institutions and even personal spiritual belief.

Blair's first publication in England as a journalist was an article, 'A Farthing Newspaper' (X.119–21), in *G. K.'s Weekly* (29 December 1928) which praised the nationalist newspaper *L'Ami du Peuple* – echoing the title of Jean-Paul Marat's radical newspaper during the French Revolution – sold in Paris for ten centimes (about one farthing). It campaigned against financial trusts and newspaper censorship, as well as advocating the lowering of the cost of living for ordinary workers. Given Orwell's strong anti-Catholicism as a writer, it seems ironic that this article appeared in a weekly founded by G. K. Chesterton, a renowned convert to Catholicism, even though their socialist views on the disenfranchisement of the poor had much in common. Similarly, his article 'John Galsworthy' (*Monde*, 23 March 1929) commended in self-reflective mode Galsworthy as a serious moralist and social philosopher, exposing the injustices and cruelties of his period and country. Blair was seeking to develop a comparable politicized authorial identity for himself, targeting 'comfortably off English philis-tines' and attacking the class systems and mentality that facilitated social oppression and inequalities (X.139). He also began to draw his suspi-cions of institutional religion into this left-wing literary stance. In a letter (24 October 1930) to his friend the journalist and poet Max Plowman, he commented on the assertion of John Middleton Murry in a recent *The Adelphi* article that, because 'orthodox Christianity is exceedingly elaborate, it presents a greater appearance of unity' than childish super-stition. While agreeing with this sentiment, he could not understand why this was so since the 'thicker the fairy tales are piled' the easier it becomes to swallow them (X.189). This seemed to him so paradoxical that he simply could not comprehend why such credulousness was so common.

This mocking reduction of the mysteries of Christian faith to the level of fairy tales fostered in Blair's writings at this period a satiric exploitation of empty religious language as a device for highlighting the soulless condi-tions of the poor and destitute of English society. In his famous essay, 'The Spike' (1931), he describes how a group of downtrodden tramps dreaded the bawling and 'blasphemous' threats of the hostel's manager, known as the Tramp Major, since you 'couldn't call your soul your own' whenever he appeared. On Sundays, after a meagre breakfast, they are locked for ten hours in the hostel's dining room, a filthy 'purgatory', during which they idly discuss 'charitable and uncharitable counties' and the militaristic ministrations of the Salvation Army. Starvation negates any possibility of finer religious sentiments since empty bellies leave no room for speculative thoughts within 'their souls'. The essay continues to foster this disjuncture between religious expectation and the reality of social hardship. A naked tramp resembles the 'corpse of Lazarus' and another indignant beggar tells of a parson who had 'peached' on him to the police, earning him seven days confinement. Next door in the workhouse, some of its paupers hide in a potato storage shed to avoid the compulsory Sunday morning service. This institution operates ridiculous rules, such as piously providing huge meals for its inmates on Sunday and then starving them for the rest of the week. As a deliberate policy to discourage itinerants, all excess workhouse food then has to be discarded rather than passed on to the equally ravenous tramps in the spike. Only a young carpenter, who claims merely to lack the necessary tools of his trade, still seems to possess the potential to transcend his currently dismal circumstances. Blair notes in characteristically mocking terms that, even though the carpenter had been a tramp for six months, he firmly believed that 'in the sight of God' he was not destined to remain a tramp. Despite his body being trapped in the spike, 'his spirit soared far away' into the 'pure æther' of middle-class aspirations (X.197–202).

Blair's correspondence at this period confirms his subversive tendency to look out for ridiculous and amusing elements within spiritual contexts. In a letter (16 August 1931) to a Southwold friend, Dennis Collings, he excitedly details seeing a ghost in the graveyard of the abandoned church of St Andrew's at Walberswick, even including a sketch map of his and the ghost's location. He then mocks a window display in the local Bible Society shop, advertising their cheapest Roman Catholic Bible at 5/6d but their cheapest Protestant one at one shilling. He notes this huge price disparity and the fact that the Catholic Douay Bible was *not* stocked there, concluding that these anomalies were helping to keep everyone 'safe from the R.C.'s'. He concludes this letter by recommending that Collings should pay a visit to this Bible Society bookshop near St Paul's to see its statue of the first Protestant bishop of India, since it will undoubtedly give him a 'good laugh' (X.211–12). In 1931, Blair also told his Eton friend Christopher Hollis that he regularly read the Catholic press because 'I like to see what the enemy is up to.' It seems ironic to note, however, that he had got in touch with Hollis after a gap of several years to seek his advice 'about the best Catholic schools' on behalf of a Southwold neighbour, a 'Catholic lady' who was 'anxious to provide a Catholic education' for her ward.[4]

Despite the irreverent tones of his letter to Collings, religious issues frequently intruded upon Blair's thoughts and private discussions during the early 1930s. In another letter (27 August 1931) to Collings he describes camping out in Trafalgar Square after finding that he would have to queue for an hour to get into the warmth of St Martin's Church. As the tramps wrap newspaper posters around themselves to keep warm during the freezing night, one of them jokes that they resemble 'fucking parsons' in their surplices (X.213). He is also amused by imagining a poetry-loving labourer reciting Henry Vaughan's 'O holy hope & high humility'; and he delights in a rendition of the traditional American hobo song, 'Alleluia, I'm a bum', sung to the tune of the Presbyterian hymn 'Revive Us Again'. Similar experiences are recorded in his 'Hop-Picking Diary' (25 August to 8 October 1931). In these private records he notes how Trafalgar Square regulars often occupied the morning by begging for food at various convents and how he always avoided St Martin's Church because of a woman there, known as the 'Madonna' (X.215), who used to ply tramps with searching personal questions. Sustaining his habitually disrespectful attitude towards institutional Christian religion, this diary also gives vent to a sporadic but ingrained anti-Semitic element in his writings. For example, he describes one young itinerant, who reappears in *A Clergyman's Daughter* as Kike, as a 'thorough guttersnipe'. This individual is a Jew of eighteen from Liverpool and Blair admits that he could not recall 'anyone who disgusted me so much as this boy'. He compares his starvation-induced greed to that of a pig scrounging around dustbins and describes how he has a face like some 'low-down carrion-eating beast'. He is no less revolted by his salacious attitude towards women and his leering expressions were so 'loathsomely obscene' as to make him feel nauseous (X.217).

This 'Hop-Picking Diary' also documents the thoughtless lack of charity shown to the poor and destitute by church officials and locals. One bitterly cold night Blair sleeps on the edge of a park and, on his way to conduct morning service, the local clergyman quickly moves him on, although 'not very disagreeably' (X.218). Then, self-consciously recalling Joseph and Mary's accommodation difficulties at the birth of Jesus, he asks a farmer if he might spend a night in his cowshed. But the former and his family, as pious churchgoers, are just setting out for evening service and insist in a 'scandalised manner' that they could not grant him even this humble shelter. Instead, Blair and his friend Ginger take refuge by the lychgate of the church in the hope that the congregation will give them a few coppers as they go in to morning service. However, they receive nothing, apart from an old pair of flannel trousers handed to Ginger by the vicar. Later, since church charity to the poor seems so meagre, there seems an alluring logic to Ginger's plan to rob the local church since in his experience there are usually some coins in the 'Poorbox' (X.226).

In keeping with the light-hearted tone of his letters to Brenda Salkeld, in October 1931 Blair describes a visit to Kensal Green Cemetery where some of the pious epitaphs leave him in 'paroxysms of laughter'. Whimsically developing this thought, he suggested that funerals should also be made more comic so as to alleviate the natural sadness of bereavement. The same letter then discusses *What Was the Gunpowder Plot?* (1897) by the Jesuit John Gerard. It proposed that William Cecil, Lord Burghley, had concocted it as anti-Catholic propaganda and he felt that its documentary evidence seemed convincing. He had also just read *The Medieval Scene* (1930) by the staunchly anti-Catholic historian George G. Coulton, commending him as an individual whose name caused 'all good Catholics' to make the 'sign of the evil eye' (X.236). This short letter usefully illustrates both the diversity of Blair's religious interests at this period and how his often satirical but engaged commentary on such matters was first honed in his private correspondence.

During the early 1930s, Blair steadily refined in both his private correspondence and his journalism a polemical tendency towards depicting Roman Catholicism as the ecclesiastical equivalent of Stalinist totalitarianism. He suspected its organization for being hierarchically structured and conservative, or even proto-fascist, in its political influences. He also despised what he saw as its authoritarian treatment of its mass of faithful but often poor, working-class adherents. Noting the public potency of Jesuits and highly educated lay converts in Catholic theological debate, especially in newspapers and periodical journalism, he tended to view the entire Roman Catholic Church as dominated by a self-serving intellectual elite, even though at this period probably less than one per cent of Catholics could be properly deemed 'intellectuals'.[5] His book reviews insistently underlined the Catholic hierarchy's desire for power and influence over social issues. He notes, for example, in a review for *The Adelphi* (May 1932) how *The Civilization of France* by the German historian Ernst Robert Curtius, an anti-totalitarian Lutheran, traced the Catholic Church's steady accumulation of power in France and how it had effectively won a resounding political victory over the State. Blair's review considers this perspective disturbing but far from surprising, given the 'Church's recuperative powers in England' (X.245).

In another review for the *New English Weekly* (9 June 1932), he commends *The Spirit of Catholicism* by the German Catholic theologian Karl Adam – first published in 1924 and translated in 1932 by Dom Justin McCann, O.S.B., then Master of St Benet's Hall, Oxford – for being generally uncontroversial in its analysis of the current revival of Catholicism.[6] This said, he launches into a savage denunciation of what he regards as the usual type of modern Catholic writers and apologists who were accomplished in debate but always wary of saying anything of genuine substance. Few of them, he thought, had any ambition beyond self-justification, resulting in them offering little more than insults directed at scientists and 'Protestant historians' and attempts to 'bluff the fundamental difficulties of faith out of existence'. In contrast, he commends Adam for not attempting to denigrate his opponents and for objectively exploring the workings of the Catholic soul, as well as ignoring what he regarded as the far-fetched panoply of its supposed philosophical basis of faith.

However, his review then turns more confrontational as he condemns the contrasting approach of the Jesuit controversialist Father Cyril C. Martindale in his study *The Faith of the Roman Church* (1927), mistitled by Blair as 'The Roman Faith'. While he commends Adam as an honest Catholic in his beliefs, he denounces Martindale as a convert who seems to be perpetually trying to justify his conversion and mocks him for attempting to float over the scientific theories of evolution in a kind of 'logical balloon-flight' with any idea of 'common sense flung overboard for ballast'. Blair readily admits that a non-believer can ultimately understand very little about the inner workings of the Catholic faith but, at the same time, he notes the 'Hebrew-like pride and exclusiveness' of the typical Catholic mentality. He strongly condemns the exclusivity of such a faith and the concept of the Communion of the Saints which seems to him to present the Church more as a 'glorified family bank' than a devotional community of religious thought. This spiritual bank acts like a limited company, which pays huge dividends to its shareholders but then ruthlessly excludes non-members from its profits. Even the smallest shareholder could supposedly benefit from the holiness of St Augustine or St Thomas Aquinas but, in Blair's eyes, the Church's insular concept of the family means that the rest of humankind, except for a few 'stray saints', is effectively excluded from the joys of eternity and patronized by the 'rigid pity' and 'dogmatic intolerance' of Catholics.

He continues by noting with scepticism Adam's claim that non-Catholics blessed with 'good will' are essentially unknowing Catholics in spirit and by (inaccurately) suggesting that Adam had argued that pagans, Jews, heretics and schismatics had all forfeited eternal happiness and were destined for Hell. In conclusion, Blair condemns the majority of English Catholic apologists (represented by Father Martindale) as so extreme in their modes of controversial debate that non-believers rarely bothered to reply to them. Instead, most contemporary anti-clericism seemed to him to be directed at the 'poor, unoffending old Church of England' with only absurd tales about intriguing Jesuits or infants' remains dug up from beneath the 'floors of nunneries' being raised against the Catholics. Father Martindale responded (30 June 1932) to this hostile review by explaining how the assertion that 'all pagans ... have forfeited eternal life' was not Adam's opinion but merely a quotation from the Council of Florence (1431–49) and that Blair's treatment of his own book had been characterized by calculated 'disingenuousness'. He offered to meet with Blair, who declined while continuing to insist that Martindale's writings were merely extreme Catholic propaganda (X.246–53).

About nine months later Blair's review (*The Adelphi*, April 1933) of *Gogol* by the biographer and translator 'Boris de Scholezer' (i.e. Schlözer) focused with distaste on Gogol's obsessive religious paranoia which had prompted him to preach endlessly to his friends, suffer self-mortification at the direction of a fanatical priest and undertake an arduous pilgrimage to the Holy Land. He describes how Gogol considered himself a 'dead soul' as a Christian because he felt cut off from any meaningful love and penitence. He also notes with curiosity that, although it was not uncommon in Calvinistic countries to find this fear of being damned for 'mere spiritual deficiency' rather than sinful deeds, it was unusual to come across it in an ultra-orthodox member of the Greek Church (X.310–11). To Blair, Gogol's form of self-mortifying faith seemed especially repulsive and contrary to a basic respect for the human spirit.

By summer 1932, Blair had found, through financial necessity, a teaching post in the Hawthorns High School for Boys in Hayes, Middlesex. As he explained in a letter (12 June 1932) to another Southwold friend, Eleanor Jacques, he found the locale a 'godforsaken' place, populated largely by clerks who worshipped at 'tin-roofed chapels'. In gently satiric mode, he described how he had befriended Ernest Parker, the local curate at the parish church of St Mary's, who was 'High Anglican' but by no means a 'creeping Jesus'. Unfortunately, this meant that he had to attend his Anglo-Catholic church services which were much too 'popish' for his tastes, especially when Parker had to dress up in biretta and cope while processing with candles, 'looking like a bullock garlanded for sacrifice'. Blair mischievously agreed to repaint a 'quite skittish-looking' statue of the Blessed Virgin Mary, hoping to make her look like one of the pictures of glamorous women in *La Vie Parisienne*.[7] He even felt under pressure to take communion but feared, jokingly, that the 'bread might choke' him as a committed non-believer. In the same letter, he proudly mentioned his review of Karl Adams's book and his spat with Father Martindale, claiming it as the first occasion on which he had successfully laid the 'bastinado on a professional R.C. at any length' (X.249).

Blair's letters to Eleanor Jacques are often filled by comic ecclesiastical phrasings and casual theological references. When planning in August 1932 a hopefully romantic rendezvous he concludes in mock piety by asking her to pray at church that Sunday for decent weather on the following Tuesday (X.262). On a Sunday one month later he describes how Mrs Eunson, the wife of the owner of Hawthorns, was disturbing the household peace by thumping out 'hymn-tunes on the piano'. He also admits to his unwavering 'obsession about R.C.s', unashamedly dismissing the Catholic convert writer D. B. Wyndham Lewis as a 'stinking RC' (X.268). In another letter (19 September 1932), he offers Eleanor a cruel comic cameo of an aged local parishioner (the model for Mrs Mayfill in *A Clergyman's Daughter*). He describes at church sitting immediately behind an old 'moribund hag', reeking of gin and mothballs, who had virtually to be carried up to the altar for communion. He supposes that she was so ancient that she took Communion as often as possible, just in case the Devil should find her in a state of mortal sin and 'carry her off to the hottest part of Hell'. He also mentions his recent reading of *Belief in God* (1921) by Bishop Charles Gore who had confirmed him at Eton, grandly deeming one of the Church's most distinguished theologians as 'quite sound in doctrine tho' an Anglican' (X.269). A few weeks later (19 October 1932) he tells Eleanor that he is now a regular reader of the *Church Times* and in June 1933 how he takes great pleasure in its 'walloping the Romans' (X.317). He admits that he will probably soon have to participate in Communion since he had passed himself off as pious to the vicar, even though he could no longer recall from his school days the correct procedure and responses. He even sheepishly admits (18 November 1932) to decorating a cigarette box for a forth-coming Church Bazaar which he had agreed to gild (X.271–3). Although the jocular informality of this private correspondence should not be taken too seriously, it confirms how deep-rooted Blair's mocking perspectives on both Anglicanism and Catholicism had become by the early 1930s.

Eric Blair becomes George Orwell, and *Down and Out in Paris and London* (1933)

The typescript of Blair's unpublished 'Clink' essay, drafted in August 1932 and describing events of December 1931, was completed when he was considering his choice of authorial pseudonym, rejecting his usual tramping name of Edward (or 'P. S.') Burton in favour of George Orwell.[8] 'Clink' is a short piece of semi-documentary reportage, based upon Blair deliberately getting drunk so that he could be arrested and experience imprisonment. As was now habitual with his lower-class characterizations, conversational obscenities are richly laced with religious references and, since Christmas is close, his fellow occupants in the Black Maria happily sing the hymn 'Adeste, fideles' (X.256) on their way to Old Street Police Court. This subversive blending of religious and secular elements provides a unifying comic framework for the narrative since the crimes committed often have religious associations. Blair meets a ruined publican who has embezzled the Christmas Club money from his establishment. Another Jewish prisoner has stolen £28 from his kosher butcher employer to spend on prostitutes in Edinburgh and is now incarcerated before facing the arbitration process of his local Synagogue, thereby hinting at the 'self-segregating tendency of Jewry'.[9]

Blair also meets 'Snouter' who makes a good living each December as a 'chanter' singing Christmas carols to passers-by, prompting another minor crook, Charlie, to burst into a rendering of 'Jesu, lover of my soul'. The duty constable sarcastically silences them by telling them that they are not at a 'Baptist prayer meeting', but this merely prompts Charlie to hum to himself the next two lines of the hymn: 'While the gathering waters roll / While the tempest still is 'igh'. He proudly boasts that he has a comprehensive knowledge of the ''ymnal' since during a sentence at Dartmoor he had sung bass in the prison choir. Charlie had ended up there because his sister had informed on his criminal activities after marrying a 'religious maniac'. He bitterly remarks that ''e's so fucking religious' that she now has fifteen children, implying that his brother-in-law is an observant Catholic who avoids contraception. The severe regime at Dartmoor had made him vow a solemn 'Bible oath' (X.259) that he would in future avoid prison sentences even though he is once again in custody. Religious references in 'Clink' are consistently utilized both for comic effect and as an irrelevant counterpoint to the grim daily hardships of the poor and criminal classes. A similar technique is deployed in 'Common Lodging Houses' (*New Statesman and Nation*, 3 September 1932), which blends satire and pathos to describe religious 'slumming parties' in which small groups of middle-class do-gooders arrive uninvited at hostels to hold impromptu and lengthy religious services which the hapless lodgers cannot avoid since they have no means of ejecting them (X.266). In both essays, institutionalized religion and its charitable activities are depicted as crassly irrelevant to the dismal daily lives of the poor and destitute of London.

Neither Jews nor (to a lesser extent) Christians fare well in *Down and Out in Paris and London* (1933), which incorporates material from an earlier draft about Orwell's experiences in Paris, 'A Scullion's Diary' (X.242, rejected by Faber in February 1932). A second-hand shop in the Rue de la Montagne St Geneviève is run by a 'red-haired Jew, an extra-ordinarily disagreeable man' and the narrator relishes the thought that it would have been a 'pleasure to flatten the Jew's nose' (I.15–16). His friend Boris, an émigré White Russian, tells him about another Jew who works as a mechanic and owes him money. He plans to steal some magnetos from his garage to sell on and then reimburse Boris who laments how tortuous it feels for a respectable Russian to be indebted to a Jew. In similar vein, he recalls how during the early months of the First World War a 'horrible old Jew, with a red beard like Judas Iscariot' tried to pimp his own daughter to him for fifty francs; and that in the Russian army it was considered bad form to spit on a Jew because a Russian officer's spittle was deemed too 'precious to be wasted on Jews' (I.34). A deep vein of anti-Semitism runs unchallenged through the Paris section of the narrative. Popular sayings are casually recalled – 'Trust a snake before a Jew' (I.72) – and the first section of *Down and Out* concludes with the farcical story of an old miser, Roucolle, who invests his money with another Jew, a 'businesslike young chap' (I.124), who plans to smuggle cocaine into England. Predictably, he is double-crossed by the Jew who gives him face powder rather than cocaine.

While Orwell was doubtless echoing the widespread anti-Semitic language of post-war Paris, there is no sense in *Down and Out* that a condemnatory view should be taken of such institutionalized racism. This tone of habitual anti-Semitism also seeps into the book's second part when, back in England, Orwell watches in a coffee-shop a 'Jew, muzzle down in the plate' who 'was guiltily wolfing bacon' (I.133), a description attributing base animalistic qualities to this character and a greedy betrayal of Jewish kosher laws.[10] In this respect, *Down and Out* remains a problematic and distasteful text for modern readers, unlike other well-known novels of the period, such as Graham Greene's *Brighton Rock* (1938), from which comparable anti-Semitic sentiments and descriptions in the first edition were silently expurgated in later printings.[11] It is also significant that *Down and Out* was published by Victor Gollancz, who had been born an orthodox Jew but later described himself as a Christian socialist. He insisted on various revisions to the typescript, mainly to obscene language and some identifiable names, but there is no record of him comme ·ing on Orwell's depiction of Jewish characters at Paris.

In contrast, aspects of institutional Christianity are more gently mocked in the Paris section *of Down and Out*. Casual oaths, such as '*Sacrée salope*' (I.1) and '*Nom de Dieu*' (I.25), inevitably lace the conversations of the lower classes, in a similar vein to the meaningless blasphemies of the petty criminals in 'Clink'. Orwell carefully stage-manages the comic tale of the waiter Valenti, whose lack of money leaves him starving for five days. In desperation, he prays to Sainte Éloise, the patron saint of the quarter, whose picture hangs on the wall of his boarding house room. Almost immediately, a kindly neighbour notices that he has an empty oil *bidon* for which he can claim a returnable three francs fifty deposit. Delighted, Valenti is about to give thanks for this saintly intecession when he discovers that the portrait is really of a renowned Empire prostitute, Suzannah May. Generally, however, Christianity plays little part in Orwell's experiences as a Parisian hotel *plongeur* since long hours of work and little money leave little opportunity for experiences beyond his room or local taverns.

Once he returns to London, however, Orwell exposes the diversity of well-meaning but generally unwelcome Christian support systems for the poor and destitute of the capital. In Whitechapel he sees 'The Singing Evangel' who offers to save his listeners from hell in return for sixpence. In the East India Dock the Salvation Army are singing 'Anyone here like sneaking Judas?' to the tune of 'What's to be done with a drunken sailor?'; and two Mormons preaching on Tower Hill are heckled by a jeering crowd as 'F— Polygamists!' (I.136). Church missionary work supporting the poor of London becomes in *Down and Out* a Babel of competing, meaningless tongues, with bland words of salvation dispensed as the obligatory cost of paltry food and warmth. Orwell tries to learn something about Mormonism but most of the preachers' words are drowned out by shouting, as happens with most street meetings.[12] He and Paddy, a wizened old Irishman, then go to a 'small tin-roofed shed' in a back street with a 'harmonium' and a 'gory lithograph of the Crucifixion'. Its exact religious denomination is never defined but a refined lady in an elegant blue silk dress and golden spectacles tells them in kindly patronizing tones that Jesus always has a 'soft spot for poor rough men'. She engages them in half an hour of prayers, endured in silence by her captive congregation who desperately want the tea and buns supplied with her gentle sermonizing. As they finally escape one man expresses the subversive thoughts of the entire group: 'I thought them f— prayers was never goin' to end' (I.140–3).

Paddy, a caricature Irish Catholic who has tramped for fifteen years, becomes an informal ecumenical guide to the various charitable Christian institutions of London. Lacing his conversation with the usual oaths, 'Christ' and 'T'ank God', he recommends Catholic convents, as well as Baptist and Church of England institutions, as always good for a cup 'o' tay', noting sarcastically: 'Ah, what'd a man do widout religion, eh?' More seriously, while admitting that he hasn't been to confession for more than seventeen years, Paddy retains certain religious 'feelin's' and becomes distraught at a copy of the devotion text *Of the Imitation of Christ* on display in a bookshop window because he thinks that it is a blasphemous parody 'to go imitatin' of *Him*' (I.152–3). Paddy's innocently ignorant concept of personal spirituality seems, in Orwell's eyes, to be the only kind of Catholicism to have any genuine meaning or value. But it remains noticeable that this humbly devout Catholic still has to be cast in *Down and Out* as a lightly sketched parody of a music-hall comic Irishman. Ordinary working- and middle-class Catholics simply do not (and cannot) exist within Orwell's polemical literary perspectives on Catholicism. Instead, a peasant-like simplicity of belief becomes the only acceptable level of Roman Catholic behaviour since it provides a conveniently sharp contrast to Orwell's obsessive *bête-noire*, the preaching and proselytizing of certain sections of the Catholic intellectual elite on behalf of a complacent, high-ranking clergy. Paddy's ingrained and unquestioning loyalty towards the religion of his birth is also contrasted with the practical but hard-edged evangelism of the English Salvation Army, founded in 1865 by Catherine and William Booth in London's East End. Their whitewashed shelters, although clean and hygienic, seem to resemble workhouses in their semi-military authoritarianism and most tramps, Orwell suggests, find these refuges less appealing than the worst of common lodging houses. He concludes bitterly that this well-meaning organization is so accustomed to regarding itself as a charitable institution that it cannot even operate basic lodging houses without making them 'stink of charity' (I.159).

And so continues the apparently unbridgeable disconnect in *Down and Out* between the charitable instincts of church institutions and the dispossessed to whom they seek to proffer good intentions and support. Finding it most effective to address this issue (like an undercover journalist) through individual case studies, Orwell encounters Bozo, a crippled street artist or 'screever' who denies his Jewish looks and, instead, professes to be the kind of atheist who, rather than disbelieving in God, feels a personal dislike for Him (I.169). When he draws a skilful copy of Botticelli's Venus outside St Martin's-in-the-Fields, an enraged man in black, probably a cleric or churchwarden, rushes out and demands that he washes it away since, perversely, he views the innate beauty of this artistic image as an 'obscenity outside God's holy house' (I.173). Orwell also recalls 'slumming parties', previously described in 'Common Lodging Houses', as he describes the intrusive arrival of three sleekly dressed gentlefolk who hold an impromptu religious service in a lodging house kitchen. The men try to ignore them and Orwell acknowledges their helpless resentment, lamenting that well-intentioned people often assume the right to preach and pray over the poor and destitute. In an evangelical church near King's Cross, the tramps deliberately misbehave, treating the religious service as a 'purely comic spectacle'. Orwell describes with distaste the conflict between the pious, well-intentioned do-gooders and the hundred or so poor men who were deliberately undermining the service (I.184–5). The only religious figure in London to engender unqualified gratitude is a young clergyman on the Embankment who silently hands out food tickets without any expectation of thanks. Consequently, he is deemed 'a — good feller' and one man calls out: 'Well, *he'll* never be a f— bishop!' (I.187), a remark intended as a compliment. But the *status quo* of this irrevocably fallen world is reasserted by the proprietor of the nearby eating-house who systematically swindles each tramp out of threepence-worth of food per ticket. Towards the end of this period of vagrancy, Orwell arrives at Lower Binfield in Oxfordshire – based on Blair's childhood Henley and later the home of George Bowling in *Coming Up for Air* – where he sprawls on the village green under the eyes of a clergyman and his daughter who stare at him and his fellow tramps for a while as though they were 'aquarium fishes' (I.196) before silently moving away. This voyeuristic image reiterates the profound and apparently unbridgeable distance between ecclesiastical institutions and the dispossessed members of an English society still rife with poverty and inequalities after the Great Depression.

Historical perspectives on religious matters, especially Catholic ones, continued to intrigue Orwell during the mid-1930s. In a review of G. K. Chesterton's *Criticisms and Opinions of the Works of Charles Dickens* (*The Adelphi*, December 1933), he identified an attempt to link Dickens with a mythologized Middle Ages 'beloved of Roman Catholics', prior to the injustices of serfdom and the Inquisition. In Chesterton's defence, he commended his restraint in not trying to claim that if Dickens had been more intelligent he would have 'turned Roman Catholic'. Unlike most Catholic apologists who, Orwell felt, demeaned their intellectual integrity in order to turn out Catholic propaganda, Chesterton was an exception in not participating in the 'great game' of insisting that all books by Protestant authors are unreadable (X.326). On a more juvenile level, the lurid details of the Catholic Inquisition continued to fascinate Orwell and in a letter (27 July 1934) to Brenda Salkeld he mentioned that he was reading Elphège Vacandard's *The Inquisition, A Critical and Historical Study of the Coercive Power of the Church* (1907), describing its detailed analysis of the use of torture in 'tribunals' (X.344). He had also perused John Swain's *Pleasures of the Torture Chamber* (1931), which went into graphic detail about the tortures used by the Inquisition.[13] His fascination with the Inquisition even led to a passing reference, incongruously, in *The Road to Wigan Pier* (V.194). Another more serious book by a Catholic convert, *Medieval Religion* by Christopher Dawson, met with his approval in *The Adelphi* (November 1934), since it seemed free of the 'humbug' which Orwell usually expected from 'English Roman Catholics', a refreshing contrast to the 'braying of Belloc and the tittering of Knox' (X.357).

In contrast to Orwell's private correspondence with young female friends – in which he tended towards the cynical and outrageous in theological matters – his steady stream of reviews for *The Adelphi* during 1934 reveals a distinctly more thoughtful attitude towards the philosophical and ethical importance of Christianity. His review (April 1934) of *Further Extracts from the Note-Books of Samuel Butler*, edited by the Cambridge librarian Auguste T. Bartholomew, noted that while Butler clearly disapproved of Christ and his teachings he did not seem to have seriously objected to either Christianity or its churches. Darwin and Huxley were more his natural enemies and Butler's writings even sometimes expressed a 'sneaking affection' for the clergy (X.340). Similarly, when reviewing (July 1934) G. T. Clapton's *Baudelaire: The Tragic Sophist*, Orwell revealed a delicate sensitivity over Baudelaire's complex attitude towards Christianity, insisting that his inner spiritual tensions and awareness of Christian ethics had made a vital contribution to his poetic creativity which remained firmly rooted in an imaginative national Christian background. Baudelaire had been raised within the Christian tradition and, Orwell argued, recognized that its concepts of sin and damnation were more substantial and meaningful ideas than anything offered by 'sloppy humanitarian atheism'. In this sense, he remained loyal to the 'Christian cosmos', even if he tended to invert its moralities and question Christian ethics from the position of an insider rather than an outsider. Such a perspective was almost to be expected in an age when religious beliefs were visibly decaying and, in Orwell's opinion, this dichotomy did nothing to limit Baudelaire's poetic spirit and, in fact, proved the 'making of him' (X.342–3). However, in a later review of Edwin Morgan's *Flower of Evil: A Life of Charles Baudelaire* (*Observer*, 31 December 1944) he disputed Baudelaire's reputed return to the Catholic Church during the last year of his life and the resulting claim that his writings may be viewed as essentially Christian.[14]

These comments were complemented by Orwell's response to Henry Miller's *Tropic of Cancer*, which he reviewed for the *New English Weekly* (14 November 1935). His opinion of this controversial novel is significant since, alongside his nuanced interpretation of Baudelaire's dark spiritual dualities, it marks a maturing in his responses as a critic and writer towards the importance of religious matters to the individual psyche. It also confirms his adult rejection of a juvenile fascination with Wells's idealistic and now distinctly passé sociological concepts in *A Modern Utopia* and the 'windy platitudes' (X.325) of G. B. Shaw, who he regarded as nothing but 'Carlyle & water' (X.307). Miller's earthy novel prompted him to contemplate the disintegration of religious belief and how it had prompted a 'sloppy idealization' of life's physicality. This process seemed logical to Orwell because, if a sense of an afterlife was now denied, basic aspects of human existence such as sexuality and birth seemed all the more disgusting. The Christian tradition had triumphantly promulgated a gloomy view of life, encapsulated in the Prayer Book's service for the dead: 'Man that is born of woman hath but a short time to live and is full of misery.' But, once a post-religious age accepts that the grave is really the end of everything, then life itself becomes infinitely more depressing. Instead, people will hopefully seek out some other form of 'optimistic lie', such as the superficial cheerfulness of *Punch* or Wells's ridiculous utopias 'infested by nude school-marms'. Miller's novel provided a welcome antidote to such trivialities since, Orwell grimly proposed, while man is not really a Swiftian Yahoo, he does sometimes resemble one and needs regularly reminding of this uncomfortable fact (X.404–5). In retrospect, Orwell regarded 1934 as the first year in which he had been able to live on his literary earnings alone (X.110). It also became the year in which Eric Blair completed his transformation into George Orwell, 'a literary man with a sociological eye and a sociological imagination'. This metamorphosis as a writer facilitated a more mature and deeper understanding of the innate human need within many (but not necessarily all) people for a spiritual direction and devotional framework to their lives. Henceforth, as D. J. Taylor explains:

> Orwell was obsessed by the problem of what might be called displaced religious sensibility. The greatest challenge facing both the state and the individual, he believed, was to recognise and put to positive use the intense human emotions that until fairly recently had been channelled into religious observance. Human beings had lost their souls, runs the argument of half a dozen of his essays, without finding anything to put in their place. When they did find something – this was a danger that became sharply apparent as the 1930s progressed – it was likely to be a form of totalitarian autocracy interested only in manipulating the past and ignoring the future.[15]

3

A Clergyman's Daughter, Keep the Aspidistra Flying and *The Road to Wigan Pier*

A Clergyman's Daughter (1935) and 'Anglican atheists'

Orwell was always dismissive of his novel, *A Clergyman's Daughter* (completed October 1934, published 11 March 1935), describing it in various letters as 'dreadful' (X.344), 'awful' (X.348), 'fragmentary' (X.349), 'very disconnected' (X.351) and 'tripe' (X.382). The only section which pleased him comprised a sub-Joycean pastiche (following his recent reading of *Ulysses* and its 'Night town' scene) of low-life dialogue among the destitute of Trafalgar Square. The novel was partly inspired by his friendship with Brenda Salkeld, who worked at St Felix's School for Girls at Southwold as the gym mistress. His letters to her reveal his often teasing attitude towards religion, prompted by her background. In late summer 1934, for example, he mischievously recommended to her Marie Corelli's *Thelma* with its potently 'licentious clergyman' (X.346–7); and in September 1934 he invoked her supplication in support of the soon to be published *Burmese Days* since he hoped that the prayers of a clergyman's daughter would receive preferential consideration in Heaven, at least in its 'Protestant quarter' (X.350).

While the novel has some major flaws – including its chaotic structuring, psychologically limited presentation of Orwell's only female protagonist and a clunking 'loss of memory' plot device to draw together disparate sections of the novel – it offers a potent exposure, in Dickensian satiric mode, of a grotesquely flawed Church of England clergyman, his repressed daughter and dispirited congregation. It is perhaps at its best when it focuses clearly upon the implications of its subtitle: 'a study of faith and the loss of faith'.[1] As with Dickens, the novel's loosely connected tragi-comic scenes embrace a deeper concern with what happens to the human spirit when it finds itself bereft of the local support mechanisms traditionally provided by a nourishing religious framework. Writing within the tradition of D. H. Lawrence's story 'Daughters of the Vicar' (1914) and Flora Macdonald Mayor's novel *The Rector's Daughter* (1924), Orwell's Dorothy Hare is the unmarried 28-year-old self-castigating daughter of a selfish father, the Reverend Charles Hare, who presides over the moribund parish of St Athelstan's, Knype Hill, Suffolk. As the younger son of a baronet's younger son who, following tradition, has gone into the Church, he represents the deadening impact of the minor aristocracy on English society. As a church minister, his introspective and alienating personality radiates the stark message that he is only their parish priest and not their friend: 'As a human being I dislike you and despise you' (III.7). Dorothy copes with her claustro-phobic life by habitually lacing her thoughts with trite biblical aphorisms, taking self-mortifying cold baths from April to November and secretly pin-pricking her arm to punish herself for negligible lapses of piety or wandering thoughts. Reduced to the level of her widowed father's unpaid skivvy-cum-secretary, mindless religious conformity deadens Dorothy's adult personality, hopes and ambitions.

Religious language in the lengthy first chapter of the novel (imitating *Ulysses* by tracing the events of a single day) conveys only farcical levels of meaning, underlining Orwell's now unremitting mockery of established religion. To the background of her idle father's 'antiphonal snoring', Dorothy's daily chores begin at five thirty in the morning because not even the 'Devil and all his angels' (III.2) can rouse Ellen, the lumpen family servant, before seven. She eschews toothpaste before Holy Communion as a gesture of fasting (the 'RCs are quite right there', Orwell sarcastically comments) and she wears only a plain gold cross, 'no [Catholic] crucifixes, please!' (III.4–5). Her father's church is cold, dreary and dilapidated. Its chancel roof is collapsing and all but one of its decommissioned bells are slowly sinking through the splintering belfry floor. This once beautiful but now decaying edifice stands as a monument to his parochial neglect since his congregation has steadily shrunk from six hundred to under two hundred parishioners. The only regular communicant at his morning service is the ancient but wealthy Mrs Mayfill, a cruel cameo lifted from a letter of September 1932 to Eleanor Jacques.

Numbed by her father's lifeless dispensing of communion, a sudden pantheistic flash of sunlight upon the churchyard's lime trees, briefly glimpsed through the open south door, revitalizes Dorothy's body and soul like a 'jewel of unimaginable splendour', reaffirming her calmness of mind, 'her love of God, her power of worship' (III.11). In similar vein, recalling Blair's and Jacintha Buddicom's childish delight in nature, one summer's day she dismounts her bicycle by the side of a meadow and breathes in the delicate fragrance of a frond of fennel. Her heart swells with unexpected joy, experiencing a delight in the very nature of things, which she half recog-nizes as a manifestation of God's love. Inspired by imagining the angels and archangels, she prays ardently, 'blissfully forgetting herself in the joy of her worship' (III.56). Such intense pastoral experiences, replacing her father's deadening ecclesiastical practices with the secular sublimity of nature itself, prepares the reader for Dorothy's spiritual rejection at the end of the novel of organized religion as merely meaningless processes and traditions.

A Clergyman's Daughter offers Orwell's first sustained exploration in fiction of the spiritual void at the heart of an increasingly industrialized and now near-Godless English society. The Blifil-Gordon sugar-beet factory dominates this East Anglian town, and its thousand employees, mainly working-class arrivals from local cities, are almost entirely 'godless' (III.12) or simply 'atheistical in a vague unreasoning way' (III.49). He also highlights the destructive sectarian tensions within the Church of England during the early twentieth century, which had created a state of semi-permanent liturgical civil war. The harvest festival-hating Reverend Hare's archaic High Anglicanism offends both the modernist and Low Church preferences of his community. His devotional tendencies seem distinctly out of place in an ecclesiastical world, which now seeks, according to Orwell, either the 'Roman fever' of 'Anglo-Catholicism pure and simple' or a vapidly liberal kind of non-denominationalism which benignly promises from the pulpit that Hell does not exist and that all 'good religions are the same'. Two thirds of his congregation have drifted away to nearby Millborough, where they can indulge in either the crudely modernist tendencies of St Edmund's (its name borrowed from the Anglican Church at Southwold) – with lines from Blake's 'Jerusalem' above the altar and wine taken at communion from liqueur glasses – or St Wedekind's, an Anglo-Catholic establishment which seems to relish being in permanent conflict with its bishop.

Predictably, the Catholics of Knype Hill are seen as a comically insidious threat. Mr Cameron, the secretary of the local Conservative Club, is a devout Roman Catholic convert and his family is rumoured to have a parrot which they are teaching to say 'Extra ecclesiam nulla salus' ('outside the Church there is no salvation', III.18–19). The rotund local Roman Catholic priest, Father McGuire – a cartoon figure who on a bicycle resembles a 'golf-ball on a tee' – is a farcically threatening presence. He has sustained a long-standing theological dispute with Dorothy's father over a burial in St Athelstan's churchyard since Knype Hill lacked a Roman Catholic cemetery. When he and Dorothy ride past one another, he simply ignores her in what Orwell describes as an un-Christian 'Cut Direct' (III.57). Orwell's publisher, following recommendations from his legal advisor, required the removal from the novel of another reference to a Roman Catholic priest, and also the revision of a description of a politician as a 'Roman Catholic Jew'.[2] The church schoolmaster, Victor Stone, an Anglo-Catholic cleric manqué (since he had not been clever enough to learn the Greek and Hebrew required for the priesthood) is represented as representative of the 'most truculent Church Times breed'. He is constantly in dispute with his own clergy, as well as all 'Modernists, Protestants, scientists, Bolshevists and atheists'

(III.63) and dreams of the 'real Catholic worship of the real Catholic Church' (III.67). Similarly, incumbents of other denominations, such as Mr Ward the Congregationalist minister, the Wesleyan Mr Foley and the elder of the local Ebenezer Chapel, are dismissed by Dorothy's father as a merely 'vulgar Dissenters' (III.57).

Orwell laces this multi-denominational clerical narrative with a selection of traditional anti-religious village caricatures. There is the poisonous Mrs Welwyn-Foster, the Rural Dean's wife, who always finds out some 'disgraceful' gossip about her diocese's clergymen and then feeds it back to the Bishop (III.27). The gloomily pessimistic Proggett is too unintelligent to hold 'any definite religious beliefs' (III.31) and instead channels his pointless piety into an obsessive concern for St Athelstan's crumbling architectural fabric. Dorothy's philandering middle-aged admirer, Mr Warburton, who both amuses and tries to seduce her (Orwell's publisher required an attempted rape scene to be removed from the printed version) supposedly epitomizes how the 'pious and immoral drift naturally together' (III.41). This phrase was added by Orwell at a late stage to justify his unlikely conjunction of these two characters in the novel. Most memorable is the odious Mrs Semprill, a voyeuristically malevolent local gossip who spreads defamation and 'purulent libel' (III.44) about her generally female victims, including Dorothy's supposed affair with Mr Warburton.

This first chapter of *A Clergyman's Daughter*, focusing on Orwell's sustained satire of moribund ecclesiastical institutions and practices, provides the most cohesive narrative element of the novel. Even so, its depiction of Anglican Church life failed to convince those who possessed first-hand knowledge of its diurnal ceremonies and customs. Christopher Hollis, the son of an Anglican bishop, wrote: 'Nor did Orwell know very clearly how Anglican parish-life is organized nor what is the degree of responsibility of a rector for the upkeep of the fabric of his church. Churchwardens and parish-councils are mysteries beyond him.'[3] Equally questionable is his dubious use at the opening of the second chapter of Dorothy's sudden and unexplained memory lapse as a crude structural device, allowing the rest of the novel to be padded out with a miscellaneous assemblage of tramping and hop-picking accounts drawn from earlier writings, diaries and private correspondence. The third chapter imitates Joyce's manipulations of disconnected dialogues in *Ulysses* but prompted the Irish playwright Sean O'Casey to remark that 'Orwell has as much chance of reaching the stature of Joyce as a tit has of reaching that of an eagle.' It sporadically springs into life through the deranged comic ramblings of the derelict Mr Tallboys, the disgraced former rector of Little Fawley-cum-Dewsbury, who perversely inverts the language of the Lord's Prayer, echoing the blasphemies of a Black Mass. He seems self-consciously to mock Orwell's own nostalgia for a lost tradition of English country parish life, with his pathetic memories of his 'red-tiled Rectory slumbering among Elizabethan yews' and his muddled delight in all forms of 'High Church, Low Church, Broad Church and No Church' (III.152) worship.[4]

Orwell tries half-heartedly to interpolate into the remaining three quarters of the novel occasional references to the first chapter's more meaningful exploration of spiritual nullity but his unsuccessful struggle to draw the novel into some form of overall structural and moral coherence (he told Brenda Salkeld that he could write 'decent passages' but could not 'put them together', X.347) remains painfully obvious. During Dorothy's brief time as a hop-picker, the ringing of distant church bells dimly evokes nostalgic recollections of how prayer had once been the source and very 'centre of her life' (III.137). But her total loss of faith amidst gruelling contexts of poverty, hunger, cold, prostitution, casual brutality and despair becomes emotionally diminished in the novel's final chapter. Defeated, she returns to her father's rectory, sadly admitting to Mr Warburton in a parody of Christian confession that she has entirely lost her religious convictions: 'my faith is gone'. Dorothy seems to echo Orwell's personal concerns over the decline of religion in Western European society as she listlessly remarks that the world seems both different and empty when an individual is devoid of personal spirituality (III.274–5). Warburton's sharp reply has the ring of authorial self-castigation when he advises that Dorothy seems to be making the worst of everything by sticking to the 'Christian scheme of things' but denying the possibility of an afterlife. Given Orwell's abiding love of the ceremonies and architecture of the Church of England – he was to be married one year later according to Anglican rites – he seems to have become a member, in Warburton's castigating words, of a new and insidious sect: 'the Anglican Atheists' who regard Christianity as an 'incurable disease' (III.277–8).

The novel's concluding chapter peters out into an unsatisfactory return for Dorothy to her father's depressing rectory, with Warburton, now in full Orwellian polemical mode, spouting nasty anti-Christian sentiments, describing the 'verminous Christian saints' as the 'biggest hedonists of all' (III.285). But all Dorothy can now feel is a deadly emptiness and she concludes that although beliefs and theological thoughts may change and faith may vanish, a personal need for faith remains undiminished. Rejecting all denominational creeds, Dorothy resorts to a child-like logic in justifying to herself the existence of a Divine Being. She argues that if one exists as a conscious being, then the God responsible must also be a conscious entity since the 'greater' cannot be made from the 'less'. She grimly concludes: 'He created you, and He will kill you, for His own purpose. But that purpose is inscrutable.' Two key religious perceptions finally crystallize in her mind: faith can never be understood but, equally, there is no realistic substitute for personal faith. Orwell endows her fictional character with a rejection of his own youthful fancies, denying the sufficiency of a 'pagan acceptance of life' or, as once enjoyed with Jacintha Buddicom, 'pantheistic cheer-up stuff' and Wellsian 'glittering Utopias' (III.292–3). Such an unsatisfactory conclusion to *A Clergyman's Daughter* confirms the novel's major weakness in that it is structured around a loosely connected series of reflections on Orwell's own disparate experiences as a tramp, hop-picker and teacher, as well as his still far from resolved personal questions and doubts about religion, belief and faith. Bernard Crick considered it a 'curate's egg' (good in parts) and D. J. Taylor notes: 'it is one of those books in which a writer's private demons contend with a mass of reportage masquerading as background'.[5] Indeed, there are probably the seeds of several interesting but different novels in *A Clergyman's Daughter*, which, while not validating its chaotic structure, confirms its fascination for readers who come to it primarily for one or more of its diverse concerns rather than its fragmented plot and narrative.

Keep the Aspidistra Flying (1936)

Aware of the weaknesses of *A Clergyman's Daughter*, Orwell assured Brenda Salkeld in February 1935 that he wanted his next novel *Keep the Aspidistra Flying* to be a genuine 'work of art' (X.375). It also came to express his now engrained disillusion with English society, arguing that it was impossible to 'achieve spiritual peace by mere defiance and hatred of the world'.[6] In an earlier letter to Brenda, written in September 1934, he had explained in jarringly Biblical terms how he was so disillusioned with contemporary life that he felt like a Jeremiah or Ezra, calling down heavenly curses on a fallen world: 'Woe upon thee, O Israel, for thy adulteries with the Egyptians' (X.349). A pervading sense of alienation from conventional middle-class society, which Orwell felt had drifted away from any meaningful concepts of the Divine, continued to preoccupy him throughout the drafting of his new novel. This jaundiced perspective was encapsulated in his gloomy review of *The Proceeding of the Society* by Katharine Williams (*New English Weekly*, 1 August 1935). He compared the modern cults of disillusionment in a world in which only self-fulfilment seemed to matter with the ancient self-mortification of Christians as a traditional route to 'sanctity'. Baudelaire's generation might have frequented brothels, he proposed, but they still lamented their lost innocence. But, nowadays, an aged man wheeled along Bournemouth seafront in his bath chair was haunted by mingling feelings of 'desolation and relief' (X.391) over adulteries he had failed to commit. This debilitating sense of moral disillusionment was accentuated by Orwell's pessimism over the escalating threat of militant Spanish and German fascism to Western European society. He observed in October 1935 to his London flatmate, the writer and later Catholic convert Rayner Heppenstall, that by 1936 he expected they might all have been 'blown sky-high' (X.399), noting how a few bombs dropped over the Thames near Greenwich could wreak havoc among London's shipping. This apocalyptic idea was echoed in *The Road to Wigan Pier* (completed mid-December 1936) when Orwell remarks that Britain may well soon be experiencing 'God knows what horrors' (V.158).

The epigraph of *Keep the Aspidistra Flying*, taken from St Paul's *First Epistle to the Corinthians* (verse 13), reflects the crass substitution within modern society of Mammon for one of the three central theological Christian virtues. Indulging in what had already become for him (and would long remain in his writings) a favoured game of subverting sacred texts, Orwell replaces the word 'charity', the greatest of the three Christian virtues which link humanity directly to God Himself, with a hard-edged adoration of money:

> Though I speak with the tongues of men and of angels, and have not money ... though I have all faith, so that I could remove mountains, and have not money, I am nothing ... Money suffereth long, and is kind; money envieth not, money vaunteth not itself ... And now abideth faith, hope, money, these three, but the greatest of these is money. (IV.vii)

This tone of biblical mockery permeates the entire first half of the novel. Orwell accumulates numerous incidental religious details and phrasings to provide a nihilistic confirmation of the loss of a communal spiritual sense within modern society. The insistent thought that civilization is 'dying' (IV.21) pervades the mind of the novel's down-at-heel philosopher-poet, Gordon Comstock, culminating in a despairing realization of his own entrapment within a world devoid of hope or spiritual meaning. He feels that the worship of money has been raised into a kind of religion, perhaps now the only 'really *felt* religion' still accessible to humankind: 'Money is what God used to be' and the only distinction drawn between 'good' and 'evil' is that of success or failure. Prefiguring the tragi-comic Seven Commandments of *Animal Farm*, the Decalogue has been reduced in Comstock's world to just two axioms: 'Thou shalt make money' for select employers, and 'Thou shalt not lose thy job' (IV.46) for downtrodden employees. Similarly, familiar biblical quotations lapse into the nightmare interior monologues of oppressed workers: 'Circumcise ye your foreskins, saith the Lord. Suck the blacking off the boss's boots' (IV.70). Comstock concludes as he ponders the novel's dystopian trinity of faith, hope and money that, without initially having the third, only saints could hope to access the first two virtues.

The first chapter opens in the gloom of a London bookshop where the determinedly poverty-stricken Comstock works as a part-time assistant because this arrangement allows time for his generally non-productive writing. He reflects Orwell's self-mocking picture of his own impractical idealism in *The Road to Wigan Pier* when he seemed to regard failure as the only true mark of virtue. The aspiring author regards any kind of self-advancement or ability to earn a few hundred pounds a year as spiritually demeaning. The bookshop is run by a Scotsman called McKechnie, a member of some kind of 'Nonconformist sect' (IV.61), and was based upon Orwell's experience as an assistant in the Booklovers' Corner Bookshop, Hampstead, owned by Francis and Myfanwy Westrope, Esperanto enthusiasts and friends of his aunt Nellie Limouzin.[7] Orwell lived above the shop in Warwick Mansions, Pond Street, and John Kimche, another young writer who shared the job with him, recalled that his casual conversation often tended to degenerate into bitter diatribes against Roman Catholicism.[8]

The narrative begins on a dismal, windy 30 November, specifically denoted as St Andrew's day (IV.2), recalling Orwell's previously published poem on 'St Andrew's Day' (*The Adelphi*, November 1935) and denouncing the 'money god' which now dominates the drab lower-middle-class decencies of urban life (IV.23). These depressing verses are quoted in full later in the novel, celebrating 'The lord of all, the money-god' (IV.168). Its sentiments constantly infect Comstock's mind and resonate because the poem was originally composed when Orwell, like Comstock, still harboured frustrated ambitions of becoming an acclaimed poet. But Comstock remains deluded enough to convince himself that only a lack of money is preventing him from writing a masterpiece. He clings to this illusion almost like a religious 'article of faith' (IV.8), a phrase again illustrating Orwell's insistent linking in his writings of self-delusion with content-devoid religious platitudes.

Sustaining this insistent jibing at religious matters, a passing customer in the bookshop has for Comstock the look of a dour Welsh dissenting Nonconformist. He imagines him as a denizen of the 'local Purity league' up in town 'on the razzle' (IV.5–6), sleazily looking for a copy of Lawrence's *Women in Love*. The shop's religious section lumps indiscriminately together 'all sects and all creeds', emphasizing the impotent redundancy of all religious denominations in a fallen secular age. Orwell indulges in mild ecumenical mockery in his range of fictional and real titles. These include *The World Beyond* by the author of *Spiritual Hands Have Touched Me* (echoing Luke 24.39), imitating the Biblical Acts and reporting how the good news about Jesus Christ had spread. Dean Frederick Farrar's renowned *Life of Christ* (1874) is also mentioned. Farrar was the author of the pious children's book, *Eric, or Little by Little* (1858) – from which Blair's own disliked first name had been derived – tracing the decline of an Indian civil servant's son who is sent to boarding school in England and eventually sinks into moral turpitude. *Jesus the First Rotarian* mocks Robert and Helen Lynd's pioneering sociological studies, *Middletown: A Study in Modern American Culture* (1929) and *Middletown in Transition* (1937), describing Muncie, Indiana, where multi-denominational churches thrived and Jesus was regarded almost as the 'first Rotarian'. Father 'Hilaire Chestnut's' most recent volume of 'RC propaganda' conflates Orwell's derision of Hilaire Belloc and G. K. Chesterton, echoing G. B. Shaw's mockery in the *New Age* magazine (1908) of the 'Chesterbelloc', a mythical creature with the hind legs of Chesterton and the front legs of Belloc endlessly waging war against the evils of modern society.[9] Comstock wearily concludes of the shop's dog-eared and worthless stock that religious books always sell, provided they are 'soppy enough' (IV.7).

Comstock's rich and supportively indulgent patron, P. W. H. Ravelston (based on Orwell's baronet friend and later literary executor Sir Richard Rees) edits the journal *Antichrist*. This ludicrously titled middlebrow monthly will soon print one of Comstock's poems about a dying prostitute, prompting him to promise sarcastically another about an aspidistra – the titular symbol of his urban entrapment. Ravelston's journal supposedly adopts vaguely socialist perspectives, implying that its allegiances had shifted from conventional religious nonconformity to radical Marxism, only for its editor to find himself ensnared by a 'gang of *vers libre* poets' (IV.88). Another influential literary journal, the *Primrose Quarterly*, to which Comstock has sent a sample of his hopeless versifications, is derided as one favoured by 'fashionable Nancy Boy' poets and the 'professional Roman Catholic' (IV.35). Orwell's habitual predilection for Catholic bashing surfaces again in Comstock's discussions with Ravelston over three possible alternatives for the future: socialism, suicide and the Catholic Church, the last offering a tempting option to the so-called English intelligentsia. They are typified by T. S. Eliot whom Orwell had also mocked in a letter of 7 March 1935 to Brenda Salkeld in relation to an Anglo-Catholic perspective on problems with servants. Eliot, according to Orwell, reminded him of a 'cracked church-bell' in sanctimoniously proposing to employ several servants so that each could do less work but still benefit from the cultured and devotional 'atmosphere' of the home in which they were employed (X.383).

Comstock's declining family background seems redolent of Orwell's distaste for his own bourgeois English ancestry and childhood amidst the dour 'middle-middle' classes (IV.39) of Henley-on-Thames, represented as Crickham-on-Thames in the novel. His ruthlessly materialistic grandfather, Samuel Ezekiel Comstock, encapsulates the humbug of God-driven Victorian plutocrats. The piously trite phrase, 'He sleeps in the arms of Jesus', carved on his vast funereal monolith in Kensal Green Cemetery provokes only 'blasphemous comments' (IV.40) from all those socially decaying descendants who had suffered the misfortune of knowing him. Gordon recalls his own schooldays, echoing Blair's at Eton, when he was 'still a believer'. He had deliberately read any books his headmaster had denounced from the pulpit and subversively fostered 'unorthodox opinions about the C of E' (IV.44–5). By the age of sixteen – corresponding to the maturing of Blair's own adolescent agnosticism at Eton – he had become determined to be '*against* the money-god and all his swinish priesthood' (IV.48).

Yet, despite the novel's dismissal of religious institutions and any meaningful spirituality in society, marriage – a Christian Sacrament – ultimately becomes both a defining social norm and a source of potential salvation for Comstock. After impregnating his loyal girlfriend Rosemary, he is faced with giving up his self-imposed impecunious lifestyle to earn a living at an advertising agency since he had previously shown an aptitude for such trivial (at least to an aspiring poet) but well remunerated work. He ponders the traditional Anglican marriage rites which render their proposed union 'indissoluble, for better for worse, for richer for poorer, till death do you part' and he half-heartedly tries to mock the 'old Christian ideal' by defining it as 'marriage tempered by adultery' (IV.115). But although Comstock has always resolutely opposed the supposedly outmoded institution of marriage, when he and Rosemary consider an abortion he suddenly feels as though they are 'joined together' and he realizes that what they are contemplating is no less than a 'blasphemy' (IV.153). Acknowledging that he must again take up advertising copywriting for the good of his unborn child, Comstock's distaste for the crudely mercenary world of merchandising is defined by the painful collision between his secular leanings and his suspicions of Divine intervention, resulting in his despairing expostulation: 'To be mixed up in *that*! ... God, God, God!' (IV.263).

Likewise, Comstock's final acceptance of his impending marriage and paternal duties, described by Christopher Hollis as 'the beginning of the story of Orwell's revolt against revolt', is expressed through an insistent blending of secular and divine concepts.[10] He recalls the axiom that the modern world is populated only by 'saints and scoundrels'. But since he cannot become a saint, he may as well be an outright scoundrel (IV.267) along with everyone else. Ordinary middle-class life is symbolized by the aspidistra that Comstock now views in mock-biblical style as 'the tree of life' (IV.268). But, finally defeated into the security of marital salvation, the novel closes with a quasi-religious iconographical image. Comstock kneels in a supplicant, prayer-like posture, with his ear pressed against Rosemary's belly listening for the beating of his child's heart – even though, as a secular doubter, he can still only hear the blood throbbing in his own ear (IV.277). Comstock ultimately becomes a socially and spiritually redeemed precursor to Winston Smith in *Nineteen Eighty-Four*. While Comstock lives in poverty and works in advertising to persuade and mislead the public, Winston lives in squalor and dupes the public through his rewriting of history for the Ministry of Truth. Comstock's world is dominated by the 'money-god' while Winston's is ruled by the 'power-god'. Similarly, Mrs Wisbeach spies on Comstock and Winston is spied on by the Parsons children and the Thought Police. The key difference between salvation and damnation for each of them seems to lie in their respective women. While Julia is promiscuous and actively seeks to subvert the sexual norms of their Ingsoc society, Rosemary is sexually chaste and seeks only conventional marriage. In this respect, Orwell seems to offer a stark and disturbing contrast: Comstock is ultimately saved by Rosemary while Winston is finally damned by Julia.[11]

The Road to Wigan Pier (1937)

On 31 January 1936, Orwell travelled via Coventry and the Potteries to Manchester, staying in a cheap lodging house. He moved on to Wigan where he lived above a filthy tripe shop, and also went down Bryn Hall coal mine. He then visited Liverpool, Sheffield and Barnsley and attended meetings held by the Communist Party and Oswald Mosley. He stayed with his sister Marjorie at Headingley, Leeds, and visited the Brontë Parsonage at Haworth. These journeys produced *The Road to Wigan Pier*, published on 8 March 1937 by Gollancz's Left Book Club and completed while Orwell stayed at a recently rented cottage in Wallington, Hertfordshire.[12] It comprised two distinct elements, as Gordon Bowker notes: 'a physical journey and a parallel journey of the soul'. The first offered documentary reportage on the dire living and employment conditions of the working class in the north of England, a locale, Richard Hoggart remarked, which was 'stranger to Orwell than Burma'.[13] The second blended autobiographical anecdotes with a highly subjective essay on the English class system and the limitations of elitist left-wing thinkers and middle-class Socialism.

The first part of the published version of *Wigan Pier* communicates little interest in religious affairs or related church activities, even though Orwell's extensive surviving notes and a 'Wigan Pier Diary' kept while he was travelling around the region reveal that he had assembled a substantial amount of factual research about such matters. Christopher Hitchens observed that his 'notebooks and research … would not have disgraced Friedrich Engels'.[14] As a polemical journalist, Orwell deliberately omits from *Wigan Pier* any elements which might lighten the tone of his unremittingly dark sketches of English working-class life. The respectable working-class are generally ignored and he excludes any descriptions of regular church worship and the importance to various denominational communities of local church schools and charities. He also makes no mention of the well-attended football and rugby matches which provided the highlight of many working men's weekends, and the strong sense of community and mutual support generated, especially by women, within the tightly packed streets of urban terraced houses. In the first part of *Wigan Pier*, such central elements of ordinary working-class northern life remain strategically absent. Instead, he concentrates on miners (specifically, unemployed ones), hapless individuals on Public Assistance and the unemployable.

Orwell does occasionally insert in this first part a scattering of trivialized religious references but, predictably, only for subversive or satiric purposes. One of the pathetic lodgers above the fetid tripe shop where Orwell stays, a garrulous unemployed Scottish miner called Reilly, occasionally babbles on about the 'conflict between religion and science' (V.6) but no-one else seems to have anything meaningful to say about spiritual matters. Even a northern Sabbath stands as a delusionary moment since all the mines seem peaceful on Sundays while for six days of the week their roaring machinery and air polluted with coal dust creates a terrifying 'picture of hell' (V.18). He castigates the Pope in distant Rome for his limp denunciations of Bolshevism and mocks the Eton-educated Rev. William R. Inge, a Cambridge Professor of Divinity and Dean of St Paul's, for his book *England* (1926) which crassly accused miners of gluttony for eating their main meal of the day as soon as they returned home after exhausting shifts. Orwell derides the idea of the worst kind of slum landlord as being a wicked fat individual, 'preferably a bishop' (V.52), and admits that the real culprits are usually poverty-stricken individuals who simply cannot afford repairs to their dilapidated properties. He also proposes that bishops, along with politicians and philanthropists, talk 'piously about "slum clearance"' (V.59) but do little or nothing to facilitate it. In this respect, Orwell's account is factually incorrect since in several major northern cities, including Liverpool and Manchester, such schemes were already well in hand by the mid-1930s with construction trades at the forefront of post-recession recovery. Surveying the conditions of the northern poor, he understandably proposes that dietary changes are often more important to ordinary people than shifts in dynasties or 'even of religion' (V.84) and, in comic mode, that black bread, 'Popery and wooden shoes' (V.92) have long been traditionally associated with Lancashire life. These superficial observations are just about all Orwell has to say about religion and local communities in the first part of *Wigan Pier*.

In sharp contrast, his carefully typed-up notes about specific locations contained several detailed sections on religious matters (X.538–84), even though he eventually chose to omit all of this information from the published version.[15] He writes about Wigan, for example, that no exact figures about its religious practices were available. Instead, he estimates that there were about forty churches and chapels of all denominations served by some sixty clergy, suggesting that there was a church for every 2,000 or 2,500 of the inhabitants. But he then notes that, even allowing for the Catholic churches holding several Masses each Sunday, it seemed likely that fewer than half of the total population of Wigan were regularly observant worshippers. He recorded (but without citing sources) that the Anglicans had about twelve churches served by twenty-two clergymen and the Catholics about six churches with seventeen priests. Nonconformity seemed uncommon in the region and the largest community was the 'Catholics with the Anglicans a fairly good second'. This was predictable, he thought, since Irish names proliferated and many of Wigan's citizens were of at least second-generation Irish descent since they spoke with strong Lancashire accents (X.547). Similarly, for Barnsley Orwell records its two Anglican parish churches of St Mary and St George, as well as six other churches and three mission churches. He then lists the town's other religious denominations, in each case citing their exact location by road or street, including Roman Catholic, Congregational, Baptist, Methodist, Society of Friends, Catholic Apostolic, Plymouth Brethren, Salvation Army, New Church

(Swedenborgian) and Christadelphian. He concludes his Barnsley notes by observing that the Roman Catholic community has recently completed a 'new church or chapel' – a minor reflection of Orwell's ignorance since Catholic churches in England are never referred to as 'chapels' (although they are in Ireland). More accurately, he also notes that religion tended to 'retain its hold only on old or middle-aged' citizens, even though Sunday schools for the children seemed popular. He concludes by recording that a few cinemas do occasionally open on Sundays but 'only in aid of charities' (X.558). Pointedly, all of this detailed information is excluded from the final version of *The Road to Wigan Pier*.

Orwell's 'Wigan Pier Diary' records his informative meeting in Liverpool with an unemployed former seaman and writer, George Garrett, who contributed to *The Adelphi* under the pseudonym 'Matt Lowe' (*matelot*). Orwell enjoyed his company, describing him as 'Liverpool-Irish, brought up a Catholic' (X.439) but now a committed Communist. This diary posits Orwell's subversive suspicion that Liverpool was 'practically governed' by the Roman Catholics, noting the Church's extensive involvements in housing issues. Characteristically (but apparently without statistical or other factual evidence), he adopts an entirely unsympathetic view, bizarrely suggesting that the church hierarchy preferred to keep its downtrodden believers in privately owned but 'insanitary' cottages rather than rehousing them in 'excellently appointed' Corporation flats built through 'Socialist legislation' (X. 440). Orwell was clearly unaware (or perhaps not informed by Garrett) of Liverpool Corporation's commitment during the 1930s – supported by the Catholic Church and its local parish priests – to exactly this kind of urban development. Following the 1930 and 1935 Housing Acts, which granted substantial financial incentives to local councils to rehouse slum dwellers, extensive council building projects were undertaken in Liverpool, including the huge multi-storey corporation developments of St Andrew's Gardens (completed 1935), Myrtle Gardens (1937), Caryl Gardens (1937), Warwick Gardens (1938) and Gerard Gardens (1939), as well as numerous other low-rise council developments in the suburbs, most notably during the late 1920s the Norris Green Estate.[16] Many of the new residents of these corporation developments were from Liverpool's Irish community and their children attended the local primary and secondary Catholic schools. But the inclusion of such information in *The Road to Wigan Pier* would have undermined Orwell's polemical antipathy towards the Catholic hierarchy.

It should also be reaffirmed here that Orwell tended to identify this Catholic hierarchy with an elite London metropolitan minority of writers and clerics rather than with provincial parish priests, bishops or other Catholic organizations. Indeed, as far as the surviving documentary evidence shows, Orwell never personally engaged in meaningful discussions with either any practising Catholics or members of religious orders during his time in Lancashire. Nor did other denominations fare any better in *The*

Road to Wigan Pier. At Sheffield, his diary records how he went to a lecture at a local Methodist hall to listen to the 'incredibly silly and disconnected ramblings' (X.444) of a clergyman. Again, his tone is entirely dismissive since he speculates that the audience was only there to sit for a few hours in a warm environment. In conclusion, when Orwell's working notes and 'Wigan Pier Diary' are held alongside the final published version of this work it is clear that he was determined to excise from the first part of his narrative the often significant presence of institutional church activities in the lives of the working classes and the poor.

The second part of *Wigan Pier* does little to address this anomaly and, instead, indulges in yet more of Orwell's anti-clerical polemics. If the first part demonstrated the potency of Orwell as a master of (selective) socialist documentary reportage, the second illustrates his tendency in argumentative prose towards partisan ranting, casual clichés and unsubstantiated generalizations. He links together the idealistic middle-class socialist and the 'sentimental democratic Catholic of the type of Chesterton' who supposedly naïvely insist that the dirtiness and grime of the poor is healthy and that cleanliness is only a 'fad' or a 'luxury' (V.121). He then dismisses an American Nonconformist missionary from the Mid-West whom he had met in Burma as a 'complete ass' and 'teetotal cock-virgin' (V.136). This section of part two concludes by ludicrously claiming that even a 'bishop could be at home among tramps', provided he wore appropriately tatty clothing (V.144). Such strained attempts at angry denunciation might have been understandable in Orwell's private correspondence, notebooks or pub chatter. But his transposing of these half-baked notions to follow immediately on from his landmark documentary account of post-Great Depression hardships in the north of England confirms his continuing inability to structure and edit cogently his own work and his sometimes determinedly slapdash approach to polemical journalism.

Victor Gollancz was nervous over publishing certain elements in the second part of *Wigan Pier* and he should have been prepared to exert greater editorial control over Orwell. At first he wished to omit entirely this second part but, as a compromise, the Left Book Club edition (but not the full-price hardback edition) was prefaced by a defensive publisher's statement, described by Gordon Bowker as 'self-righteous' and 'hand-washing'.[17] While Gollancz praises the first part's 'burning indignation against poverty and oppression', he tries to suggest that Orwell is writing in the second part primarily as a 'devil's advocate' and, therefore, is 'exaggerating violently'. He admits that some of the most contentious sections are intended to be 'highly provocative' not only in 'general argument, but also in detail after detail'. On more persuasive ground, Gollancz claims that Orwell only writes in this way so as to expose how someone brought up in his privileged middle-class background is likely to think of the poor and the working classes. But even Gollancz has to admit that Orwell denoting 'Socialists as a whole', with only a few exceptions, as 'a stupid, offensive and insincere lot' bears little resemblance to the reality of 1930s politics. He picks out as unjustifiable Orwell's nasty 'sneers' against anyone supporting feminism, pacifism, vegetarianism or advocating birth control as 'cranks' (V.217–20) since these kinds of people represented for Orwell everything he despised about the left-wing intelligentsia. He also readily admits that 'Mr Orwell does not once define what he *means* by Socialism; nor does he explain *how* the oppressors oppress, nor even what he understands by the words "liberty" and "justice"' (V.224). In the Left Book Club edition of *Wigan Pier* Orwell blusters and rants while Gollancz fumbles and fudges over his favoured author's difficulties in creating a cogent and sustainable structuring for his literary journalism.

Significantly, Gollancz does not comment at all on Orwell's treatment of established religions in *Wigan Pier*, perhaps because, as he notes, he writes as a Jew who had passed the years of his 'early boyhood in a fairly close Jewish community' (V.219), isolated from the spiritual aspects of a still predominantly Christian English society. But a closer analysis of the treatment of such subjects in the second part of *Wigan Pier* is certainly merited. Orwell begins with the broadest of generalizations by claiming that, as with Christianity, Socialism's worst form of publicity was its own adherents. He goes on to caricature two typical types of current Socialists: a 'youthful snob-Bolshevik' who within five years will marry a wealthy woman and convert to Roman Catholicism; or a 'prim little man with a white-collar job' (V.161) from a Nonconformist background. Such trite writing should have prompted an editor's red pen and throughout the second part of *Wigan Pier* a firmer guiding hand from Gollancz could well have saved Orwell from this kind of intellectually lazy attempt at polemical writing.

Predictably, Orwell's commentary on Roman Catholics at this point in *Wigan Pier* is subversively partisan in its perspectives. He claims that an important analogue between Communism and Catholicism lies in his view that only the so-called educated classes can be regarded as entirely orthodox. He briefly acknowledges the existence of 'real Catholics' but never bothers to clarify or expand upon what he means by this pointed phrase. His only other comment on such individuals comes when he asserts that both working-class Socialists and Catholics are always 'weak on doctrine' and rarely speak without uttering a 'heresy' (V.206). But what, exactly, does this statement mean? He presses on to condemn the self-consciousness and fanatical orthodoxy of such prominent Catholic converts as the Jesuit Monsignor Ronald Knox and the Catholic apologist Arnold Lunn, the founder of the eponymous Travel Agency. Their writings, Orwell claims, are defined absolutely by the simple fact that 'they *are* Roman Catholics'. From this act of authorial identity, Orwell proposes, both writers ooze self-commendation and fashion from it the 'entire stock-in-trade of the Catholic literary man'. Whether Knox's writings are riddled with self-praise may remain a matter for personal judgement but the fact that a Jesuit priest's writings are firmly rooted in his Catholicism hardly seems unexpected. In more comic vein, Orwell claims that G. K. Chesterton viewed tea-drinking as 'pagan', beer-drinking as 'Christian' and coffee as the 'puritan's opium'. As Orwell notes, such a perspective is unfortunate in that Catholics are often members of the Temperance movement and Irish Catholics are the world's most notable 'tea-boozers'. However, this argument remains problematic – despite its frequent citation in studies of Orwell's writings – since no direct source seems traceable for such a quotation from Chesterton.[18]

In the second part of *Wigan Pier* Orwell at least credits working-class Catholics with being able to appreciate the comic triviality of Chesterton's supposed statement. If an 'Irish dock-labourer' in slumland Liverpool is told that his cup of tea is 'pagan', Orwell proposes, he would certainly respond by calling you a 'fool'. He also approves of how in many working-class Catholic homes in Lancashire it is common to find a crucifix on the wall and a copy of the *Daily Worker* on the dining table (V.165–6). However, he then makes the unsubstantiated statement that ordinary northern Catholics did not spend much time brooding on their faith and were not especially conscious of being much different from their 'non-Catholic neighbours'. The close conjunction of this statement with Orwell's reference to the Catholic Irish of Liverpool is unfortunate since it reveals his lack of first-hand knowledge of religious sectarianism in Northern England. During the mid-nineteenth century the Potato Famine had occasioned a huge influx of poor Irish immigrants into Liverpool and other Lancashire towns, resulting in serious hostilities between Catholic and Protestant communities for the next eighty or so years. Entire rows of streets around the docks at the north of the city of Liverpool were largely Catholic with Great Homer Street marking the divide from the Protestant areas in the south of the city and the Everton district. These tensions had culminated in the notorious street riots of June 1909 in the Scotland Road area. They were triggered when a proposed march from a local Catholic Church was opposed by members of the Protestant community, resulting in widespread violence and Liverpool being dubbed in a later official enquiry as the 'Belfast of England'. It was only the post-war clearance of slumland and war-damaged properties which finally broke up these tightly knit communities, thereby reducing the opportunities for sectarian clashes.[19]

It remains problematic that neither part of *Wigan Pier* provides any substantial first-hand observation or informed analysis concerning the majority of Lancashire's Roman Catholics, who at this period sometimes comprised twenty-five per cent or more of the workforce in manual and lower-middle-class occupations. If Orwell had paid the same level of attention to, say, a local community of Irish immigrant Catholics in Liverpool as he did to unemployed miners in Wigan and Barnsley then his commentary in this second part of *Wigan Pier* could have been rendered much more meaningful and accurate. Although he spent only a few days in the company of miners, he diligently researched additional newspaper and statistical information on their pay, conditions, diet and physical health. So thorough was this research that it led to Special Branch keeping him under surveillance from 1936 until 1948.[20] By hinting that he was at least aware of the existence of 'real Catholics' in the north-west of England, but then not bothering to familiarize himself with their living conditions and personal views, Orwell's *Wigan Pier* indulges in biased and sometimes downright inaccurate polemic masquerading as informed political thought.

Occasionally, Orwell's leaps of illogicality seem barely credible. He cites the *Intelligentsia of Great Britain* (1935) by Dmitry P. Mirsky as a 'viciously malignant book'. Its author was an aristocratic White Russian émigré to London who had converted to Communism and returned to Russia. He then denounced from a hardline Marxist perspective what he viewed as the shortcomings of the British bourgeois intelligentsia who had previously welcomed and supported him. But Orwell seems to mention this book primarily as a means of setting up yet another bout of Roman Catholic baiting. He claims that it illustrates the 'queer resemblance' between the Roman Catholicism of converts and Communism, suggesting that the likeliest place to discover another such evil-spirited book is among the 'popular Roman Catholic apologists'. In both Mirsky's work and that of the Catholic apologists, Orwell argues, it is possible to find comparable levels of antisocial venom and the same indulgence in moral dishonesty, although he admits that Catholics do not usually show the same level of 'bad manners' as Mirsky. Such a qualification merely implies that Catholics are even more devious and underhand in their literary tactics. He then offers a semi-censored statement which would have baffled most of his ordinary readers but, nevertheless, implied guilt through undefined association: 'Queer that Comrade Mirsky's spiritual brother should be Father —— ——!' The identity of this priest has never been conclusively established, although Mirsky and Ronald Knox moved in similar London circles, both being warmly acknowledged, for example, in *Translations Ancient and Modern* (1925) by the Catholic convert Maurice Baring. Mirksy also knew personally other Catholic writers despised by Orwell, including Chesterton and Belloc. This shameful literary technique seems little different from Orwell claiming that a mysterious 'Father —— ——', who can be neither identified nor defended but anonymously represents all intellectual Catholics, is the kindred spirit of some disreputable, threatening or criminal figure. Orwell concludes this crude anti-Catholic diatribe by arguing that to an outsider Communists and Catholics seem very much alike, even though they certainly preach difference messages and 'each would gladly boil the other in oil if circumstances permitted' (V.168–9), again implying that both are always nasty, bigoted and vicious. This passage of *Wigan Pier* illustrates the worst aspects of Orwell's not unfamiliar tendency in his writings towards hectoring and factually hazy polemic in which documentary truth and factual accuracy become distinctly secondary to the angry, sneering rhetorical impact of his denunciations.

In contrast, Orwell's concerns in *Wigan Pier* over the rise of English Fascism initially seem more cogently presented. He denounces the violent fanaticism of Oswald Mosley and his followers as little more than a joke to most English observers. Similarly, his 'Wigan Pier Diary' roundly dismisses Mosley's acclaimed public-speaking skills as offering only the familiar 'claptrap' about Empire free trade, Jews, foreigners and working conditions. He mocks how the Blackshirts blame most of England's ills on shadowy international Jewish conspiracies which supposedly finance both the Soviets and the British Labour Party (X.456). Although Orwell's first-hand exposure to Mosley was brief, his extremist perspectives played a pivotal role in clarifying Orwell's fears over both the rising tide of Jewish persecution and the incipient dangers of Western-European Fascism. Such issues were clearly on his mind when he wrote a review for the *New English Weekly* (12 November 1936) of the novel *The Calf of Papers* about German society during the post-war inflation of the 1920s. He criticizes its Jewish author, the US-based Scholem Asch, for his overly formulaic approach towards German society. In Orwell's opinion, the novel included too few Jewish families to reflect the beginnings of anti-Semitism. Instead, Orwell proposed that the best book to read to gain a clearer understanding of the roots of anti-Semitism was the 'Old Testamemt' (X.516).

The political vision of *Wigan Pier* then seems to lose both its focus and momentum when, instead of offering a clear-cut condemnation of all forms of Fascism, Orwell seeks to highlight what he views as the insidious dangers of a far less clearly defined Fascist way of thinking which, he argues, seeks to do whatever seems the opposite of the 'mythical' (V.197) socialist viewpoint. Yet again, it seems as though this convoluted reasoning is adopted primarily as a means to facilitate a standard Orwellian anti-Catholic polemic. He claims that a similar thought process may also be identified in the writings of such Catholic converts as D. B. Wyndham Lewis, the South African poet Roy Campbell, and, in a sweeping gener-alization, many 'su-superior conservative highbrows' such as T. S. Eliot and his countless admirers and the majority of 'Roman Catholic writers' (V.198). Claiming as proof for his suspicion of the latent Fascism of both Catholicism and High Church Anglicanism, Orwell cites the supposed howls of glee issuing from both Anglican and Catholic pulpits over the rise of Fascism in Spain, referring his readers (but without quotation) to articles and editorials in the 17 August 1936 issue of that perennial bane of liberal opinion, the *Daily Mail* (V.198).

During the 1930s, Orwell clearly felt that Catholicism and High Church Anglicanism had grown too remote from the daily lives of their ordinary worshippers. Many working-class Catholics and Anglicans would have agreed with this perspective, especially when they viewed the luxury of their bishops' private residences and the construction of hugely expensive cathedrals such as Liverpool's vast Anglican cathedral (begun in 1904) which took over seventy years to complete. Similarly, the city's Catholic cathedral was begun in 1853 to grandiose classical designs by Edward Pugin, radically revised during the 1930s by Giles Gilbert Scott and only completed to a third modernist design in 1967. Both of these edifices – each in different ways magnificently impractical, expensive to maintain and a severe drain for decades on parish budgets – were built not only upon the burgeoning profits of the Port of Liverpool but also, more reprehensibly in the eyes of many of the city's working-class citizens, through countless small donations and levies from the local parishes. But to avoid falling into the mode of Orwell's own one-sided reportage, the crucial social role should also be noted – especially among the working classes and the poor – of hardworking clerics and parish community groups, along with the enlightened educational work of religious orders such as the Irish Christian Brothers and the Jesuits, and the medical care given by orders of dedicated nuns to the sick and elderly. Orwell shows no interest in (or knowledge of) such activities in his writings and, instead, determinedly casts traditional institutional religions as either the enemy of, or an indifferent opposition to, humanitarianism and democratic socialism. But such a crudely polemical stance, as evidenced by the second part of *Wigan Pier*, tends to disrupt the logic, structuring and political impact of his writings by deflecting attention away from the potency of his denunciations of all forms of Fascism and totalitarianism into his parochial, sneering dislike of Catholicism and High Church Anglicanism and his idiosyncratic suspicions over what he viewed as the flaws of bourgeois middle-class socialism.

4

Homage to Catalonia, Coming Up For Air and the Outbreak of War

Homage to Catalonia (1938)

During 1936 Orwell continued to view England's established churches as out of touch with the majority of their communicants and a generally pernicious influence on public life. Such hostility, however, did not impede his marriage to Eileen O'Shaughnessy on 9 June 1936 in a traditional church ceremony. Her family's former vicar, John Woods, who had christened her and prepared her for confirmation in South Shields, came to conduct the service at St Mary's Church in the Hertfordshire village of Wallington where Orwell was now resident. The bride and groom regarded themselves as non-practising members of the Church of England and, in a pointed secular touch, the Rev. Woods agreed to omit the word 'obey' from their marriage vows.[1] On the morning of the wedding Orwell wrote to an Eton contemporary, Denys King-Farlow, saying that he had been studiously perusing the Prayer Book for several days in order to prepare himself for the 'obscenities' of his forthcoming wedding service (X.485).

Orwell's book reviews during the latter half of 1936 continued to raise a wide range of intriguing religious perspectives, both serious and light-hearted. He reviewed for *Time and Tide* (11 July 1936) James Stead's *Treasure Trek*, recounting his pursuit of supposedly buried Jesuit gold in Bolivia (X.486–7); and for *The Listener* (15 July 1936) Mark Channing's *Indian Mosaic*, tracing his spiritual pilgrimage towards Hinduism (X.488). He was amused in *Time and Tide* (18 July 1936) to have read in the memoirs of a Liverpool-born craftsman, *Rolling Stonemason* by Fred Bower, how he had secreted deep in the foundations of Liverpool's Catholic Cathedral a copy of *Clarion*, a weekly Socialist newspaper, and a revolutionary speech which he had personally composed for the occasion (X.490). In terms of fiction, he offered an equivocal response to *The Rock Pool*, a fey novel tracing the dissolute lives of Riviera bohemians by his Eton friend Cyril Connolly. He also digressed in this review (*New English Weekly*,

23 July 1936) to consider how many Christian writers sought to escape
the mundane qualities of ordinary life by hiding under the 'moulting wing
of Mother Church' and he proposed that the only way of escaping the
all-encompassing demands of money was via either religion, endless work
or 'sluttish antinomianism' (X.491).

In a review of *Coconuts and Creoles* (*Time and Tide*, 21 November
1936) by the Anglican clergyman J. A. F. Ozanne, a former chaplain to the
Crown Colony in the Seychelles, Orwell condemned the islands' religious
bigotry, lax morality and poor education system. Dubiously, he attributed
these failings almost entirely to the pernicious influence of the Catholic
Marist Brothers whom, he claimed, habitually threatened to excommu-
nicate children who attended the government's secular secondary schools.
Predictably, Orwell also warmly commended Ozanne's 'unmistakable
prejudice' against Roman Catholicism (X.523–4). In a more thoughtful
review of Philip Henderson's volume of Marxist literary criticism, *The
Novel Today* (*New English Weekly*, 31 December 1936), he raised the
problem of superficially judging a book by its ostensible religious or moral
tone. This kind of approach, he felt, was typical of both Catholic and
Communist extremists, who tended to judge the worth of a publication
only in terms of whether it preached the 'right sermon'. Lapsing into a more
whimsical mode, he proposed that this habit was most apparent in book
reviews published by Roman Catholic journals and in many other religious
newspapers. He imagined how the editors of the *Church Times* 'gnash
their false teeth and quake in their galoshes' whenever they hear the term
'modern' and yet they remain happy to praise the modernist poetry of T. S.
Eliot because he was revered as an 'Anglo-Catholic' (X.533).

This review was published on the last day of 1936 when Orwell had
already left England, probably on 23 December, to travel via Paris to
Spain to support the Republicans in the Civil War which had erupted in
the previous July. The next six months in the Aragon trenches and the
streets of Barcelona proved 'the defining experience of Orwell's life'.[2] It
also served to radicalize his perspectives on the political significance of
Catholicism. Christopher Hollis wrote in 1956 that, prior to his experiences in Spain, Orwell had not really considered that the 'Catholic Church,
could be a serious factor in modern politics'. Instead, Hollis believed that
he had regarded its teachings as 'clearly false' but not a 'matter of much
importance'. His explanation of how radically Orwell's views were altered
through his Spanish experiences emphasizes that he was increasingly
alienated by the escalating power of the Catholic Church:

Neither the Catholic unemployed nor the Catholic literati were very
important features in the shaping of English opinion in the 1930s, and
Orwell might well have continued to leave Catholicism alone, as he had
on the whole left it alone up until then. But it was while preparing *The
Road to Wigan Pier* that the Spanish War broke out, and the Catholic

Church, which had up till then been for him a quaint and unimportant survival, now showed itself for the first time as one of the great claimants to power – a force much stronger and therefore, as it appeared to him, much more evil than any of its Protestant rivals.

In Spain on the Aragonese front, Hollis records, Orwell 'for the first time came face to face with organized religion as a strong force. He disliked it intensely.' Henceforth, he seemed determined to regard 'Catholicism as an evil political force'.[3]

Orwell wished to fight against Franco's Nationalist forces which were supported by Nazi Germany, Fascist Italy and the local Falange. As an adherent of the Independent Labour Party, Orwell joined in Catalonia the affiliated Workers' Party of Marxist Unification (POUM, *Partido Obrero de Unificación Marxista*). He was wounded in the throat by a Fascist sniper in May 1937 and declared unfit for military service. In *Homage to Catalonia* he took mischievous pleasure in finding that the Sanatorium Maurín where he was treated was near the mountain of Tibidabo (from '*illi haec **tibi** omnia **dabo** si cadens adoraveris me*', 'all these things I shall give thee, if thou will fall down and worship me', Matthew 4.90), traditionally assumed to have been the location from where Jesus was shown the 'countries of the earth' by Satan (VI.152). In the following month, POUM members were outlawed by the pro-Soviet Communists and Orwell and his wife, denounced as Trotskyists, had to escape by train from Spain (XI.30–1).

Although he was often ill informed about the Spanish political situation, Orwell's eye-witness experiences undoubtedly hardened his personal form of socialism and, at the same time, confirmed his anxieties over the escalating Western European threat of both Fascism and Communism. When completing the second part of *Wigan Pier* in late 1936 he had affirmed that the spread of Fascism was ruthlessly sweeping aside the worthy tenets of international socialism. He noted that, while he was completing this book, Spanish Fascists were bombarding Madrid, and by the time of its publication most of Spain would probably have fallen to the Fascists, giving them control over the Mediterranean region and, in turn, greatly increasing Mussolini's influence over British foreign policy (V.159). However, despite Spain's long tradition of Roman Catholicism, his essay 'Spilling the Spanish Beans' (*New English Weekly*, 29 July and 2 September 1937) and *Homage to Catalonia* (published 25 April 1938) make surprisingly few references to religious affairs. Nor is there any mention of religious matters in his 'Notes on the Spanish Militias' (XI.135–45). Orwell thereby implies that this apocalyptic civil conflict had already reduced the country – especially in the eyes of its warring factions and foreign combatants – to a secular and Godless state.

'Spilling the Spanish Beans' opens with a mocking reference to 'hecatombs of nuns' being 'raped and crucified' in front of *Daily Mail* reporters (XI.41) and dismisses outright the 'huge, parasitic church' and its repressive 'clericalism'. But this essay's primary purpose was to expose the inherent dangers not of the Church but of Communism and the tensions set up in Spain between revolution and count-revolution. He regrets how English public opinion had not yet realized that Communism had become essentially a counter-revolutionary force and that many communists were secretly in league with bourgeois reformists and intent on ruthlessly crushing any nascent signs of revolt against their self-interested authoritarianism (XI.42). In a private letter (1 August 1937) to a literary admirer, Amy Charlesworth, Orwell describes Franco's supporters as fascists and mainly standing for 'feudalism' and the Roman Catholic Church (XI.61). Generally, however, he seems surprisingly uninterested in the role played by the Church in either Spanish daily life or Franco's regime. He savagely reviewed in *Time and Tide* (11 December 1937) *Spanish Rehearsal* by the pro-Franco Catholic convert Arnold Lunn for claiming that the 'burning of a nun in petrol' (XI.103) was now commonplace in 'Red' Spain. In contrast he commended (XI.102–3) the well-informed analysis offered in *Storm Over Spain* by the Irish writer Mairin Mitchell and later approved of her sympathy for Spanish anarchists (XI.114), despite her Catholicism.

Homage to Catalonia, as befits a literary text from a warzone, offers an essentially Godless landscape and yet it has also been described as offering a highly personal vision of a form of socialism, 'inspired more by Christianity than Marx'.[4] It is striking that its non-believing author selects a biblical epigraph from Proverbs 26.4-5 (cited inaccurately as '5-6'):

> Answer not a fool according to his folly,
> lest thou be like unto him.
> Answer a fool according to his folly,
> lest he be wise in his own conceit.

These apparently contradictory lines have caused uncertainty for generations of biblical readers but may be interpreted in an Orwellian context as suggesting that sometimes it is wise simply to ignore the words of a fool but on other occasions, when the issues are serious, they should be firmly addressed and the fool reproached. Orwell's introduction of his own political commitment in Spain within such an overtly biblical context is curious and has even facilitated the identification of a broadly spiritual structuring of the work. For example, the political journalist Stephen Schwartz proposed that the book possesses a distinctly Dantesque framework, offering a brief glimpse in its opening pages of the Paradise of Barcelona thronging with idealistic volunteers, leading inexorably to the Purgatorial conditions of trench warfare and, ultimately, to a Hell of Communist and Fascist genocide.[5]

At the hellish end of things, the wrecked ecclesiastical architecture of Spain firmly impressed on Orwell the mindless iconoclasm of war. He records how by early 1937 virtually all of the country's churches had been gutted and had their images desecrated and burnt before being demolished by workmen (VI.2–3). The wrecked church at Monflorite was used as a military store (VI.53) and in La Granja, the church's walls were riddled with shell-holes and its floor covered in dung (VI.54).[6] Despite the deep-rooted Catholicism of Spain, Orwell detected the signs of a decline in the relevance of religion to the common people even before the Civil War had begun. He claimed surprise to see how rarely gravestones in the local cemeteries bore any religious inscriptions and even those with a cross or some kind of reference to Heaven had been recently vandalized by some 'industrious atheist with a chisel' (VI.56). Such systematic destruction echoed the iconoclasm of the sixteenth-century Tudor Reformation and, in his review of Edgar Allison Peers's *The Church in Spain, 1737–1937* (*New English Weekly*, 24 November 1938), Orwell compared the ruination of Spanish churches with Thomas Cromwell's despoliation of English ones during the 1530s (XI.233). This historical conjunction prompted him to ponder the speedy obliteration (or at least temporary repression) of generations of Spanish religious feelings and customs by internal political conflicts. He assumed that the traumatized locals must have lost any sense of orthodox religious feeling and, throughout his time in Spain, he never saw anyone make the Sign of the Cross even though he felt that such a gesture in a supposedly Catholic nation should be ingrained and constantly visible. While not doubting that the Spanish Church would one day reassert itself, in keeping with the saying 'night and the Jesuits always return', it seemed clear that the outbreak of civil war had led to its rapid collapse and to an extent that simply could never have happened to the likes of the 'moribund C of E'. In Catalonia and Aragón, he thought, the Spanish people now regarded the Catholic Church as deeply complicit with Franco and a despicable 'racket pure and simple', with its once all-encompassing influence replaced by a self-destructive brand of Anarchism tinged by religious fervour (VI.56–7).

Orwell's perspectives on a possible post-war Republican government are cast in *Homage to Catalonia* in specifically anti-religious tones. He is confident that it would prove hostile to both feudalism and clericalism and would seek as a priority to control the Catholic Church. In contrast, Franco stood for the Republicans as a repressive form of 'stuffy cleric-military' authoritarianism (VI.133). In a political chapter included in the first edition, Orwell expanded on his views of Franco. He was careful to distinguish the Generalissimo from Hitler and Mussolini because Franco's uprising had been a predominantly military mutiny, supported by the Church and aristocracy, which sought not to establish Fascism but rather to reaffirm feudalism. The Catholic Church's close collaboration with Franco inevitably hardened Orwell's anti-Catholicism and, henceforth, he regarded Catholicism's brand of authoritarianism as implicitly fascist, a charge which he never levelled at Anglicanism because he felt that it was characteristically undoctrinaire and did not seek to impose specific political perspectives on its followers. Spanish Fascism, it seemed to Orwell, had become an inevitable by-product of Franco's personal and pragmatic religiosity. As Republican forces systematically wrecked churches and drove out or murdered their priests, Orwell claimed that the *Daily Mail*, egged on by the 'cheers of the Catholic clergy', presented Franco to its English readers as a nobly patriotic nationalist, saving his besieged country from barbarous hordes of 'Reds' (VI.190). In what Orwell regarded as a highly centralized English press catering for a facile and easily deceived readership, two equally distorting perspectives on the Spanish Civil War had been promulgated: the right wing's view of 'Christian patriots' heroically opposing blood-soaked Bolsheviks, and the left wing's depiction of 'gentlemanly' Republicans suppressing an unfortunate military revolt (VI.192).

The fate of the established Catholic Church preoccupies Orwell in this section of *Homage to Catalonia*. He was at pains to denounce the lie of some foreign anti-Fascist newspapers in suggesting that only churches used as Fascist bastions were attacked since, in reality, churches were pillaged everywhere because the Spanish Church had already been long hated by the populace as a key collaborator in the 'capitalist racket' (VI.194). He notes that during his six months in Spain he saw no more than two undamaged churches and only a couple of Protestant churches in Madrid were allowed to hold religious services. One of Orwell's closest companions during his time in Spain was Stafford Cottman who, as the youngest member of the ILP contingent, fought alongside the POUM in Catalonia and escaped with him when the Communists began their purge of independent Marxists and the POUM. He described in an interview in 1984 how he and Orwell had once come across a desecrated church where the 'altar cloth had been torn across and was left lying on the floor. There were very crude slogans written in human excreta on the walls'. Orwell seemed unconcerned by this sight and Cottman recalled how his attitude towards the Catholic Church had always seemed to him 'extremely critical', explaining that Orwell distrusted their hierarchy because 'they always identified with the oppressors rather than the oppressed'.[7] The total ruination of the Catholic Church in Spain was potently confirmed for Orwell when, attempting to flee the country, he was obliged to seek refuge one night in the shell of a gutted and burnt-out church with only 'four roofless walls surrounding piles of rubble' (VI.167). The memory of such iconoclastic destruction remained with Orwell for the rest of his life and pointedly resurfaced in *Nineteen Eighty-Four* as one of the secret places where Winston meets his illicit lover Julia – in the belfry of a 'ruinous church' destroyed by an atomic bomb thirty years previously (134). Orwell finally escaped from Spain into France on 23 June 1937 and was back in Wallington in the first week of July.

Inevitably, Orwell's experiences in Spain generated a wide range of books on the Civil War being offered to him for review and he remained keen to utilize such opportunities to castigate the perspectives of both the Catholic Church in Spain and Catholic authors writing about the conflict. In a review for the *New English Weekly* (23 June 1938) of Robert Sencourt's *Spain's Ordeal* (misprinted in his review as *Spanish Ordeal*) he mentioned that virtually all of the books currently being published on the subject, with the notable exception of a study by the Anglican scholar Allison Peers which he reviewed in following November, had been penned by Roman Catholics, implying that they tended to distort the facts for pro-Franco propaganda. He wrote that while Sencourt's study did not sink to the same level of propagandist crudity as Arnold Lunn's *Red Rehearsal*, its central message was identical in claiming that Franco was a 'Christian gentleman' and that Guernica had not been bombed but, instead, had been 'wantonly burnt by Red militia men' (XI.166). In contrast, he praised Frank Jellinek's *The Civil War in Spain* in a review for *The New Leader* (8 July 1938) as the best book available on the Spanish Civil War from a Communist perspective. Predictably, he approved Jellinek's highlighting of the Church's corruption and his chapter on its power, wealth and repression of the ordinary people left no doubt in Orwell's mind as to why virtually all the churches in Catalonia and eastern Aragon had been vandalized as soon as war broke out. In conclusion, he suspected that the Jesuits could still formulate the ideal totalitarian regime since, if Jellinek's statistics were correct, there were only about 22,000 Jesuits worldwide but their power and business sense were immense. Orwell drily noted that their 'man of affairs' in Spain was a director of no less than forty-three commercial companies (XI.172).

In a separate review of Peers's *The Church in Spain, 1737–1937* for *New English Weekly* (24 November 1938), Orwell described him as a 'Franco partisan' (XI.233) and, mistakenly, as a Catholic. He later acknowledged this error, admitting that his testimony in favour of the Catholic Church was strengthened by him not being Catholic, but he reasserted the view that the book had been written from a pro-Franco perspective (XI.236). Orwell focused on his account of the destruction of Spanish churches, dismissing outright the propagandist rumour that they had only been demolished when used in street fighting and as fortresses. Instead, he insisted that, apart from a few Protestant churches, none was able to hold religious services until about August 1937. He also denied the view that both anarchists and Marxist socialists were 'hostile to all religion' since in Spain hostility towards the Church was driven primarily by the economic oppression of ordinary people by landowners, industrialists and the Church. Contrary to Peers's view, Orwell argued that the destruction of local churches had been instigated while the proletariat was still in control but, once the Cabellero Government had been overthrown, leading to a resurgence of the middle classes, some churches had reopened as their priests came out of hiding. He concluded that the most violent aspect of Spanish anticlericalism was an indigenous and populist movement among Spaniards themselves. It grew, Orwell insisted, not from Marx or Bakuin (a Russian anarchist and opponent of Marx) but from the repressed social conditions of the ordinary Spanish people. Supporting this perspective, he recorded how during the first year of the war he felt in both Catalonia and Aragón that there was a tangible absence of any 'religious feeling whatever' among the ordinary people of Spain, perhaps partly due to the dangers of admitting to religious belief but also because religion had grown remote and exploitative rather than supportive of their lives since the Church always seemed to side with the wealthy.[8]

To Orwell it was especially reprehensible that Catholic apologists had been consistently denying this state of affairs, claiming that the Church was neither corrupt nor wealthy and that many of its priests were committed Republicans. According to Orwell, most rural Spaniards regarded the Church as a cynical 'racket' and its priests as uncaring cronies of their bosses and landlords since it had callously failed in its central duties to its flock. He concluded unequivocally that it would be best for Catholics simply to face up honestly to this failure rather than trying to attribute the chaos of the Civil War to either 'mere wickedness, or to Moscow' (XI.234–5). Orwell's experiences in Spain confirmed his theory that the Catholic Church had long been part of a capitalist conspiracy to exploit its ordinary people for the benefit of an elite few. This perspective facilitated his maturing concept of all organized religions, but especially the centuries-old politicized potency of the Catholic Church, as approximating to a ruthless form of repressive totalitarianism. From these contexts, Orwell's personal distaste for Roman Catholicism – intensified by his experiences in Catalonia – would feed directly into the dystopian power politics of *Nineteen Eighty-Four*.

Orwell's Spanish experiences remained vividly in his mind during the Second World War even though his health limited him to office-bound BBC work, reviewing and journalism. In 'Looking Back on the Spanish War' (written c. 1942 and first published, in truncated form, in *New Road*, probably June 1943) he recalled how the Nazis and Fascists had tried for propaganda purposes to represent themselves as 'Christian patriots' actively protecting Spain from Russian Communism. They pretended, Orwell argued, that they were intervening to prevent governmental massacres of the people and he felt that both the *Catholic Herald* and the *Daily Mail*, along with the continental Fascist press, had taken a disgracefully sympathetic line to this travesty of the truth.[9] In particular, he denounced how reactionary and Catholic presses had constructed a 'huge pyramid of lies' (XIII.503), such as their blatantly false exaggeration of the presence of a Russian army in Spain to justify military support for Franco. As Orwell explained soon after the defeat of Nazi Germany in 'Why I Write' (1946), the Spanish Civil War had marked a watershed in his political experience and from then on all his writings had been aimed either indirectly or directly '*against* totalitarianism and *for* democratic Socialism' (XVIII.319). The poet and novelist John Wain summed up the political and creative importance of these searing experiences:

Up to 1937, Orwell saw the world struggle as between Left and Right, with the good will and the good arguments on the side of the Left ... After

1937 he saw it in terms of democracy *versus* totalitarianism, and he no longer cared whether the totalitarianism called itself Left or Right. What changed his outlook was his Spanish experience. *Homage to Catalonia* is the most important book for anyone who wants to understand Orwell's mind. It is a book that describes the hinge of a man's life.[10]

Marrakech and *Coming Up For Air* (1939)

After returning to England from Spain, the Orwells first stayed in Greenwich at the O'Shaughnessy family home and then returned to their cottage at Wallington where Orwell's aunt Nellie had been living while they were abroad. He began to plan *Coming Up for Air* in about December 1937 but by the following March his health had seriously deteriorated. He was admitted to a sanatorium near Aylesford, Kent, where Eileen's brother Laurence was a consultant surgeon, remaining there as a patient until September. By 1 June he had recovered enough to be transferred to the Sanatorium's ancillary hostel from where, despite his lack of religious faith, he undertook constitutional trips to the Aylesford parish church of St Peter's and bus rides to Rochester Cathedral.[11] After his discharge in September, the Orwells travelled to Marrakech in Morocco for him to recuperate in a warmer climate, the costs borne by an anonymous gift of £300 (later repaid by Orwell) from the wealthy Old Etonian Marxist novelist Leopold H. Myers.[12] The day after the Orwells arrived in North Africa Neville Chamberlain flew to Munich for discussions over Hitler's demands to draw the Sudetenland into German territories.

Settled in a rented property near Marrakech, Orwell focused on familiarizing himself with the lifestyles and culture of the native population. His 'Morocco Diary' records a marked interest in local religious customs at Marrakech, noting in October 1938, the beginning of Ramadan and how most Arabs, despite their poverty, endeavoured to be reasonably strict over their religious observances (XI.230). He observed how their devout servant, Mahdjoub Mahommed, surreptitiously secreted scraps and leftovers from their meals, presumably to eat after dusk. In a letter to Charles Doran (26 November 1938) he described most of the locals as still living a feudal lifestyle and 'fairly strict Mahommedans' (XI.239), although he admitted in another letter (26 December) to the working-class novelist Jack Common that sheer hunger sometimes prompted them not to be overscrupulous about their eating regimes, despite being 'pretty strict Mahomedans' (XI.261).

The primitive funeral customs of the Arabs and Mohammedans fascinated Orwell, even though he described them in his 'Morocco Diary' as the 'wretchedest' that he had ever seen (XI.258), with the corpse of the typical peasant wrapped in cheap cloth and squeezed into a shallow hole with no tombstone or other commemoration. He again detailed these dismal ceremonies in an article, 'Marrakech', for *New Writing* (Christmas 1939), beginning with a potent image lifted directly from one of Eileen's letters (XI.217). He described how, when the corpse was carried past, the flies departed from the restaurant in a 'cloud' to rush after it, returning to the diner's food a few minutes later (XI.416). Only richer citizens could afford more care for the afterlife and he carefully examined one such interment set within a mud enclosure. It had a small oven near the head of the grave for burnt offerings and on a nearby tree various charms and bunches of wool had been hung. He removed one of these offerings in the form of a small leather purse and found inside some wool and a scrap of paper with writing on it (XI.315). He was more impressed with Berber burials at Taddert high in the Atlas Mountains about 95 kilometres from Marrakech where the graves of devout Mohammedans (XI.326) were constructed mainly of rocks with a small cairn placed on top, but again without any name or other means of identification.

Orwell's 'Moroccan Diary' also reveals a significant interest in the depressed living conditions of the country's Jews. He considers the levels of poverty in the Jewish quarter at Marrakech to be worse, or at least more noticeable, than those found in the Arab quarter (XI.209). Although Arabs and Jews apparently did similar work (XI.219), there seemed everywhere a great hostility towards them, not only from Arabs but also from Europeans who claimed that the Jews were undercutting them in business, cheating, and taking the jobs of others (XI.230). In contrast, in the Berber villages of the Atlas Mountains he spotted only the occasional Jew, who blended in well with other members of the community (XI.326). In a letter (15 January 1939) to Francis Westrope, his former employer at the Booklovers' Corner bookshop in Hampstead, he noted how most of the Moroccan Jews were poverty stricken and lived very much as the Arabs did, sharing in the sustaining of distinctive Moroccan trades such as 'coppersmithing' and making other cheap products (XI.230). These fragmentary private observations formed the basis of his essay, 'Marrakech' (*New Writing*, Christmas 1939), offering a potent warning from his North African exile over the age-old problem of anti-Semitism. He explained for his Western European readers, now directly threatened by the aggressive militancy of Nazi Germany, how Moroccan Jewish quarters – prefiguring the Warsaw and other European Jewish ghettoes of the early 1940s – had hardly moved on from the overcrowded, unhygienic living conditions of medieval ghettoes. Eking out little more than a subsistence living, huge orthodox Jewish families worked in the Marrakech bazaar in dark, fly-ridden booths resembling caves. His essay concluded ominously by noting that it was a 'good job Hitler isn't here' since rumours abounded over Jews supposedly taking employment from both Arabs and poor Europeans. Locals, Orwell recorded, frequently claimed (echoing words which had led to the rise of anti-Semitism in Western Europe) that the Jews were the 'real rulers of this country' and ruthlessly controlled the 'banks, finance – everything' (XI.417–18).

Orwell's Marrakech novel *Coming Up For Air* – a work of exile both geographically and mentally from his own past – was pessimistically elegiac in tone and, to date, his most cogently constructed work of fiction. It is suffused with nostalgia for a soon to be lost rural England in which local church life and county communities played a reassuringly unchanging role. Its middle-aged, overweight anti-hero, a nondescript insurance salesman called George Bowling (echoing H. G. Wells's Mr Polly), resides unhappily at Ellesmere Road in the North London suburbs, trapped in a loveless marriage with a shrewish wife and two young children to support. Any lingering sense of local community in his neighbourhood has been usurped by the secular 'god of building societies' (VII.11) since the Ellesmere Road houses are only leasehold, not freehold, and can never be permanently owned by their residents even when they have finished paying off their mortgages. As in *Keep the Aspidistra Flying*, money now presides as the god of the middle classes – an absolute dictator demanding unending dependence and working servitude. Comically revitalized by a new set of false teeth and a seventeen-pound win on the horses, Bowling decides on impulse to revisit his childhood home at Lower Binfield, Oxfordshire, modelled upon Orwell's memories of Henley-on-Thames.

Even before he returns there, Bowling's mind is pervaded with dreamy glimpses of this lost pastoral world. His memories drift back over thirty-eight years to the dank and decaying aromas of Lower Binfield's parish church, representing the very 'smell of death and life'. He can still clearly recall how as a small child he stood on the hassock to look over the pew, listening to the wheezing organ. Two voluble locals, Shooter the fishmonger and Wetherall the undertaker, are vividly remembered loudly singing psalms in competing voices. The young Bowling relished the psalms about King Sihon of the Amorites and King Og of Bashan; and as an adult his mind remains replete with Biblical passages about Asher, Dan, Beersheba, Shimei, Nebuchadnezzar, Ahithophel and Hashbadana, names all subtly blended with the 'sweet graveyard smell', the serge dresses of parishioners and the 'wheeze of the organ' (VII.30). In this world of childishly fascinating Bible stories, he remembers how he was reassured by knowing that 'God's in heaven' and 'Christ's on the cross' (VII.31), with Jonah inside his whale, the piously loyal Jewish youths Shadrach, Meshach and Abednego saved from cruel Nebuchadnezzar's fiery furnace, and Kings Sihon and Og safely ensconced on their thrones.

Leaving school to support the family's dwindling finances, the young Bowling began working for a local grocer, old Grimmett, a staunch Baptist who worshipped in the small local chapel, known as the 'Tin Tab', and began each shop-day with morning prayers for his staff. He also joined the vicar's Reading Circle, and poignantly recalls how in those days belief in religion was still prevalent. His mother had been brought up as a 'decent God-fearing shopkeeper's daughter' and had become a 'decent God-fearing shopkeeper's wife', even though the young Bowling knew that he had never really met anyone who seemed to really believe in a 'future life' (VII.111). His memories of Lower Binfield in 1900 – in contrast to war-threatened London and the shimmering heat of Marrakech – are permanently locked into a reassuring world of social order, spiritual meaning and community spirit, centred upon the diurnal rhythm of church life and a traditional knowledge of the scriptures.

When Bowling finally makes his clandestine visit back to Lower Binfield he finds that the old cemetery is now full, with the ardent psalm-singers Shooter and Wetherall lying either side of the path and other stone slabs bearing the names of once well-known local figures. Much is changed in the town but the church itself remains unaltered with the same pews and 'dusty, sweetish corpse-smell' presided over by the now aged vicar, the Rev. Betterton.[13] Even though he had confirmed Bowling and led the Reading Circle, he no longer recognizes him and thinks that he is merely a tourist fascinated by church architecture and local history. While everything else in Lower Binfield seems to have been subject to the transition of time, only the parish church – its architecture, liturgy, graveyard, monuments and, above all, its smells – provides a sense of social and psychological continuity which Orwell so prized as quintessentially English and which by the late 1930s seemed precariously balanced on the edge of a fascist abyss.[14]

The outbreak of war

While Orwell claimed in retrospect to have anticipated since about 1931 the likelihood of a pan-European war (a fear all but confirmed by the signature on 30 September 1938 of the Munich Pact by Germany, Britain, France and Italy, surrendering the Sudetenland to Germany's Third Reich), much of his anger was directed at a now familiar opponent – the British intelligentsia.[15] In 'Political Reflections on the Crisis' (*The Adelphi*, December 1938), he deplores how so-called Western 'civilization' was producing ever increasing numbers of two categories of individuals, derided as the 'gangster' and the 'pansy'. Whenever a Trotskyist is liquidated somewhere in Eastern Europe, he speculates, a 'pansy' in Bloomsbury writes to justify it. He mocks, in particular, W. H. Auden's naïve insistence upon accepting guilt for a 'necessary murder'. Orwell's essay concludes with a damning indictment of an irresponsible British intelligentsia which had keenly embraced Roman Catholicism in the previous decade before taking up Communism and which, doubtless, would adopt an English variant of Fascism in a few years' time (XI.244). This sophistic linking of Catholicism, Communism and Fascism in late 1938 is telling since it provides a significant key to understanding how throughout his literary career Orwell insistently chose to equate a two-thousand-year-old, worldwide religious faith with the more temporal political extremes of Communism and Fascism. To confirm this unholy trinity of connections Orwell simply sidelined approximately three million ordinary adherents to Catholicism at this period in England, Wales and Scotland. Instead, he focused his venom upon a minuscule minority of contemporary Catholics (especially converts from High Church Anglicanism) who took it upon themselves to speak for the mass of their fellow worshippers. This said, it should be noted that the majority of working- and middle-class Catholics in cities such as London, Liverpool and Manchester or in England's agricultural communities probably also felt little kinship with the wealth, privilege and intellectually rarefied utterances on Catholic affairs of the likes of G. K. Chesterton, Arnold Lunn, Hilaire Belloc and Monsignor Ronald Knox. Nevertheless, Orwell's polemical selectivity during the late 1930s in so insistently linking Catholicism, Communism and Fascism is deeply misleading and a striking confirmation of his ingrained religious bigotry.

Orwell clearly suspected that most of these élite Catholic apologists were guilty of the subversive sin of aspiring to a kind of totalitarian democracy, in which a self-selecting and supposedly enlightened minority justified authoritarianism and even coercion against those who did not conform to their standards of virtue in order to encourage man's spiritually utopian progress towards virtuous behaviour and social harmony. The superficially liberal tendencies of some of these apologists, to Orwell's eyes, were merely camouflaging calculated repression and bullying, ostensibly as a form of 'caring' or as a necessary response to oppressive bigotry from others. He systematically sustained and developed these polemical perspectives throughout the 1930s and 1940s. In a letter, written on Boxing Day 1938 to Jack Common, he cynically mulled over the religious conversion of John Middleton Murry, the founder and editor of *The Adelphi* and an early supporter of Common's literary ambitions. Murry, formerly the Marxist author of *The Necessity of Communism* (1931) and then the pacifist author of *The Necessity of Pacifism* (1937), had just become a communicating member of the Church of England with the intention of training for the Anglican priesthood (although ill-health and marital problems eventually prevented him from doing so). Viewing him as a typical intellectual and wavering extremist, Orwell mockingly speculated that this spiritual conversion was likely to produce in a few years' time a book from Murry called 'The Necessity of Fascism' (XI.261). In a later letter to Common (23 February 1939), he even joked that it would be wonderfully comic if Murry eventually became a bishop (XI.331).

In a review for *The Adelphi* (January 1939) of Bertrand Russell's *Power: A New Social Analysis*, Orwell lamented the lack of a truly liberal and enlightened intelligentsia, thereby enabling various manifestations of crude force to become dominant in Western European societies and ensuring that 'Bully-worship' in various forms had become a kind of 'universal religion'. He strongly agreed with Russell's forensic analysis of various kinds of despotic power – 'priestly, oligarchical, dictatorial' – and (in words that might well describe his own aspirations as a writer), commended Russell as an 'essentially *decent* intellect' which was far less commonly found than 'mere cleverness' (XI.311–12). Significantly, another review for *Peace News* (January 1939) demonstrated that Orwell was not necessarily hostile to all Roman Catholic commentators. He warmly commended *Communism and Man* by Frank R. Sheed, an Australian-born Catholic convert, writer and publisher, for the objectivity of its refutation from a Catholic perspective of Marxist Socialism. This praise was doubly surprising because Sheed was the publisher of Chesterton, Belloc and Knox, but Orwell insisted that the Church would have far fewer enemies (including himself) if its apologists were more like Sheed. Orwell accepted the view that the essential difference between Catholicism and Communism, both of which espouse humanitarian principles, lay in the issue of 'personal immortality'. But he also explained that, while the Catholic Church readily denounced mindless Capitalism, its materialistic upholding of the right to private property became problematic to reconcile with purely economic justice. Property, Orwell argued in his review, remained at the heart of the still largely unresolved tensions between Catholicism and socialism and he proposed that the Church urgently needed to review its stance on property in order to regain its former spiritual influence. Ultimately, he argued, it must decide whether it really believed that its 'kingdom is not of this world' and that feeding and supporting humanity is of little significance compared to 'saving souls'. He concluded by highlighting the irony of the Pope denouncing capitalism while at the same time awarding high decorations to General Franco (XI.322–3). Sheed seemed to Orwell a noble exception to his generally disapproving view of the Catholic press and its literary apologists. His 'Diary of Events Leading Up to the War', for example, noted under 12 July 1939 how the Catholic *Universe* had finally come out as firmly against the Nazis but, seemingly, had little to say about Italian Fascism and remained strongly 'anti-red as regards Spain' (XI.370) – conclusions drawn from Orwell's close reading of this newspaper's 7 July issue.

Orwell increasingly linked in his reviews a fourth element with his established interest in the associations between Catholicism, Communism and Fascism – the repressive treatment of the Jews and other minorities in Western Europe. In a review of Marion Block's *Gypsies* for *The Adelphi* (December 1938) he pondered what Hitler and Stalin were planning for the Jews since totalitarian regimes invariably seemed to persecute them on the pretence of 'civilising' them, even though Jews had survived numerous previous attempts to eradicate them from European society. His review then broadened its perspective to include out of favour revolutionaries, while also taking a swipe at the Roman Catholic Church by claiming that, although the Inquisition had finally failed, it seemed less likely that the threatened 'liquidation' of both Trotskyists and Jews would fail. He speculated that both gypsies and Jews were already being regarded as 'corpus vile' (of no value) and little publicity was being given in the Western press to their dire situation because they did not possess friends and supporters who owned newspapers (XI.247).

In a thoughtful analysis of John MacMurray's *The Clue to History* for *The Adelphi* (February 1939), Orwell ultimately rejected the book's fanciful thesis but still managed to utilize it to warn of the potentially lethal dangers threatening Jews through the rise of Fascism. MacMurray proposed that human society should move towards world communism but also argued that the major obstacle to such progress was a persistent dualism which, he claimed, only the Jewish consciousness had managed to avoid. His book proposed that the 'Jewish mind, chiefly *via* its offspring, Christianity' had been the 'sole agent of human progress' and that Hitler's version of Fascism was the 'last effort of the western world to escape its destiny'. Understandably, Orwell viewed with deep scepticism MacMurray's idealistic hope that even if Hitler succeeded in destroying the normative values of capitalist society he would still, unintentionally, facilitate the 'Jewish Kingdom of Heaven' based upon a free and equal society. His review brushed aside these wild utopian fantasies, pointing out MacMurray's basic omission of Hinduism when claiming that Hebrew culture should be regarded as the only global religious culture. He also questioned MacMurray's assertion that the Jewish consciousness had managed to avoid the familiar dualisms of the world since, for Orwell, it had been a slave to the most profound dualism of all, that of consistently casting itself against Gentiles. He went on to describe the books of the Old Testament as primarily manifestos of 'hatred and self-righteousness', advocating the extermination of enemies as a religious duty and Jehovah as a violent 'tribal deity'. But far more importantly, Orwell argued, 1939 was the worst possible time for a writer to be airing fanciful theories about the Jews as mysterious and, from a Western perspective, sinister entities. Above all, it was now paramount to remember that they should be regarded as fellow humans rather than merely Jews (XI.327–9).

The Orwells arrived back in England in late March 1939 and George's father, Richard, died in the following July, prompting several brief visits to Southwold.[16] With his access renewed to English friends and newspapers, Orwell resumed collecting scraps of second-hand information on the position of Western European Jews for his reviews and journalism. In a private 'Diary of Events Leading Up to the War' he recorded under 2 August 1939 an informal report from (probably) Cyril Wright, a friend from Spain, that London was receiving an influx of wealthy German Jewish refugees who were buying up houses in certain areas such as Golders Green (XI.384). He also noted on 31 August, after reading about foreign affairs in *The Daily Telegraph*, *News Chronicle* and *Daily Mirror*, the erroneous speculation that the Nazis' persecution of the Jews was 'slightly diminished' (XI.403). His review of *Foreign Correspondent* for *Time and Tide* (12 August 1939) sought to look beyond the current crisis in the hope of finding a more permanent solution to the age-old problem of Jewish persecution. The book's author was the civil servant and academic

Lewis B. Namier who had been born a secular Jew in Poland but in 1913 became a naturalized British subject. His book argued persuasively that the dilemma of the Jews would remain unresolved until they were granted a country of their own. This thesis prompted Orwell to wonder whether uncontrolled immigration into Palestine was either possible or desirable, a point over which Namier himself remained unclear (XI.390–1). In a later 'News Review' (8 August 1942), written by Orwell and read for the BBC's Indian Service by an Indian law student at Oxford University, he noted the encouraging news that a Palestinian regiment had been raised which incorporated both Jews and Arab soldiers serving alongside one another. Such a combination demonstrated how the threat of Fascist aggression could bring together peoples who had previously been enemies for countless generations for the common purpose of 'defending their country' against invaders (XIII.456).

Inside the Whale (1940)

After the outbreak of war in September 1939, Eileen worked at the Censorship Department at Whitehall in London while Orwell struggled to find any meaningful war work. Disheartened, he was often isolated at Wallington, carrying on with reviewing, journalism and completing his first essay collection, *Inside the Whale* (published 11 March 1940). His long associations with *Horizon* and the non-Stalinist left-wing *Tribune* (founded in 1937 by George Strauss and Stafford Cripps), in which he had his own column 'As I Please', both began in February 1940. By the following April he was also planning a never completed saga of three novels with the alternative working titles of 'The Lion and the Unicorn' or 'The Quick and the Dead' (XII.148). He joined the staff of the BBC on 18 August 1941 and worked there until 24 November 1943 in the BBC's Eastern Service where he compiled and directed broadcasts to India as counter-propaganda to German attempts to destabilize the longstanding Anglo-Indian loyalties of the British Empire (XIII.xxiii).

Orwell's suspicions over what he viewed as the authoritarian impulses of Catholicism, especially among the London intelligentsia and popular writers, continued to preoccupy his mind during the 1940s. In a communication (c. 28 January 1940) with the libel lawyer scrutinizing the typescript of *Inside the Whale*, a collection of three essays in which the first blended a review of Henry Miller's *Tropic of Cancer* with broader thoughts on contemporary literature, he admitted that, in view of his previous comments on Evelyn Waugh's conversion to Catholicism, it would be wise for him to adjust a section of his text comparing Waugh's early comic novels to the nihilistic cynicism expressed in the semi-autobiographical French novel, *Voyage au Bout de la Nuit* (1932), by Louis-Ferdinand Celine, satirizing various aspects of contemporary European and American life (XII.10). The potency of Catholicism – in both attracting its adherents and repelling its opponents – pervaded the entire texture of *Inside the Whale*.

Orwell deemed Joyce's *Ulysses* the product of a distinctive vision of the world and human life, the vision of a 'Catholic who has lost his faith', telling his readers: '"Here is life without God. Just look at it!"' (XII.97). He reiterated this view of Joyce in a BBC India broadcast (10 March 1942) on 'Literature Between the Wars', depicting him as a lapsed Catholic who retained the 'mental framework' of his youth. He concluded that the modern world had no great meaning for Joyce now that the Church's teachings lacked credibility (XIII.215). *Inside the Whale* also proposed that Ezra Pound, T. S. Eliot and Aldous Huxley had harboured some 'tenderness' for the Catholic faith although of a non-orthodox variety (XII.98); and that an illusory dawn had risen when a small but significant group of talented writers, including Waugh and Christopher Hollis, had 'fled' to Catholicism (XII.102). However, he thought it significant that the only recent convert of 'really first-rate gifts', T. S. Eliot, had adopted Anglo-Catholicism rather than Roman Catholicism, which he regarded as the 'ecclesiastical equivalent of Trotskyism'. Orwell seemed to be implying that the Catholic Church offered a haven to the popular but intrinsically second-rate writer – something of a contradiction given Orwell's longstanding admiration for Waugh. Even as he lay dying in a hospital bed in 1950, he was planning an essay on Waugh's distinctive contribution to English Literature.

Similarly, Orwell felt that with the decline of organized religion many youthful writers of the 1930s had gravitated towards the Communist Party, looking for meaning in their lives. Equating its superficial appeal to the allure of Catholicism, he suggested that Communism had simply offered something vague to believe in: 'Here was a church, an army, an orthodoxy, a discipline' (XII.103). But in Orwell's world picture, orthodoxy – a term inevitably recalling Chesterton's renowned volume of Christian apologetics, *Orthodoxy* (1908) – was something which authors should rigorously avoid. *Inside the Whale* proposes that the prevalence of orthodoxies would always prove damaging to creative prose writing, especially the novel which, he argued, should aim to be the most 'anarchical' of all literary forms. Pointedly, but without naming names (perhaps at the advice of his publisher's libel lawyers), he questioned how many Roman Catholics could be deemed good novelists, adding that even the few that could be named were usually 'bad Catholics'.

Frustratingly, Orwell does not define what he means by a 'bad' Catholic or, for that matter, a 'good' Catholic. Might Graham Greene – a self-confessed adulterer (as Orwell was himself) fall into this category? Or might Evelyn Waugh qualify with his lack of Christian charity in his wickedly amusing but often cruel depictions of 1920s life? Instead, Orwell concludes with the grand assertion that the English novel should be regarded as an essentially 'Protestant' art form (XII.105), produced by minds untrammelled by orthodoxy. Again, without names or specific novels, it is impossible to judge the validity of this resonant statement. Returning to more familiar ground, Orwell insists that 'Catholic critics' – apparently in his mind a single amorphous group – tended to see good in books only when a clear Catholic quality could be attributed to them (XII.108). His now familiar anti-Catholic diatribe culminates in a reassertion of his fixed view of a world plagued by the disintegration of laissez-faire capitalism and of a 'liberal-Christian culture'. His apocalyptic conclusion reads almost as a proposal for *Nineteen Eighty-Four* as he claims that the Western world was moving inexorably into a time of 'totalitarian dictatorships', a period during which freedom of thought will first become a 'deadly sin' and ultimately no more than a 'meaningless abstraction' (XII.110). This point is reaffirmed by the title *Inside the Whale*, recalling the Biblical story of Jonah and the whale and how it stands as a metaphor for accepting experience without seeking, or being able, to change it. By hiding away inside the whale – like Miller safely ensconced in Paris and puzzled why Orwell was bothering to head out to participate in the Spanish Civil War – Jonah preserved his isolation from the trials and tribulations of the outside world.

A central problem with Orwell's estimation in 1940 of the momentous decline of organized religion in England lies in the noticeable lack of evidence in his surviving papers to demonstrate that he ever conducted any serious statistical research to back up these claims. In a letter (11 April 1940) to the academic Humphrey House he frankly admitted that he did not know how many active religious believers were in England but he guessed that the figure was somewhere between ten and six million, the former probably being, in his opinion, the more likely figure. Among these, he speculated, there was only an 'active minority' who would be seriously offended by his idea that the churches rarely 'put their professions into practice'. He concluded by affirming that the established churches no longer exerted any significant hold over the minds of the working class, apart perhaps from 'Catholic Irish labourers' (XII.139–40). Once again, the many thousands of working- and middle-class English citizens who were devout Catholics but whose employment hardly equated to that of 'labourers' simply did not figure in Orwell's imagination or researches as a journalist.

Some salient facts about the vitality and spread of Catholicism at this period should be recorded at this point. During the latter half of the 1930s the Catholic population of England and Wales stood at approximately 2,350,000 (from a total population of about 40 million), supported by some 4,500 priests and 2,400 churches. In Scotland, there were about five million citizens of whom some 615,000 were Catholics. Most were lower-middle-class or working-class, often of Irish ancestry, and many lived within the conurbations of London, Glasgow and the north-west of England, especially Liverpool, Manchester and the Lancashire cotton towns. A much smaller grouping, largely drawn from the upper-middle and upper classes, were descendants of the 'Old English' Catholic families whose religious heritage often stretched back before the Reformation and who possessed strong links to the great Catholic public schools, such as Stonyhurst, Ampleforth and Downside, and overseas vocational establishments such as Douai in northern France and the English College at Rome.[17] Such information was easily verifiable, for example, from the annual *Catholic Directory*. But for a writer who systematically collected in his diaries and notebooks (as befits a working journalist) a miscellany of information from newspapers, journals, reviewed books, radio broadcasts and private conversations and correspondence, Orwell's apparent indifference to verifying his facts about Catholicism and other established religions in England is nothing short of astonishing. It seems that in his mind members of the upper classes who were practising believers could be written off as over-privileged elitists. No less negatively, the devout were more sympathetically, if patronizingly, viewed as mindlessly loyal drones or mere 'Irish labourers', recalling Winston's entry in his diary in *Nineteen Eighty-Four*: 'If there is hope ... it lies in the proles' (IX.56). By far the largest number, the religiously observant working and middle classes, were simply to be ignored or dismissed as occasional users (like himself) of church facilities for births, marriages and deaths but generally only through a desire to please parents or a nostalgic delight in the picturesque aspects of English devotional traditions.

The second essay of *Inside the Whale*, 'Charles Dickens', detailed how some Catholics had sought to identify Dickens as 'almost' a Catholic (XII.20), a point reiterated in May 1942 when Orwell noted in a review of Edmund Wilson's *The Wound and the Bow* that G. K. Chesterton had sought to depict Dickens as a 'Catholic medievalist' (XIII.35). While Orwell readily admitted that Dickens had in the past been appropriated, variously, by Marxists, Catholics and Conservatives (XII.47), he admired his resolute 'Christian morality', especially in his habitual siding with the poor and oppressed against their oppressors. For Orwell, Dickens was a kind of zealous missionary, like himself always supporting the underdog, and even though he considered him to have loathed the Catholic Church, as soon as Catholics seemed under persecution (as in *Barnaby Rudge*) he was 'on their side' (XII.54).

In the month following the publication of *Inside the Whale*, Orwell's 'Notes on the Way' column in *Time and Tide* (6 April) reviewed *The Thirties* by the then left-wing agnostic journalist and later Catholic convert Malcolm Muggeridge, who, like Orwell, had worked in India during the 1920s.[18] Many of Muggeridge's social and religious perspectives chimed with Orwell's scepticism over the decline of organized religions during the early twentieth century. He agreed that a conviction had steadily grown that it was necessary for the soul of man to be cut away because traditional religious belief had commonly become a device of repressive social control and had had to be abandoned. Even in the Victorian period, it seemed, religious institutions peddled what was essentially a lie, a 'semi-conscious device for keeping the rich rich and the poor poor'. The poor were expected to tolerate their poverty in return for eternal happiness beyond the grave since both rich and poor alike were, supposedly, spiritually united in being the 'children of God'. Orwell saw this lie as running throughout the fabric of capitalism and insisted, with Muggeridge, that it must be eradicated. The unforeseen problem with such views was that a world without religion invariably regresses to a state of 'savagery' (XII.124). His review explains how the essential qualities of Muggeridge's book were encapsulated in two famous quotations from Ecclesiastes: 'Vanity of vanities, saith the preacher; all is vanity'; and 'Fear God, and keep His Commandments, for this is the whole duty of man'. He then parodies the Gospel command to 'Render to Caesar the things that are Caesar's and to God the things that are God's' (Matthew 22.21, Mark 12.17, Luke 20.25) with the view that Western society was now experiencing nightmarish horrors because, through a hubristic belief in progress, humanity had tried to set up an 'earthly paradise'. This meant that by trusting only to human leadership, society now 'rendered unto Caesar the things that are God's'. If the soul, Orwell argued, is excised from an individual's being, then, like surgical procedures, there is always a risk of the wound turning 'septic' (XII.125).

Orwell acknowledges and respects Muggeridge's agnosticism and agrees with him that belief in God has been steadily vanishing from Western societies for several generations. The consequences of this loss are huge for countries now drawn into international military conflict. If the Bible once taught that only supernatural sanctions should prevail, then a belief that the only true wisdom lay in a 'fear of God' must have naturally followed. But, Orwell reasons, if nobody any longer fears God, then there cannot be any fundamental wisdom still possessed by humankind. Furthermore, even if an old-style belief in the 'Kingdom of Heaven' has been lost, 'Marxist realism' must also be judged to have failed (XII.125). Instead, Orwell envisages the return of a kind of Spanish Inquisition but one which is to be even more dreaded (especially by ordinary Winston Smiths) due to the all-pervading power of radio transmissions and secret police surveillance. He proposes that only the reinstatement of the secular concept of human brotherhood without a dependence upon a belief in another eternal world would provide a sense of renewed meaning to Western European societies. In effect, he argues, we still need to feel as though we are the 'children of God', despite the traditional God of the English Prayer Book no longer holding much validity for most people.

Within these pessimistic perspectives lie the seeds of thought which ultimately stimulated the creation of Orwell's fictional dystopias in *Animal Farm* and *Nineteen Eighty-Four*, as illustrated by his careful reiteration of the crucial (but usually overlooked) first phrase in Marx's famous axiom: 'Religion is the sigh of the soul in a soulless world. Religion is the opium of the people'. Orwell is keen to emphasize that Marx never claimed that religion was merely a drug imposed upon the people by their superiors but rather that they create it for themselves in response to a 'real' and

where comes an argument

heartfelt need (XII.126). As this review eloquently illustrates, the welfare and health of the individual soul became for Orwell central to his concern for humanity during wartime conditions. He reiterated these ideas in a later review in *Tribune* (21 June 1940) of the novel *A Hero of Our Own Times* by the Russian Romantic writer and painter Mikhail Yurevich Lermontoff. This novel demonstrated to Orwell how during the last century the breakdown of Christianity and the dissipation of belief in the immortality of the soul lost any sense of spiritual meaning from European life, resulting in many leading nineteenth-century figures being 'haunted by a sense of futility' (XII.190).

Inside the Whale also enabled Orwell to return to his increasingly sympathetic treatment of the Jews – a far cry from his callous references to them in *Down and Out in Paris and London*. In his essay on Dickens he categorically asserts that he reveals anti-Semitic prejudices, although he seems on shakier ground when he tries to argue that Dickens merely assumes that receivers of stolen goods in both *Oliver Twist* and *Great Expectations* will be Jewish because during this period such an assumption was justified. Clearly, Orwell did not wish at this point in his essay to be drawn into a potentially lengthy and difficult digression over the prevalence of anti-Semitic characterizations in nineteenth-century literature (and his own writings of the late 1920s). Instead, he commends Dickens for being remarkably free from the folly of treating nations as individuals and for rarely making jokes based upon nationality. In particular, he admires the judicious depiction of the French in *A Tale of Two Cities*, remarking that there is not a single line of the novel that could be interpreted as saying: 'Look how these wicked Frenchmen behave!' (XII.35). Clearly, Orwell was overlooking Dickens's vicious *tricoteuse* Madame Defarge in this novel, as well as his malevolent French murderer Blandois (alias Langier and Rigaud) in *Little Dorrit*.

Inevitably during 1940, the fate of European Jews tended to draw Orwell's attention away from purely literary considerations of the anti-Semitism of earlier periods. But his attitude to Hitler also remained highly idiosyncratic, at least from the evidence of his review for *New English Weekly* (21 March 1940) of an unabridged English translation of *Mein Kampf*. Although the review recognizes this manifesto as the product of the obsessive thoughts of a 'monomaniac' he admits that he had been unable to 'dislike Hitler', given that (like many others during the 1930s) he had at first underestimated his political threat and brutal methodologies. He describes a photograph included in the volume of Hitler in his early Brownshirt days as conveying the pathos of a downtrodden outsider with the pathetic expression of a man burdened with great injustices. While this perspective is perhaps understandable, given Hitler's nondescript physique, Orwell then bizarrely suggests that this image conveys in a 'rather more manly way' the impression conveyed by traditional images of the crucified Christ and he concludes that this is exactly how Hitler now views himself. Quite how

Hitler appears more 'manly' than Christ on the Cross is not elucidated but Orwell concludes by asserting that he would certainly assassinate Hitler if he could, even though he felt no 'personal animosity' (XII.117) towards him. No less provocatively, in an August 1941 *Horizon* article Orwell tentatively compared Hitler to an Antichrist or the Holy Ghost (XII.538).

In his 'Notes on the Way' column for *Time and Tide* (30 March 1940) Orwell condemns with distaste the views of Dr Robert Ley, a virulently anti-Semitic leader of the German Labour Front who later committed suicide in 1945 while awaiting trial for war crimes at Nuremberg. Ley argued that 'inferior races', including Poles and Jews, did not need to eat as much as Aryan Germans; and Orwell's review recognizes that the current prevalence of such anti-Semitic hatred meant that it was virtually guaranteed that somewhere a German was 'kicking a Jew' – an understated caricature of what was actually happening to German, Polish, French and other Jews during spring 1940. He explains that age-old concepts of racial supremacy – from which the colonial English had hardly been innocent – lay behind the current escalation of the violence of Nazi Germany towards Jews, Poles and all other national groupings viewed as alien to the genocidal ambitions of the Third Reich. Orwell proposes that authorities or, as he denotes them, 'aristocracies' with tangible political powers, historically exploited differences in race, including Normans conquering Saxons, Germans ruling over Slavs, Englishmen suppressing the Irish and, most commonly, white races dehumanizing blacks. The aristocrat, Orwell proposes, had always found it preferable to be ruthless towards those who differed from himself in 'blood and bone' and such views were sadly central to human nature. He even recalls hearing extreme racial theories in Burma which were less brutal than Hitler's treatment of the Jews but no 'less idiotic' (XII.121–2).

Throughout much of the war Orwell carefully monitored news of the treatment of European Jews, for instance including in one of his BBC radio 'English News Reports' for India (12 December 1942) details of the Polish government's reports about the systematic massacres of Jews in occupied Poland. He also notes that the Nazis in France were now beginning to put into place strict anti-Jewish laws and that numerous French Jews were being deported eastwards. Although it is uncertain exactly how much Orwell knew by late 1942 about the horrors of German concentration camps, his talk details how thousands of deported men, women and children had been packed into cattle-trucks by the German militia without either food or water, thereby ensuring that many had died by the time the trucks were opened in Russian territory. He also cited Polish estimates that of the three million Jews living in the country before the war over one third had been either killed, had starved to death or had perished through 'general misery'. These haunting images lingered in Orwell's mind, resurfacing in his grim description in *Nineteen Eighty-Four* of the prisoner with a 'tormented, skull-like face' who was 'dying of starvation' (XI.247). He concluded this talk – and BBC notes indicate that he personally read this India broadcast

– by emphasising that he was not merely seeking to repeat horrific accounts of the treatment of Jews but rather that he considered that such clinically calculating cruelty, utterly unlike the violence of the battlefield, confirmed the true evil of Fascism as the enemy 'we are fighting against' (XIV.234).

It is noticeable, however, that Orwell's broadcast and published utterances on the Jews tended to strike a very different tone to various notes made for his private reference and research. For example, in his personal 'War-time Diary' (15 October 1940), written from Wallington, he recorded rumours among the local community about the growing population of Jews in Baldock, an historic market town in north Hertfordshire; and that an unidentified source had advised him that Jews predominated among citizens taking shelter in Tube stations. In response, he added as a note to himself: 'Must try and verify this' (XII.273). Such notations in no way imply anti-Semitism on Orwell's part but rather confirm his wish to act as an objective and accurate documentary reporter (a quality, however, never much in evidence in his utterances about Roman Catholics). Nevertheless, the tone of his research findings as recorded in this diary ten days later (25 October 1940) remains more troubling. When he visited the crowds taking shelter in Chancery Lane, Oxford Circus and Baker Street tube stations he noted that they were certainly not all Jewish but that there seemed a larger number of Jews than might normally be expected in such a crowd. He suggested that what was most unattractive about Jews was that they were not only 'conspicuous' but seemed to seek consciously to be so. Describing a 'fearful Jewish woman, a regular comic-paper cartoon of a Jewess', who battled her way out of a tube train at Oxford Circus and hit anyone who stood in her way, he wryly recalled that such behaviour reminded him of Jewish individuals on the 'Paris Métro' during the 1920s (XII.278). In the same diary entry, he notes the views of another unidentified left-wing source, recorded only as 'D.', who tended to confirm current anti-Semitic feelings. This individual had even claimed that some Jewish businessmen were 'turning pro-Hitler' or about to do so. Orwell records his own incredulity at this claim and notes that 'D.' had justified it by resorting to the old smear that supposedly masochistic Jews 'always admire anyone who kicks them'. But he then compounds the problematic nature of this diary entry by musing over whether some European Jews would actually prefer 'Hitler's kind of social system' to Britain's, if only they had not been so systematically persecuted during the 1930s (XII.278).

On a more positive note, Orwell enthusiastically reviewed Charlie Chaplin's satirical comedy film '*The Great Dictator*' for *Time and Tide*, briefly on 14 December and then at more length on 21 December 1940. In the preliminary notice he described how an insignificant Jewish barber (played by Chaplin) had escaped from a political 'concentration camp' – an early usage of this term in the British media since the United Nations' *Joint Declaration* confirming and condemning the Nazi camps was not published until December 1942 – and is then mistaken for the Dictator of Tomania,[19]

Herr 'Heinkel', who bears a striking resemblance to Hitler. He commended the film's powerful conclusion, culminating in a fine speech supporting democracy (XII.308), and provided more specific detail about the film in the second review. Here he describes how the barber first escaped from a mental asylum where he had been confined for some twenty years with amnesia after heroic service in the German Army during the First World War. When he returned to his familial ghetto to resume his trade as a barber, he finds that Herr 'Hynkel' (the correct spelling) is conducting a ruthless purge against the Jews and he is arrested and thrown into a concentration camp. He manages to escape in a stolen uniform but is then mistaken for Hynkel. Surrounded by Nazi dignitaries and soldiers, he delivers his renowned speech advocating political democracy based upon common decency and tolerance. Orwell describes this speech as a Hollywood version of Lincoln's Gettysburg address and commends it as a powerful piece of anti-Fascist propaganda, demonstrating Chaplin's ability to represent the simple wisdom of the common man. This kind of ordinary individual, unlike pompous intellectuals who had concocted supposedly logical reasons for suppressing and torturing Jews, works only from instinct and tradition and knows intuitively that it simply 'isn't right' to vandalize the homes of insignificant Jewish 'shopkeepers' (XII.313–15).

5

The Second World War

The Lion and the Unicorn (1941) and the Second World War (1941–2)

Subtitled *Socialism and the English Genius,* Orwell's *The Lion and the Unicorn* was published on 19 February 1941 as the first in Secker & Warburg's Searchlight Books series, planned by Fredric Warburg, Tosco Fyvel and Orwell as a means of bringing writers together to consider key wartime issues. This hastily written sixty-four-page pamphlet eloquently expressed Orwell's implicit affection for the benign religious traditions of English society, encapsulated in the dreamy image of 'old maids biking to Holy Communion through the mists of autumn mornings'. But it also voiced Orwell's characteristic desire to secularize traditional religious institutions since he claims that the 'common people' – a sweeping generalization conveniently undefined in this pamphlet – lack any specific religious beliefs and have quietly been so for several centuries. He dismisses the increasingly ineffectual Anglican Church as now merely the territory of the English landed classes. Similarly, the Nonconformist sects have become little more than 'influenced minorities', an indeterminate phrase which, again, is never specifically defined. English Roman Catholics do not merit any mention at this point in *The Lion and the Unicorn.*

Despite an overwhelming sense of spiritual decline, Orwell argued that the English people still retained a deep strain of Christian sentiment, even though they had now almost completely forgotten about the 'name of Christ'. More positively, he celebrated the view that the new secular European religion, which he denoted as 'power-worship', had not managed to contaminate the thinking of ordinary people, even though, predictably for Orwell, it had seemingly infected the metropolitan intelligentsia (XII.393–5). His solution to this socio-spiritual dilemma is a loosely defined one, blending elements of democratic liberalism and tolerant humanitarianism with a patently unattainable form of utopianism. Orwell's resolutely secular brand of English socialism could now steadily come to the fore (provided the Germans did not invade and conquer Britain), leading to a disestablishment of the Church while also ensuring that religious persecution would not be tolerated. At the heart of this new model society would be a vague respect for the moral tenets of Christianity and, as toleration of difference finally reigns supreme, it would even be acceptable for England occasionally to be described as a 'Christian Country'. Nonconformists and most Anglicans would be able to live with such an arrangement and, inevitably, only the 'Catholic Church will war against it' (XII.427).

Given the pamphlet's alluring but ultimately whimsical socialist perspectives – advocating the retention of the monarchy but the abolition of the House of Lords, greater political powers for skilled workers, a judicial system reconstituted along sternly benign lines and the nationalization of all major industries – it is understandable that in the grim post-war world of 1949 Orwell recommended that it should not be reprinted (XII.391). Ultimately, *The Lion and the Unicorn* stands as an eloquent expression of an Orwellian socialist dream world but one which was ultimately swept away not by invading Fascists but by the unavoidable circumstances of the harsh social reality of the later 1940s. It is interesting, however, to see how some of its axioms, especially the policies of nationalization and international collaboration, prefigured the central policies of Sir Richard Ackland's left-wing egalitarian Common Wealth Party, founded in July 1942. Orwell was generally supportive of this new party's political perspectives, noting in the *Partisan Review* (July–August 1943) that several Anglican priests were already prominent among its membership while it was generally opposed by the 'Catholics' (XV.103–6, 108–9). *The Lion and the Unicorn* should also be read alongside his seminal essay 'Fascism and Democracy', published in *The Left News* (February 1941), in which he highlighted the dangers posed by British Fascists and Communists and his categorical assertion that Communism had always been a 'lost cause' in Western Europe. Crucially, this essay underlines Orwell's firm belief in the need for an absolute 'faith in Democracy' (XII.381) and confirms his attempts to cast democratic socialism as a viable substitute for (or at least a parallel framework to) traditional religious spirituality (XII.380–1).

Orwell's 'War-time Diary' reveals just how much the involvement of religious institutions in public affairs tended to annoy him, often on a superficial or petty level. On 23 March 1941 he took part in a semi-compulsory Home Guard church parade to mark a national day of prayer. He recorded how he had been appalled from the outset by the sheer 'jingoism' and pompous self-righteousness of the event, even though he readily accepted that the Church had a significant role to play in any nationally declared war. While he understood the morale-boosting role of bishops blessing regimental colours and the Church condoning Parliament's commitment to war in a time of national emergency, he detested the apparent lack of any form of self-criticism within church ceremonies. Prayers were automatically invoked for the assistance of God for the British and Allied cause simply because, Orwell speculated ironically, 'we are *better* than the Germans'. His anger prompted him to dismiss the entire day of national prayer as no more than a self-deluding 'box barrage fired at the angels' (XII.456). Similarly, he recorded in the same diary how he had attended an open-air church parade in Regent's Park on 27 September 1942. He listened to a sermon packed with the usual 'jingoistic muck' which was almost enough to render him pro-German during its delivery. He dismissed a special prayer for the besieged residents of Stalingrad as no more than a 'Judas kiss' and noted how the purity of the clergyman's white surplice looked entirely wrong when surrounded by military uniforms (XIV.61).

Despite such feelings, Orwell was also at pains under wartime conditions to draw a clear distinction between what he deemed the totalitarianism of the Church and that of the Nazis and other Fascists. In one of his BBC India talks, on 'Literature and Totalitarianism', he argued that literature as it is generally known probably could not survive under the incipient secular totalitarianism of Western European Fascism.[1] In previous centuries literature had thrived because the totalitarianism of the Church was essentially unchanging or only ever changed very slowly. The medieval Catholic Church had dictated for centuries exactly what should be believed and he felt that the same was true for any 'orthodox Christian, Hindu, Buddhist or Moslem today'. Hence, writers knew what could and could not be said with clear parameters set for intellectual and theological debates. But the peculiarity of modern godless totalitarianism is that, although it constantly seeks to control thought, discussion and publications, it does not necessarily fix the limits of what it defines as conformist or acceptable. Secular totalitarianism promulgates and imposes questionable dogmas which may change from day to day. But the point of such dogmas is never to establish truth but merely to enforce absolute obedience from its subjects, even though these changes are driven by the transient requirements of power politics (XII.504). The critic Alex Zwerdling describes how ideological political elites, even socialist ones, reflected for Orwell the tendencies of the 'Catholic Church, with its emphasis on dogma and its domination by a priest caste that interposes itself between the ordinary man and truth'. In contrast, Orwell always sought to adopt the stance of a decent 'Protestant socialist', arguing that every man should have 'access to the Word' and be 'considered competent to understand the world around him without the benefit of a socialist priesthood'.[2]

In the same 'War-time Diary' (6 July 1941) Orwell recorded his scrutinizing of several Catholic papers and the Catholic journal *Truth* to assess the English Roman Catholic Church's attitude towards Britain's potential military alliance with Russia. It seemed to him that most of these Catholic publications had not gone pro-Nazi and seemed unlikely to do so, but, in worrying contrast, he felt that some Irish Catholic papers were expressing 'frankly pro-Nazi' sentiments and, if so, there would probably be similar sentiments expressed in the US (XII.525). This kind of *aide-memoire* note was often used to support his 'London Letter' columns, written for the

Partisan Review (January 1941–summer 1946), an influential American journal founded in 1934 and encompassing both liberal and conservative viewpoints. In one 'Letter', written in August 1941 and published in the November issue, he began with his familiar (if factually incorrect) assertions that there were approximately two million Catholics in England, mostly 'very poor Irish labourers', while the middle- and upper-class Catholics were 'extremely numerous' in both the Foreign Office and the Consular Service, as well as exerting undue influence over the press. He considered members of the old English Catholic families or, as he called them, 'born' Catholics, as less 'ultramontane' (papist) and more traditionally patriotic than converted intellectuals, naming Monsignor Ronald Knox and Arnold Lunn as examples of the latter elitist category. More provocatively, he regarded the majority of these intellectual converts as having essentially the same mental framework, '*mutatis mutandis*, as the British Communists'. He condemned their earlier pro-Fascist activities but noted that since the outbreak of war they had not dared to express open support for Hitler. Instead, he argued, they preferred to disseminate such propaganda implicitly via by their fulsome praises for Marshall Pétain and General Franco.

However, it was within the context of potential English responses to the still developing Russian military situation that the virulent extremity of Orwell's hostility towards the Catholic Church was given its most intense and disturbing expression. He notes in this same 'Letter' that as soon as Hitler invaded the USSR, the English Catholic press recommended taking advantage of the respite which the Germans opening up a Russian front should bring to the British war effort. But, at the same time, their hierarchy was insistent that there should be no talk of an alliance with the Communists of 'godless Russia'. Indeed, in Orwell's opinion the Catholic press had become much more anti-Soviet when their military resistance towards Hitler's invading forces seemed to be having some success. Orwell's sombre conclusions over the essentially Fascist political stance of the Catholic elite offer a clear reflection of his hatred of what he regarded as the controlling forces of a self-serving minority then active within the Catholic Church. He begins by claiming that anyone who was familiar with Catholic literature (no specific references are supplied) of the previous ten years could not doubt that the majority of the Church's 'hierarchy and intelligentsia' would choose ultimately to ally themselves with Germany rather than Russia. Such a decision was firmly rooted, Orwell proposed, in their inherent hatred of communist Russia that was virulent enough even to alienate a hardened anti-Stalinist like himself. Much of the Church's anti-Soviet propaganda, such as its pious denunciation of Bolshevik atrocities, seemed to him retrospectively focused and of little relevance to the British working classes. Moreover, regardless of whether Hitler's forces reached Moscow or the Russians gathered to invade Europe, he suspected that the Catholic hierarchy would soon openly support Hitler. Disturbingly, he concluded that they would also be keen to seek some sort of compromise peace. He speculated that if an English equivalent of the Pétain government was ever established it would have to depend heavily upon the Catholic authorities, concluding that they were the only 'conscious, logical, intelligent enemies' of English democracy and that it would be a serious error merely to despise and denigrate them (XII.548–9). In another entry in his 'War-time Diary', dated 14 March 1942, Orwell again reiterated his conviction that anti-Russian feeling was being subversively fostered by the 'Catholics' (XIII.230). Such incendiary views remained private but not intentionally so since the diary still exists in two forms. One draft is in manuscript, clearly written at the time, and another in a lightly edited form, typed up later that same year by Orwell himself so that it might be published with the war diary of his friend, the novelist and journalist Inez Holden. Eventually, however, only Holden's diary was published as *It Was Different at the Time* (1943).[3]

Due to the sheer pressure of his commissioning, writing and editorial commitments at the BBC, along with his occasional journalism, Orwell suspended work on any larger projects, although he retained a keen interest in how other authors had responded to the challenges of faith, spiritual belief and, to his eyes, the declining authority of the established churches of England. In an essay for *Tribune* (18 September 1942), 'Thomas Hardy Looks at War', he discussed his poetic drama, *The Dynasts*. Orwell saw in Hardy's vision of life a desire to confirm that experience is predetermined and that all humans are merely animated automata buoyed up by the 'illusion of free will' and the potency of suffering. Almost enviously, Orwell analysed how in Hardy's world everything seemed to be controlled by something externally omnipotent called the 'Immanent Will' whose purposes can never be understood or defined by common humanity. He felt that it told readers of the 1940s a great deal about Hardy. He had firmly believed in a God but always referred to Him as an 'It' whose purposes can never be understood by ordinary mortals (XIV.43). Similarly, in an essay on 'T. S. Eliot' for *Poetry* (October–November 1942) he joked that even he would find it too crude to state that every contemporary poet is faced with the choice of dying young, entering the 'Catholic Church' or joining the Communist Party. Instead, in Eliot's choice of conversion to High Church Anglicanism, Orwell saw an attempted escape from the loneliness of urban secular individualism into a spiritual community which did not necessarily impose upon its adherents the all-constricting conformity of the Catholic Church since Anglo-Catholics did not seek to force any specific political line on its adherents. Nevertheless, he still firmly believed that all Christian churches demanded from their faithful an adherence to ancient doctrines to which credence could no longer be readily given. To Orwell the most obvious example was an unwavering insistence in Christian creeds upon the immortality of the soul. More cynically, he concluded that if a man seeks some kind of purpose in life, especially one which is progressive rather than reactionary, then the obvious and immediately comforting refuge is the Church, which merely asks in return an acceptance of harmless but comfortingly traditional 'intellectual absurdities' (XIV.65–6).

Ironically, December 1942 closed with Orwell in the guise of the homely promulgator of the traditional Christian Christmas Message, via his poetry magazine 'Voice' which he wrote and directed for the Indian section of the BBC's Eastern Service. The 29 December episode comprised a Christmas special, with hymns, readings and discussions seeking to define the essential qualities of the festival of Christmas as something central to Western culture and spirituality. Along with William Empson and Herbert Read, Orwell endeavoured to explain to his Indian audience its key concepts, which he catalogued as wintery snow, family feasting, Christ's nativity and the exchanging of gifts. In scripted dialogue with Herbert Read, Orwell pondered the Biblical story of Christ's birth, with Read replying that it encapsulated the concept of 'power and wisdom abasing themselves before innocence and poverty'. Verses from Matthew's Gospel (2.1-4, 7-15) were read by Venu Chitale of the BBC's Indian Section and Read recited an edited down version of John Milton's 'Hymn on the Morning of Christ's Nativity'. After a choral 'Gloria in Exclesis', and a pre-recording of T. S. Eliot's 'Journey of the Magi', the broadcast concluded with William Empson reading Robert Bridges's moving poem, 'Christmas Eve 1913', and closed to the sounds of the Royal Choral Society's 'In Dulci Jubilo', conducted by Sir Malcolm Sargent (XIV.262–4).

1943: A wasted year

During 1943 Orwell's duties at the BBC, commissioning and drafting talks for the India section of the Far Eastern service, occupied most of his working days. Other essays and journalism were sidelined (as well as being limited by his BBC contract) with no time left for beginning a new novel. Although often exhausted, he tolerated this situation because he believed that the war might be concluded within twelve or so months. He wrote optimistically on 3 January 1943 in his 'A Letter from England' for the *Partisan Review* (March–April 1943) that the defeat of Germany was now expected during either 1943 or 1944. He continued to insist, however, that both the Church and the literary intelligentsia held a special responsibility in defending the country from the incursions of Fascism. In the same *Partisan Review* 'Letter' he noted the growth of a more extreme faction of left-wingers within the Church of England, centred not, as might be expected, on the modernists but rather on the dogmatic Anglo-Catholics whom he denoted as the Church's 'extreme "right-wing"'. He also claimed that sections of the Roman Catholic press had become distinctly more pro-Fascist since the death of Admiral Darlan, formerly a deputy leader of the French Vichy

Government and a German collaborator who had controversially gone over to the Allies when they invaded North Africa, only to be assassinated in Algiers on Christmas Eve 1942. This apparent shift in the Catholic press, Orwell argued, was indicative of a divide forming within the Catholic intelligentsia over the dangers of Fascism, noting that they had previously avoided public attacks on one another (XIV.295–6). Written in late May 1943, another of Orwell's reports for the *Partisan Review* (July–August 1943) stated that the left-wing English intelligentsia were in awe of Stalin (Orwell's word is 'worshipped') because they were bereft of both the spirit of patriotism and religious belief but had not shaken off their psychological necessity for a 'god and a Fatherland'. He even repeated his incendiary view that in the spiritual void of such a world many of them, in the event of a German victory, were likely to transfer their loyalties to Hitler (XV.107).

In one of the few book reviews published by Orwell at this period (*Horizon*, January 1943), he insisted that the political and religious beliefs of a writer would always be traceable in even the minutest details of his work. The author in question was W. B., Yeats whose poetry had been depicted by V. K. Narayana Menon, an employee of the BBC Indian Service, as revealing an 'exultant acceptance of authoritarianism'. For Orwell, Menon's study confirmed that Yeats's tendency was indeed towards Fascism but via the so-called 'aristocratic route'. He saw Yeats as longing for a new 'aristocratic civilization' – an accusation which he later also levelled against Evelyn Waugh in the 1940s – in which the Emperor is a 'God dependent upon a great God'. He considered that Yeats's fascination with magic implicitly linked him with Fascism since both expressed a deep hostility towards Christian ethics (XIV.281–2). Inevitably, this review generated a range of angry responses, but Orwell remained firm in insisting that a writer's political and religious views would always impact directly upon his 'aesthetic achievements' (XIV.285).

In contrast, Orwell was far more ready to defend the reputation of T. S. Eliot with whom he shared a productive literary relationship, even if their religious and political views were divergent. In an equivocal review (*The Observer*, 7 November 1943) of *I Sit and I Think and I Wonder* by Sidney Dark, a recent editor of the gently left-wing *Church Times*, Orwell recommended his book to any left-wingers who had failed to understand the political perspectives of the Anglo-Catholic movement and to readers who still considered all religious believers to be reactionaries. Dark's diligent attempts to present himself as an orthodox left-winger, Orwell argued, prompted him to accept simplistic solutions to complex political problems such as the Palestine question.[4] Equally reprehensibly, Dark clearly wished to be seen 'walloping his co-religionist' Eliot, even though his book revealed, in Orwell's opinion, no real understanding of Eliot's motives as a High Church Anglican (XV.304).[5]

During 1943 the rise of Western European anti-Semitism increasingly preoccupied Orwell's radio broadcasts and the still limited range of his other publications. He had begun the year in a cautiously positive frame of mind by suggesting on 3 January in his 'A Letter from England' for the *Partisan Review* (March–April 1943) that, although there was still some anti-Semitism in Britain, there seemed to be no sign of its escalation (XIV.296). Just under two months later his BBC 'Weekly News Review' for India, broadcast and read by Orwell himself on 27 February, noted how Hitler had not personally attended the celebrations to mark the anniversary of the founding of the Nazi Party in February 1920, supposedly because he was preoccupied with military duties relating to the Russian front. But a scripted speech read out on his behalf, Orwell noted, was made up almost entirely of his ranting against the Jews, Bolsheviks and other supposed traitors within Germany. Reports of the grim implications of this second-hand oratory accentuated Orwell's awareness of the genocidal horrors now unambiguously posed by German anti-Semitism. Two chillingly totalitarian threats were promulgated by this hectoring diatribe: one was that Hitler's regime intended to murder every European Jew and, second, that Germany could not afford to be 'over-scrupulous' in its handling of 'aliens', implying that reduced rations and more forced labour remained the fate of already subjugated European nations (XIV.361).

In late May news began to filter through to England of the massacre of Jews in the Warsaw ghetto which took place between 20 April and 16 May 1943. At least 56,000 people were killed and survivors were transported to their deaths in concentration camps. In his 'London Letter', drafted in late May for the *Partisan Review* (July–August 1943), Orwell confirmed – in a striking understatement – that anti-Semitism could now be deemed as something of a 'problem'. Although he noted that British radio was reporting the dire situation in the Warsaw ghetto, it is unlikely that he possessed at this stage any detailed knowledge of the full extent of German atrocities against Jews. Instead, Orwell's literary focus remained primarily on the rise of anti-Semitism in England since it seemed to him that everyone was now very much aware of it, given how it was being analysed 'interminably' by the British press. In this substantial and potentially influential (especially in the US) analysis of the problem, Orwell noted that Jews had long been regarded as socially inferior in England and had been effectively debarred from various professions, citing the Royal Navy as an employer which was unlikely to engage Jews as senior officers.

This 'Letter' also conveys Orwell's personal uncertainties and inconsistencies over the specific causes and spread of anti-Semitism in 1940s England. For example, his sweeping statement that anti-Semitism was mainly a 'working-class thing' and that it was most commonly found among 'Irish labourers' seems to have been based purely on anecdotal and fragmentary observation. Such a claim merits closer scrutiny, not least because the term 'Irish labourers' in Orwell's journalism invariably implies Catholics. But were working-class Irish Catholics at this period significantly more hostile towards Jews than, say, Protestant working men or, for that matter, other social groupings such as the middle classes, the aristocracy or the London intelligentsia? Orwell cites no evidence to support this claim and he seems unaware that not only in London but also in major northern cities, such as Liverpool (Childwall and Aigburth districts), Manchester (Cheetham Hill and Prestwich) and Leeds (Chapeltown and Moortown), communities of first- or second-generation immigrant Irish Catholics and Jews often lived alongside each other without any major social problems. While hostility towards Jews and anti-Semitism was far from uncommon during the early 1940s, it was by no means the Irish Catholic working classes who led the way in such racial discrimination. Individuals from various levels of British society were no less guilty of such attitudes, despite many others (including even some of those who tacitly harboured such racial resentments) experiencing little problem in frequenting Jewish shops and consulting Jewish doctors and lawyers.

In writing about urban life and class issues during the early 1940s Orwell often reveals an ingrained narrowness in his perspectives on English social life. Nor at this period did he have any first-hand experience of social, political or religious issues in Wales, Scotland or Northern Ireland. By the time of his fortieth birthday in June 1944 virtually all of Orwell's British life experiences had been based within the parochial confines of Henley-on-Thames, Eastbourne (St Cyprian's), Windsor (Eton), a remote village in Hertfordshire (Wallington) and London. By neither attending university nor serving in the wartime army, as well as only ever working within either the overseas colonial service or London (apart from brief periods as a schoolteacher), Orwell had experienced very limited personal contacts with ordinary British citizens. Indeed, his reputation as an egalitarian social commentator was based upon a few weeks' strategically planned sojourn in the north of England during the late 1920s and, again very briefly, in down-at-heel parts of London during the 1930s.

Within this context, Orwell's comments on the spread of anti-Semitism in England remain worthy in intention but sometimes suspect in specific detail. He proposed, for example, that while the middle classes would sometimes discriminate against Jews, it was primarily the working classes who fostered the crudely populist view of cunning and sinister Jews who existed by exploiting Gentiles. The anecdotal basis for such a sweeping conclusion seems, at best, unsubstantiated, and at worst, irresponsible hack journalism. To support his view on the growing prevalence of English anti-Semitism, he merely recalls hearing a single working man saying, 'Well I reckon 'Itler done a good job when 'e turned 'em all out', noting that such an individual seemed entirely indifferent to, or ignorant of, the Nazi pogroms, deportations and exterminations. More substantially, he asked whether Jews were treated badly because they were Jews or simply because they were foreigners and he was certain that religious considerations played no part in such attitudes. A strictly orthodox English Jew who was anglicized, Orwell thought, usually attracted less enmity than a non-observant

European Jewish refugee: and he had heard with astonishment some people objecting to Jews because they were German. He went on to explain in this *Partisan Review* 'Letter' how anti-Semitism had spread among the English middle classes, with even those who proclaimed themselves as generally tolerant of their immediate Jewish neighbours still suspecting Jews of avoiding military service, contravening food rationing and pushing to the front of queues. Others accused Jewish political refugees of exploiting England for temporary asylum but, Orwell surmised, such attitudes were merely a convenient way of rationalizing racial prejudice. Similarly, he claimed to have heard members of the British intelligentsia promulgating the view that Jewish refugees were 'petty bourgeois', thereby seeking to cloak their anti-Semitism under a more respectable guise. It even seemed that some British pacifists and other opponents of the war found themselves pressured into anti-Semitism by either popular opinion or their peer-groups.

Hence, by the end of this 'Letter' Orwell had apparently contradicted his initial assertion that anti-Semitism was primarily rooted among working-class Irish labourers, in favour of delineating a far broader spread of anti-Semitic attitudes throughout English society. But he then seemed to dilute his warnings by insisting that his readers should not be tempted to overstate the risks of such behaviour. He stated that in 1943 there was probably less anti-Semitism in England than thirty years earlier, since novels no longer habitually contained depictions of Jews as inferior figures and the 'Jew joke' had been generally absent from theatres, the radio and comic publications since 1934 (following Hitler's rise to power in the preceding year). Nevertheless, while emphasizing that the milder forms of hostility towards Jews found in England in no way matched the genocidal horrors of anti-Semitism under the Nazi regime, he viewed all such tendencies as reprehensible because they tempted the Allied powers to ignore the escalating European refugee problem and to remain conveniently distant from the dangerous circumstances of surviving European Jews (XV.109–11).

Continuing to explore the issue of anti-Semitism, Orwell noted in a BBC India Broadcast on 'Modern English Verse' (13 June) how an average adult person in 1900 would have been astonished to find over forty years later that Jews were being persecuted more severely than they had been even during the Middle Ages (XV.135). Similarly, in a review for *The Observer* (7 November 1943) of *Lest We Regret* by the political journalist and novelist Douglas Reed, Orwell attacked what he viewed as Reed's rabid anti-Semitism. Although Reed had originally been regarded as an opponent of Fascism, Orwell condemned his admiration for one of the early founders of the Nazi Party during the 1920s, Otto Strasser, known as the 'Black Nazi' and 'Hitler's Trotsky'. Strasser, in Orwell's opinion, had merely offered a diluted version of Hitler's extremist views, advocating the persecution of Jews but a 'little less viciously'. Reed even claimed that the Jews had never been systematically persecuted in Germany and that stories about pogroms were merely Zionist propaganda. His implication that Britain had also now become a 'Jew-haunted plutocracy' (XV.303–4) understandably triggered Orwell's angry disgust.

Orwell continued to denounce such crass anti-Semitic views, for example, in his first 'As I Please' *Tribune* column (3 December 1943) in which he memorialized the year soon about to end as an age of 'concentration camps and big beautiful bombs' (XVI.14). He had left the BBC on 24 November and also resigned from the Home Guard (on medical grounds) so that he could take up a post as literary editor of the left-wing newspaper *Tribune*. This new employment gave him considerable time for reviewing, essay writing and more considered politico-religious commentaries, as well as for working on drafts of *Animal Farm* which occupied him from November 1943 until February 1944. He personally regarded 1943 as a wasted year in view of how little other writing he had been able to complete due to his BBC duties. Nevertheless, his commentaries on anti-Semitism, despite at times being uneven and ill informed, played a major part in the formulation of his later views in *Animal Farm* and *Nineteen Eighty-Four* on the dehumanizing threat of all totalitarian regimes and their characteristic persecution of specific groupings viewed as a threat to the ruthless political ambitions of an elite minority.

1944: A productive year

During 1944 Orwell's anxieties over anti-Semitism solidified into a formulating element of his writings, not only through his horror at the persecution and extermination of the Jews but also because in his mind it encapsulated the dangers to humanity of all totalitarian regimes. As he remarked in his tenth 'As I Please' column for *Tribune* (4 February 1944), the most terrifying quality of totalitarianism was not only that it instigates atrocities but that it also seeks to control the 'concept of objective truth' and, thereby, manipulates both the past and the future (XVI.89). In his review for *The Observer* (30 January 1944) of *The Devil and the Jews* by the historian and folklorist Joshua Trachtenberg he proposed that Mass Observation or some such organization should be commissioned to compile a full assessment of the current levels of anti-Semitism which, he proposed, could be viewed as essentially a 'magical doctrine' (Trachtenberg had also written *Jewish Magic and Superstition: A Study in Folk Religion*) rather than just xenophobia and an expression of financial and economic discontent. The latter explanation, Orwell argued, was usually favoured by liberal left-wing thinkers who regarded the persecution of Jews as a manifestation of how a society's authorities sought to blame others for their own mistakes and mismanagement. In contrast, Trachtenberg argued that contemporary anti-Semitism was firmly rooted in a long tradition dating back to the Middle Ages when Jews were denounced, tortured and murdered for a wide range of alleged crimes, including such ridiculous accusations as drinking the blood of Christian children, riding broomsticks and giving birth to piglets. Despite his obvious interest in this line of argument, Orwell still questioned whether tracing medieval and other historical anti-Semitic practices was relevant to modern-day pogroms and racial genocide and, instead, reiterated his view that the whole issue urgently required 'cold-blooded' and objective investigation (XVI.83–5).

Orwell carried over this debate into his next 'As I Please' column (11 February 1944), noting that two kinds of journalism always generated bristling responses from his readers: 'One is to attack the Catholics and the other is to defend the Jews.' It is noticeable, however, that while his responses to anti-Semitism were continually evolving during the 1940s, the tenor of his hostile rants against Catholicism barely changed. Orwell reiterated his scepticism over left-wing attitudes towards anti-Semitism as being essentially an economic conspiracy by the ruling classes. He also noted with concern the increasing prevalence among apparently reasonable and well-balanced individuals of a belief that somehow Jews brought persecution upon themselves through their business practices. He again called for a detailed examination of the specific causes of anti-Semitism, and whether or not it was still increasing, or perhaps decreasing, in England. He concluded by noting that tendencies towards anti-Semitism had long been prevalent among literary types, citing Villon, Shakespeare, Smollett, Thackeray, Wells, Huxley and Eliot as authors whose pre-war writings contained passages of hostile terminologies towards Jews which would be deemed distastefully anti-Semitic if they had been published after Hitler's rise to power in 1933.

In terms of Catholic writers Orwell specifically pointed to Belloc and Chesterton as individuals who had 'flirted, or something more than flirted' with the spirit of anti-Semitism (XVI.91–2). Chesterton remained a *bête noire* for Orwell, so much so that in another 'As I Please' column for the *Tribune* (25 February 1944) he commended Chesterton's informative introduction to the new Everyman edition of Dickens's *Hard Times* and, at the same time, condemned his statement that there are no new ideas (referring to the origins of the French Revolution) as one of the meaningless stock arguments of reactionary Catholic apologists. In one of his most sweeping anti-religious generalizations, Orwell linked together Catholic and Hindu intellectuals in a supposed community of reactionary thought. He argued mockingly that every scientific thought or theory, according to the 'popular Catholic press', supposedly had been anticipated by Roger Bacon – a thirteenth-century philosopher and Franciscan friar – and, even more mischievously, that some Hindus claimed the material products of scientific advancement, such as aeroplanes and radios, had been first invented by the Hindus in ancient times who then abandoned them as 'unworthy of attention' (XVI.104). By the early 1940s it seems that derision rather than debate had become a standard trope in Orwell's approach to Roman Catholicism.

He also grew increasingly preoccupied at this period over the validity of the once traditional relationship between civilization and organized religions, especially Christianity. In a review of *The Edge of the Abyss* by the Catholic convert Alfred Noyes he was attracted by his proposition that Western civilization was running the risk of annihilation not only through warfare and economic crises but also because of the decline of a fundamental belief in the presence of good and evil. Noyes's ideas eventually fed into the dystopian world of *Nineteen Eighty-Four*, and Orwell noted with approval his suspicion that the intelligentsia were now even more contaminated by totalitarianism than ordinary people. At the same time, he strongly disagreed with Noyes's conviction that a humane and tolerant society could only ever be founded upon 'Christian principles', pointing out that most of Asia was non-Christian and yet it might reasonably be supposed that some Eastern countries should be deemed capable of forming humane and democratic societies. He also denied the likelihood of Noyes's hope that the Christian faith, as it had once existed in Europe, could ever be restored to the modern world. Instead, Orwell argued that the real crisis facing their times was to re-establish concepts of 'absolute right and wrong' when the philosophical system upon which it used to rest – a firm conviction in the possibility of personal immortality – had been almost entirely lost (XVI.106).

In his fourteenth 'As I Please' column (3 March 1944) Orwell sought to address how currently nebulous approaches to Christian doctrine carried potentially serious difficulties which neither Christians nor well-meaning socialists had previously encountered. A recent correspondent had assured him that whether or not saintly miracles really did occur, and even whether Jesus had ever really existed, should be regarded as only minor matters of personal belief. In contrast, voluble Catholic apologists, including Ronald Knox, insisted that Christian doctrine always meant exactly what it stated and should not be reinterpreted in a 'wishy-washy metaphorical sense'. The problem with such views, Orwell felt, was that many modern day Christians, both Catholics and Anglicans, were sincerely devout in their religious observances but now seemed far less interested in following Church doctrines to the letter. Similarly, the steady removal from Western civilization of the once central belief in life after death had exerted a major spiritual impact upon modern man, leaving disturbing political consequences which still remained unresolved within British society.

Crucially for Orwell's argument, Western civilizations had always previously been based upon a firm conviction in personal immortality, perhaps even more so than a belief in God Himself. This concept had been intrinsic to humanity's understanding of the differences between good and evil. If death is really the end of everything, Orwell argued, it is far more difficult for the defeated to retain a belief in their essential righteousness. Consequently, the modern 'cult of power-worship' becomes instead a dominant element in justifying how the material world is now the only one which counts. Orwell concluded that this apparently irreversible decline in a belief in personal immortality had proved just as significant to modern society as the rise of the 'machine civilisation'. While not personally wishing for the return of a belief in life after death, he argued that modern humankind had a momentous responsibility to develop a 'system of good and evil' independent of ideas of heaven and hell. Otherwise, the ruthless regimes of Hitler's Third Reich and Stalin in Russia, as well as a few years later the pig Napoleon in *Animal Farm* and Big Brother in *Nineteen Eighty-Four*, would relentlessly move in to fill the void. Even Orwell had to conclude that it was impossible to formulate a worthwhile and decent sense of the future without a clear realization of what had been lost by the irrevocable 'decay of Christianity' (XVI.111–13).

One of Orwell's most interesting meditations upon potential links between the Christian Church and secular dictatorships is found in his review of *Faith, Reason and Civilisation* by the former Marxist Harold J. Laski, who was a co-founder of the Left Book Club and became Chairman of the British Labour Party in 1945. It was written (13 March 1944) for the *Manchester Evening News* but rejected and never published. Laski's central theory, Orwell explained, was that the modern USSR could be equated to the Christian Church during the collapse of the Roman Empire, acting as a source for fresh doctrines which could both rescue civilization and facilitate new social advances. Laski traced parallels between how early Christians had created the potential for a new world after the crumbling of the Roman Empire and how Russian ideals might now 'revivify' society in the West, replacing outmoded religious beliefs. The dangers in such an approach seemed to Orwell deeply insidious. Laski, he felt, was willing to tolerate Russian totalitarianism because similarly extreme qualities – 'Heresy hunting, persecution, mental dishonesty' – had all been found among early Christians and yet they still managed to act as the founders of modern civilization. There were, Laski admits, some 'thoughtful pagans' who opposed the 'crudity and superstition' of Christians but, generally, they were only looking after their own interests, just as opponents of Stalin's totalitarianism could be dismissed as self-focused defenders of *laissez-faire* capitalism.

While it may be debated whether this was essentially what Laski had sought to promulgate in *Faith, Reason and Civilisation*, Orwell – never averse to overstating his opponent's intellectual position – insisted that his political premise was erroneous in all particulars. Some obvious flaws in Laski's perspective were immediately highlighted, especially his sense that Stalin's political aims were broadly compatible with Lenin's and that the early Christians were merely a persecuted minority sect. But, most importantly for Orwell, Christianity had remained through the centuries a relatively stable and unchanging doctrine, providing its adherents with the qualities of continuity and clarity of conviction so essential to all productive societies. In contrast, Orwell viewed Communist doctrine as constantly evolving, so frequently and dramatically that a firm belief in it required an abandonment of any sense of intellectual integrity. Orwell concluded in terms that clearly prefigured the central political message of *Animal Farm* which had been completed in the previous month and sent to his agent only a few days after drafting this unpublished review. He proposed that if a dictatorship is established, there are never any guarantees that it will necessarily act as it has promised to do. All extreme, non-democratic forms of Socialism place immense power under the control of an elite clique of self-interested figures who invariably develop as keen an interest in retaining their privileges as British or American capitalists or any other kind of oligarchy (XVI.122–3).

Soon after completing the typescript of his new novel, Orwell read *Tolstoy: His Life and Work* by Derrick Leon. His review for *The Observer* (26 March 1944) marked in his writings an intensified focus – in the shadow of both worldly (Nazi and Stalinist) and fictional (*Animal Farm*) totalitarianism – on the meaning of Christianity from an historical perspective and, specifically, how it had been variously interpreted by other writers. Tolstoy, he proposed, had cultivated for over fifty years a highly idiosyncratic and steadily more extreme form of 'Christian Anarchism', in which all material concerns, revolutionary politics and even national laws and governments were to be regarded as intrinsically evil. Happiness (an ambiguous term when applied to the depressive Tolstoy) could only be derived in such a creed from 'self-abnegation' and absolute obedience to the 'will of God' (XVI.136). Although Tolstoy professed to have based these views on his reading of the Gospels, his outlook seemed to Orwell to be contaminated by two extremist doctrines that could only be regarded as 'doubtfully Christian'. In the first instance, Tolstoy appeared to believe that all human actions were predetermined; and, second, that physical pleasures invariably led to wickedness and that earthly life is defined ultimately by its miseries and sufferings. In Tolstoy, whose novels and pamphlets he greatly admired, Orwell found a writer who had created (anticipating the despairing tones of *Nineteen Eighty-Four*) his own internalized form of hellish totalitarianism in which the human condition was viewed as intrinsically flawed, sinful and possibly beyond redemption.

Orwell's thoughts on Tolstoy's masochistic interpretation of Christian ethics stimulated his interest in how other disparate groupings had adapted the central tenets of Christianity. He reviewed *Coming of Age in Samoa* by the American anthropologist and devout Anglican Episcopalian Margaret Mead for the *Manchester Evening News* (6 April 1944) – which this time chose to publish his review. He was fascinated by her finding that, although the native Samoans were generally Christian, having been converted by Congregationalists from the London Missionary Society, they had readily adapted Christian doctrine to suit their own needs and inherited cultural values. The concept of Christian eclecticism clearly appealed to Orwell and he commended how the Samoans simply ignored the concept of 'original sin' (XVI.144) and rejected most aspects of Western Christian materialism, except for a few basic domestic essentials such as matches and cotton cloth.

It would have been interesting at this point to explore further Orwell's perspectives on his suspicions of the totalitarian tendencies of Roman Catholics but some of the key documentary evidence is missing. This is because his 'As I Please' column of 14 April 1944 elicited a detailed response from the novelist and journalist Antonia White, who had converted to Catholicism at the age of seven with her father. A detailed correspondence ensued but, unfortunately, Orwell's side is now lost and his clearly provocative perspectives on Catholicism can only be reconstructed from a single surviving letter from White, dated 27 April 1944. She expressed scepticism over Orwell's claim that most 'ordinary' people no longer believed in immortality and doubted that there was any reliable means of testing out such a view or, for that matter, even defining the meaning of 'ordinary'. She explained that the deathbed repentance of an unbeliever was not a strict Catholic Article of Faith but merely a traditional belief, noting that even when consciousness seems to have been extinguished, a soul may still have a 'true apprehension of God' and, therefore, make a 'final acceptance or rejection'. White's comments on this issue may well have been in Orwell's mind when he considered the death of Lord Marchmain in Evelyn Waugh's *Brideshead Revisited* in an unpublished essay (XX.74–7) which he began to draft in about April 1949 during his own terminal illness. She strongly supported Orwell's views that a belief in Hell had never proved to be a spur to virtue and that the modern cult of 'power-worship' was directly linked to a decline in a religious faith in immortality. The Church's loss of the allegiance of the common people (as Orwell had apparently argued in his letter) seemed to White to have become a genuine crisis and a 'terrible responsibility'. But she also reminded Orwell of Pope Leo XIII's renowned 1891 encyclical, *Rerum novarum* (Rights and Duties of Capital and Labour), condemning the 'monstrous exploitation of man by man', noting that in many dioceses the parish priests had refused to read it to their congregations because it seemed to be 'sheer socialism'. She also disagreed with Orwell's derogatory insistence upon the Catholic Church's defence of private property by emphasising the Church's support for man's 'natural right to enjoy the fruits of his labour' which, she noted, was 'not at all the same as approving of unbridled capitalism'.

In his lost letter, Orwell had referred to the French Catholic novelist Georges Bernanos, claiming that he was (White quoted Orwell's words) 'no more typical of Catholics than an albino Negro is typical of Negroes'. While agreeing that Bernanos's intense commitment to his faith was probably now only true of a minority of modern-day Catholics, she felt that he was one of the 'truest representatives of the real Catholic spirit' and that he represented a devotional resurgence that was steadily 'growing stronger in the Church'. She agreed with Orwell that it would be desirable to see this level of spiritual commitment more obviously expressed by the 'majority of our bishops' and insisted that it could readily be found among the Dominicans, 'innumerable obscure parish priests' and many members of the laity. However, she dismissed Orwell's suggestion that the Catholic Church should adjust its beliefs to accommodate them to the temper of the 'modern mind' since its message had been entrusted to it by Christ Himself and could not be revised to fit with humankind's changing social or political circumstances. She was struck by Orwell's apparent claim in his letter that either Hinduism or Buddhism might offer alternative religions to Christianity for the 'plain man' (Orwell's term) since she viewed both religions as philosophically complex and 'not native to the western mind'. For White, Christianity offered the only true option for the modern Western European since at 'baptism the soul receives the potentiality of being adopted into a higher order' and of 'sharing the vision of God'. She considered ridiculous Orwell's speculations on the importance of inculcating a 'religious attitude' into modern society without insisting upon the presence of definite religions. Quoting the philosopher and novelist George Santayana, she noted that to 'attempt to be religious without a religion is like trying to speak without a language' (XVI.169–71). It is regrettable that Orwell's contribution to such a thoughtful (on both sides) correspondence has not been traced since the details that can be teased out from White's reply suggest that he was re-engaging constructively with his views on both Christianity and Catholicism as the war began to draw to a close.

Orwell's preoccupation with the cult of 'power-worship' figured prominently in his booklet, *The English People*, commissioned in September 1943 for Collins's series 'Britain in Pictures' and completed by May 1944 (but not published until August 1947). In this analysis of English life, which Orwell regarded as little more than propaganda for the British Council, he insisted that for virtually a century and a half organized religion or, as he described it, 'conscious religious belief of any kind' had been of little significance to ordinary English people. He estimated that only about ten per cent of nominal church members regularly attended services, except (like himself) for births, marriages and deaths. He sensed that a 'vague theism' and a somewhat 'intermittent belief in life after death' was probably still prevalent but most of the principal Christian doctrines were no longer recalled in modern society. Christianity, he argued, was now usually defined by the ordinary man in vaguely ethical terms, such as 'unselfishness' or 'loving your neighbour'. He traced such sentiments back to the early days of the Industrial Revolution when the disruption of traditional village life had destabilized the role of the Established Church in the lives of ordinary people. Orwell was drawing here directly from Jack London's dystopian novel *The Iron Heel* (1908) – a potent influence on *Nineteen Eighty-Four* – which had explained:

With the introduction of machinery and the factory system in the latter part of the eighteenth century, the great mass of the working people was

separated from the land. The old system of labor was broken down. The
working people were driven from their villages and herded into factory
towns. The mothers and children were put to work at the new machines.
Family life ceased. (31)

Similarly, Nonconformist sects had lost much of their potency and Bible
reading had lapsed, with many young people no longer familiar with basic
Bible stories. Nor had Calvinism's 'dismal theology' ever substantially
impacted on the English people, in contrast to its greater success in Scotland
and Wales. This said, he felt that the English common people had remained
more Christian than other social classes, and probably more so than any
other European nation, because of their cultural rejection of the 'modern
cult of power-worship'. While the age-old doctrines of the Christian Church
probably now meant little to these individuals, Orwell felt that they had at
least retained a strong sense of 'might is not right' (XVI.204–6), an axiom
which lay at the very heart of both Christian behaviour and his hatred of
totalitarianism as expressed in *Animal Farm* and *Nineteen Eighty-Four*.

He again picked up on these ideas in his essay about the journalist,
novelist and anti-totalitarian writer Arthur Koestler, completed in September
1944 and published in *Focus, Critical Essays* (1946). Koestler became for
Orwell, in Gordon Bowker's words, 'a looking-glass self' and writing about
him facilitated and enhanced Orwell's powers of self-analysis.[6] Noting
that civilized societies may be uplifted by the inspiring concept of a just
and egalitarian world – denoted spiritually as a heavenly kingdom or in
more secular terms as a classless society or Golden Age – Orwell warned
that all such political aspirations were doomed to failure within modern
societies. Instead, he proposed that the only easy solution afforded to the
religious believer was to treat earthly life merely as a 'preparation' for the
next world. But, since such beliefs in the afterlife had markedly declined,
he suspected that most Christian institutions would not survive if their
economic or financial resources were seriously eroded. Orwell reiterated
that a central challenge for post-war societies would be to revitalize some
form of 'religious attitude' (XVI.399) even if death would still be generally
accepted as final.

Despite the seriousness of Orwell's discussions with Antonia White
and his essay on Koestler, his journalism retained an edgy and often light-
hearted attitude towards religious matters. In a letter of 1 May 1944 to
Philip Rahv, co-founder of the *Partisan Review*, he mockingly suggested
that Stalin had seemingly become comparable to Franco who was so often
treated by politicians and churchmen alike as a 'Christian gent' beyond
criticism (XVI.174). Similarly, when reviewing a biography of General de
Gaulle for the *Manchester Evening News* (5 May 1944) he wryly suggested
that de Gaulle's austere political style and firm policies boiled down to
little more than 'religion and tanks' (XVI.179). Writing about Salvador
Dali, he noted how the artist had combined his distinctly idiosyncratic

Catholicism with accumulating considerable financial wealth (XVI.235). Of course, such facetious tones – damning with faintly patronizing smiles – had long been a staple element in Orwell's critical approaches to institutional religion. In September 1938 he had written in a book review that a communist reverting to liberal values and democracy was about as common as a conversion from 'Catholicism to Protestantism' (XI.202); and in an 'As I Please' column (14 April 1944) he mocked the liberal dispensing of advice on birth rates by 'childless Roman Catholic priests' (XVI.151). Similarly, in a later 'As I Please' column (31 January 1947), he noted that occasionally a person may dye their hair or even convert to Roman Catholicism but humans simply cannot fundamentally change their own natures (XIX.35).

Orwell justified such mocking tones because of his intense dislike of a Catholic intelligentsia which seemed to dominate public debate. In his 'As I Please' column for 23 June 1944, he savagely attacked the newspaper columns of 'Timothy Shy' (D. B. Wyndham Lewis, a 'professional Roman Catholic') in the *News Chronicle* and Beachcomber (J. B. Morton, a 'fellow-Catholic') in the *Express.* He accused both columnists of blindly championing virtually every current reactionary cause, including Mussolini, appeasement, Franco and literary censorship. Both Wyndham Lewis and Morton, he felt, had been committed propagandists against Socialism and the League of Nations. His comments on the two men remain central to an understanding of why Orwell remained so rabidly anti-Catholic. It is clear from his denunciations that the true object of his attacks was what he perceived as their reactionary and pro-Fascist perspectives, in contrast to the far more tolerant and politically indifferent attitudes (which did not really interest him) of the majority of ordinary Catholics. Wyndham Lewis and Morton were both dangerous individuals, Orwell insisted, and should not be regarded as 'comics, pure and simple' but rather as sophisticated propagandists. Their most vociferous co-religionists, such as Chesterton, held them in unduly high regard and approved of their insistent tone of denigration towards England and other largely Protestant countries. Catholic apologists, Orwell felt, systematically claimed superiority not only for Catholic countries (perhaps a reasonable accusation) but also for the Middle Ages as compared with present times (a characteristically Orwellian exaggeration), just as British communists always felt duty-bound to support the Soviet cause.[7] Consequently, in Orwell's eyes, these two columnists systematically sneered and sniped at the most revered of English institutions – tea and cricket, Wordsworth and Chaplin, Nelson and Cromwell – and Wyndham Lewis even lamented the failure of the Spanish Armada and the rise of the modern novel which Orwell regarded as a post-Reformation form of writing intrinsically alien to the Catholic spirit (XVI.263). For Orwell, the retrogressive ultramontanism of these two representatives of a socially privileged group of literary English Catholics rendered them guilty of a treacherous lack of patriotism towards their Protestant homeland. Such a betrayal seemed to Orwell all the more reprehensible during a time of global military conflict and the threatening encroachment into Britain of Western European Fascism and totalitarianism.

Nor were Wyndham Lewis and Morton alone in attracting Orwell's hostility towards their overt commitment to religious faith. In a review of *Beyond Personality* by the academic C. S. Lewis – written for *The Observer*, probably in mid-October 1944, but never published – Orwell aggressively attacked various ideas promulgated by Lewis, a committed Anglican convert, in this collection of his radio broadcasts on theology. Orwell objected to another reviewer having compared Lewis's *The Screwtape Letters* to Bunyan's *Pilgrim's Progress*, mocking the former's frequent use of emphatic italics, its colloquial asides, *faux* geniality and Edwardian slang as a subterfuge to persuade the reader that a Christian could also be a 'decent chap'. This self-conscious style of delivery, Orwell suggested, conveyed the impression that even Lewis realized that the Christian Church had managed to alienate the majority of his potential readership by its stiff traditionalism. As his review turned into a sustained rant, Orwell made no attempt to disguise his distaste for Lewis's tactics in making theology accessible to the masses, claiming that he belonged to a polemical tradition of 'silly-clever apologists' who effectively patronized their audiences with facile styles of delivery. He compared Lewis's style to that of W. H. Mallock who had popularized an easy-reading form of the religious novel. Orwell did at least acknowledge that Lewis never denied the existence of the many millions of good and virtuous non-Christians and he commended the fact that Lewis sought to tone down St Augustine's inflexible doctrine of *extra ecclesiam nulla salus* ('no salvation exists outside the Church'). Nevertheless, Lewis's idea that there are many different routes to salvation and that an individual could be a 'Christian without knowing it' was dismissed by Orwell as merely lax thinking since it apparently denied the centrality of an established Christian Church to which Lewis seemed so loyally committed. His conclusions about Lewis's (remarkably successful) attempts to popularize Christian theology were damning. Orwell claimed that his books were irrelevant to the modern world since the growing insignificance of the churches and the 'decay of the religious attitude to life' were now unstoppable and some fifty years of religious polemic had, to his eyes, amounted to very little of substance (XVI.439).

Since this review remained unpublished, Orwell recycled most of it in his next 'As I Please' column (27 October 1944) and also took the opportunity to enrich its denunciations of other Catholic apologists. Alongside Lewis's mawkishly 'simplified religion' for the masses, he placed the writings of Monsignor Ronald Knox and the popular religious novelist and preacher Monsignor Robert H. Benson. He especially disliked a form of theological writing which he felt had been endemic in England for over sixty years and which (borrowing again from his unpublished review) he christened the 'silly-clever religious book' which steered clear of scaring its readers about Hell but gently reminded them that an unbeliever must be an 'illogical ass', unaware that all of their simple doubts had long before been experienced and dismissed by previous generations. He traced this line of anti-rationalist theological writing back to W. H. Mallock's *New Republic or Culture, Faith and Philosophy in an English Country House* (1877), a satire on the aestheticism and High Church views of Oxford intellectuals, and its vapid descent (in Orwell's opinion) into banality through the writings of Benson, Chesterton, Knox, Wyndham Lewis and Morton. Such writers, he argued, adopted the same pseudo-logical position by claiming that all heresies have been previously stated and readily refuted and that the ordinary person should leave the complexities of theology to trained theologians, implying that it was always best for ordinary folk to hand over their 'thinking to the priests' (XVI.440–1).

Orwell's hostility towards C. S. Lewis's popular theological works carried over into 1945 when he reviewed for the *Manchester Evening News* (16 August 1945) his novel *That Hideous Strength*, the concluding volume in a theological science fiction space trilogy. However, he at least admired its wildly dystopian qualities in portraying a group of mad scientists from NICE (National Institute of Co-ordinated Experiments) who were plotting to conquer first Britain, then the whole Earth and eventually all other planets, to become masters of the universe. But he balked at what he saw as Lewis's Chesterton-like qualities in setting the 'eternal verities' of Christianity against scientific materialism and his eventual resolution of the plot by supernatural intervention. His mad scientists were not content with merely conquering the terrestrial universe but also sought immortality for themselves, enabling Man not only to 'storm the heavens and overthrow the gods' but finally to become a god himself. Orwell linked this nightmarishly destructive fantasy with the recently exploded atomic bombs over the Japanese cities of Hiroshima and Nagasaki (6 and 9 August), commending Lewis's prescience in imagining mankind to be capable of such nightmarish horrors. Lewis's scientists were depicted as secretly in touch with the forces of evil and, to Orwell's eyes, this element seriously diminished the drama and suspense of the novel since whenever a Christian writer placed God and Satan in opposition it was always clear 'which side is going to win' (XVII.250–1). For Orwell the only viable solutions to the world's problems had to be secular ones but his firm dismissal of organized religion seemed by 1945 only to be accentuating his anxieties over the future of both domestic and global politics in this new atomic age.

6

1945–6 and *Animal Farm*

1945: Anti-Semitism

The year 1945 proved to be a momentous one for Orwell when his wife Eileen unexpectedly died during surgery on 29 March, a loss reflected in his essay, 'A Good Word for the Vicar of Bray' (*Tribune*, 26 April 1946), which offers a 'poignant meditation on death, guilt and immortality'.[1] From 15 February until late March, and again from 8 April until 24 May, he worked as a war correspondent for *The Observer* and the *Manchester Evening News*, viewing at first hand the post-war desolation of France, Germany and Austria.[2] His international reputation as a writer and political satirist was confirmed over the next two years by the publication of *Animal Farm* on 17 August in the UK and 26 August 1946 in the USA (XVI.126). By 25 June 1945 he had also completed the first twelve pages of *Nineteen Eighty-Four*. In September he stayed for the first time in a fisherman's cottage on the desolate Isle of Jura in the Inner Hebrides where he was to complete his new novel.

Even before the full horrors of the Holocaust were widely known, Orwell continued to scrutinize the reasons for anti-Semitism in Western Europe. In a review of *Der Führer* by the exiled German historian and journalist Konrad Heiden for the *Manchester Evening News* (4 January 1945) he referred its origins back to the notorious pamphlet, *The Protocols of the Elders of Zion*, first published in Russian in 1903 and then translated into numerous languages and circulated throughout Western Europe. Outlining plans for Jewish hegemony and world domination through their control of the press and economic subjugation of Gentiles, *The Protocols* was exposed as a fake by *The Times* in 1921. But by then it had already exerted a strong influence over the young Hitler and he decreed it required reading in German classrooms after the Nazis' rise to power in 1933, viewing anti-Semitism as both a devious political device and a social delusion (XVII.5). The world conspiracy theory expounded in the *Protocols* may have partly inspired the repressive controlling mechanisms of the totalitarian State in *Nineteen Eighty-Four*, with its voyeuristic spies, secret police, censorship, and exploitation of history as propaganda. Significantly, Orwell agreed with Heiden's view that Hitler's Fascism had filled a political and social vacuum created by the decline of established religion in Germany. His review quoted two key statements from this biography which concurred with his own theories over the loss of a religious ethos in Western European society:

> Hitler was able to enslave his own people because he was able to give them something that even the traditional religions could no longer provide – the belief in a meaning to existence beyond the narrowest of self-interest. The real degradation began when people realised that they were in league with the devil, but felt that even the devil was preferable to the emptiness of an existence which lacked a larger significance.
>
> The problem to-day is to give that larger significance and dignity to a life that has been dwarfed by the world of material things. Until that problem is solved, the annihilation of Nazism will be no more than the removal of one symptom of the world's unrest. (XVII.7)

Orwell traced the origins of the decline of the established churches back to the early nineteenth century. While he saw the rise of the Industrial Revolution as having destroyed numerous local village communities centred round their parish churches, he also felt that the modes of Christian indoctrination traditionally used to educate children in religious and spiritual matters had been seriously flawed. In his 'As I Please' column for 5 January 1945, he discussed his re-reading of *The History of the Fairchild Family: or The Child's Manual, being a collection of stories calculated to show the importance and effects of a religious education* (1818–47) by Mrs Mary Sherwood. Combining sanctimonious sadism with religious repression, the children in the stories supposedly delight in poems about the 'bad hearts' of mankind and accounts of a young girl being locked for several days in a darkened room with only bread and water because one Sunday she had gone out with her nanny and picked some cherries without her mother's permission. While her nanny is duly flogged, the repenting girl's aunts kindly explain that retribution was fully deserved because she had not only broken the Fourth Commandment ('Remember the Sabbath and keep it holy') but also the Fifth ('Honour your parents') and Eighth ('Thou shalt not steal'). Each chapter of the book is laced with Biblical verses and hymns, and concludes with a sanctimonious prayer for general recitation. Similarly, when the Fairchild offspring have a childish quarrel, their mother takes them to see the rotting corpse of a murderer hanging from a gibbet to remind them of the tragic outcome of an argument between two brothers. When they forget to say their prayers, they fall into a trough full of pigswill; and stealing a few damsons results in pneumonia. Fascinated and repelled by this grotesque world of religious humbug, Orwell concluded by noting that Mrs Sherwood had several children of her own and, remarkably, 'they did not actually die under her ministrations' (XVII.15).

Returning to his preoccupation with anti-Semitism, Orwell recorded in his 'As I Please' column (12 January 1945) visiting a grubby London waxworks exhibition, showing German brutalities and advertised as: 'HORRORS OF THE CONCENTRATION CAMP. COME INSIDE AND SEE REAL NAZI TORTURES' (XVII.18). That morning's newspapers were also beginning to cover the official British Army Report on Nazi atrocities. Prompted by the growing public awareness of these persecutions, Orwell completed on 26 February his most substantial and enlightened analysis of the problem, 'Antisemitism in Britain', for the New York *Contemporary Jewish Chronicle* (published April 1945). He outlined the English situation, drawing his conclusions primarily from his observations of daily life in London, coupled with some secondary statistical research about other (unspecified) English cities. He estimated that there were already about 400,000 resident Jews in England and since 1934 many thousands more Jewish refugees had arrived. Most lived in large towns and worked in the food, clothing and furniture trades, either for major companies such as ICI or for national newspapers or Jewish-owned (or co-owned) department stores such as Marks & Spencer or Lewis's. He concluded that there was no evidence of Jewish businessmen seeking to dominate aspects of British merchandise and trade; indeed, the wealthier Jews seemed averse to the modern tendency towards large amalgamations.

Orwell insisted that there was no real Jewish problem in England and it was only within intellectual circles that they seemed to have a noticeably strong influence. Yet he suspected that anti-Semitism was steadily increasing and, although usually non-violent, it remained ill-natured, and rooted in hostilities which often took the form of individuals considering themselves not to be anti-Semitic but quietly harbouring various minor resentments against Jewish people. Orwell cited how otherwise law-abiding citizens would avoid Jewish areas, such as Golders Green, and often refer in derogatory fashion to Jews as the Chosen Race. He recalled hearing stories of Jews pushing to the head of food queues, being selfish and too clever for their own good and, most disturbingly, pro-German and secret admirers of Hitler's ruthlessness because Jews will supposedly 'always suck up to anyone who kicks them'. The key issue, Orwell sensed, was that many English men and women would readily deny anti-Semitic feelings but still consider it acceptable to admit disliking Jews. This enabled such individuals to rationalize the patently irrational nature of xenophobic prejudices. The war had aggravated this situation, prompting some to view the Jews as amongst those who had most to gain from an Allied victory. Given the sheer size and heterogeneous diversity of the British Empire, it had become problematic to praise, for example, the heroism of Jewish soldiers and the large Jewish army in the Middle East for fear of triggering hostilities in South Africa and the Arab countries. But such hesitancy inadvertently gave the man in the street the impression that most Jews had managed to dodge active war service. Air raids on the Whitechapel Jewish quarter had caused disproportionate suffering for Jews but some commentators simply exploited this situation to claim that Jews had sought to monopolize refuges set up in the Tube and other air-raid shelters. Orwell cited the tragic example of a crush of panicking people at Bethnal Green Underground Station as the air-raid siren sounded, resulting in the loss of 178 lives. Jewish civilians were widely blamed for this incident, even though such claims had been proved erroneous. In this respect, Orwell proposed with a dogged sense of objectivity that wartime conditions had provided an understandable and quasi-logical reasoning to anti-Semitism in that it was at least sometimes based upon entirely mistaken assumptions.

It seemed to Orwell, however, that anti-Semitism was a far more complex and deep-rooted problem than merely the misinterpretation of inaccurately reported incidents. Above all, it was a manifestation of human nature in that some individuals inevitably tended to dislike one another. For Orwell, anti-Semitism seemed to be different from other forms of inter-racial hostilities but the recent atrocities in Germany had prevented any serious anthropological or sociological studies of the problem. In fact, trivial adjustments, such as the suppression after 1934 of Jewish jokes in theatres and on postcards and the avoidance of unattractive Jewish characters in fictional works, had only aggravated the situation by suggesting super-ficially, but misleadingly, that anti-Semitism was disappearing from English society. Due to Hitler, Orwell argued, a paradoxical situation had arisen in which the press and public entertainments were self-censored in favour of the Jews while in private 'anti-Semitism was on the up-grade' even among educated and usually compassionate people. The assumption that anti-Semitism was something that the civilized and thinking person simply did not countenance, was an insidious perspective in that it prevented society from recognizing the true extent of the problem and taking measures to tackle its still vicious tendencies in post-war Western Europe.

While anti-Semitism had existed during the early 1900s in England, Orwell argued that generally it had been milder in form. There was little bigotry against intermarriage or talented Jewish people occupying prominent roles in public life. Nevertheless, it was still acceptable for Jews to be treated as figures of fun and some professions, such as the Navy and the smarter Army regiments, were effectively closed to Jewish recruits. Many wealthy Jews found it expedient to minimize or even disguise their Jewish heritage, and casual violence against Jews in working-class areas was tacitly expected. 'Jew-baiting' had been common in English literature with Orwell's familiar targets, Belloc and Chesterton, accused of an almost 'Continental level of scurrility' and hostility towards Jews by importing from France into Britain the racial malevolence of the anti-Dreyfusards. He noted that anti-Semitic passages could be found in the works of Shakespeare, Smollett, Thackeray, Shaw, Wells, Eliot and Huxley. Orwell remained sceptical over the two most common theories used to explain anti-Semitism – economic envy and an historical legacy from the Middle

Ages – and instead believed it to be a kind of semi-rationalized neurosis which had turned the Jew into a convenient scapegoat, even though it was far from clear exactly why Jews had been placed in this role. It seemed as though some 'psychological vitamin' was missing from modern nationalism which created an irrational 'lunacy' through which supposedly civilized societies drew strength from the alienation of persecuted minority groupings. Orwell concluded this searching essay by insisting that anti-Semitism could never be definitively eradicated without first treating the 'larger disease of nationalism' (XVII.64–70).

Orwell's short period as a newspaper correspondent in France and Germany served to broaden his perspectives on both Jewish issues and the destruction wrought by Fascism. He noted at Cologne, for example, in a report for *The Observer* (25 March 1945) that the new Chief of Police was a Jew who had occupied the same position until 1933 when the Nazis had ejected him from office. On 8 April he commented in the same newspaper that the levels of ruination of Germany cities were so extensive that he had begun to doubt whether traditional Western civilization was capable of recovering (XVII.122). In his essay, 'Notes on Nationalism', for the journal *Polemic* (October 1945) Orwell claimed that ardent nationalism (which tends to suppress any sensitivity towards the dilemmas of other races) had blinded many in the rest of Western Europe to the atrocities of the Nazis' 'Final Solution'. He was struck by the fact that English admirers of Hitler had supposedly contrived throughout the war to know nothing about the horrors of Dachau and Buchenwald; and even those who volubly condemned German concentration camps still seemed generally unaware of similar camps in Russian-controlled territories. In this respect the inherent but unadmitted anti-Semitism of such individuals had allowed this horrific crime to 'bounce off their consciousness'. In a footnote to this essay, Orwell condemned the *Star* newspaper for voyeuristically reproducing photographs of half-naked female collaborators being paraded through Paris as no better than Nazi photographs of Jew-baiting by the 'Berlin mob' (XVII.147). He made a similar point in his 'London Letter' of 5 June 1945, remarking that post-war it was now possible to elicit outrage at the horrors of Dachau and Buchenwald but in the pre-war period little interest had been shown in such repressions outside Germany. By 1939, Orwell surmised, the majority or at least a 'very big minority' of English citizens still had no knowledge whatsoever of Nazi concentration camps (XVII.163).

In his *Polemic* essay Orwell also focused upon Zionism as a nationalist movement and its resurgent desire to re-establish a Jewish homeland within the historic territories of Israel.[3] Orwell had an inbuilt antipathy towards small nationalist movements (such as Irish nationalism) and he noted that American Zionism seemed notably more threatening and 'malignant' than that of British Jews. He defined this phenomenon as 'Direct' rather than 'Transferred' nationalism (also categorizing 'Political Catholicism' under this term) because it thrived virtually only among Jews themselves. He noted that most English citizens in 1945 felt well disposed towards a Jewish desire for their own land because of Nazi persecution and that the British intelligentsia were also predominantly supportive of Jews regarding the Palestine issue (XVII.150). He was sure that the Nazis had ensured that all right-thinking people would naturally sympathize with the Jews against their oppressors. But although anti-Jewish remarks had been almost entirely purged from contemporary literature, he suspected that a deep current of anti-Semitism still flowed through the British consciousness and that a general silence in the media was unfortunately allowing it to increase. Even left-wingers were not immune to such bigotry, not least because some Trotskyists and Anarchists were Jews. However, Orwell argued that the real risk for the continuation of anti-Semitism came from Conservative-leaning individuals since he felt that 'Neo-Tories and political Catholics' were especially prone to occasional anti-Semitism because they feared that growing communities of Jews would ultimately dilute the British national identity (XVII.152).

Orwell again discussed the problematic issue of Palestine in his 'London Letter' of 15–16 August 1945 for the American readers of *Partisan Review*, following the unexpected landslide victory of Clement Atlee's Labour Party in the May General Election (with results declared on 26 July after allowing British forces still based abroad to vote). He considered various aspects of the new government's likely foreign policy but, in particular, focused on Palestine as a likely source of future trouble. Orwell explained that both the Labour Party and most left-wingers were firmly committed to supporting the Jews against the Arabs in Palestine, even though this was probably because only the Jewish cause was widely voiced in England. He emphasized that most white Britons were ignorant of the fact that the Palestine question was partly a colour problem and, for example, an Indian nationalist might well 'side with the Arabs' (XVII.248).[4]

In an article on 'The British General Election' for *Commentary* (1 November 1945), Orwell felt that anti-Semitism had not played any significant role in influencing national voting and the press had not attempted to stir up such bigotries. He was inclined to believe that, although anti-Semitism was still increasing, it had not become a dominant political issue in England because it usually first required a Fascist or totalitarian regime to become established in a country. He also noted positively that there were now Jews in all the main British political parties, with slightly more in those of the left wing, and there had been 'Jewish candidates on all the tickets' (XVII.336). In his concluding paragraph Orwell returned to the thorny question of Palestine, reiterating views previously expressed in his *Partisan Review* article. He regarded Palestine as the one political question over which the new Labour Government might well diverge from the views of its Conservative predecessor. In his opinion Labour remained generally committed to establishing a Jewish homeland and a high proportion of the radical intellectual classes also supported this view. However, he doubted whether Atlee's cabinet would necessarily sustain these commitments as firmly as they had been expressed during election campaigning when his party was in opposition. Reiterating his ideas about the problem being partly a colour question, he noted that unquestioning British support for a Jewish state in Palestine might well have 'repercussions in the other Arab countries', including Egypt and India (XVII.341). David Walton records how Tosco Fyvel confirmed to him in private correspondence that Orwell strongly disapproved of his overt support for Zionism. Similarly, Arthur Koestler told Walton that he had only ever discussed the 'Palestine Issue' once with Orwell. His support for the Arabs seemed so exclusive that he decided to drop the subject rather than endanger their friendship. Fyvel told Walton in a letter of 14 April 1978:

> Concerning the Holocaust, Auschwitz, the desire of the survivors of the death-camps to get to Israel – on all this he had something of a blind spot. He rather agreed with Ernest Bevin that there was no reason why the Jewish survivors should not after 1945 live peacefully in Europe – weren't they getting on peacefully in Britain?[5]

In a *Tribune* article, 'Revenge is Sour' (9 November 1945), Orwell tackled the complex issue of how war criminals should be punished and, in particular, how Jewish people might respond to their liberation from Fascist tyranny. He recalled from his time as a war correspondent being shown around a concentration camp by a Viennese Jew who was assisting the American army with the interrogation of Nazi prisoners. This young man was clearly an intelligent and civilized individual but when he came across a sleeping former SS officer with horribly deformed feet he savagely kicked this prostrate man on one of his feet. This incident, typical of many such encounters between the formerly repressed and their defeated oppressors, made Orwell wonder whether the young Jewish man had gained either pleasure or catharsis from his actions. He acknowledged that it was absurd to criticize a German or Austrian Jew for 'getting his own back on the Nazis' (XVII.362) since the horrors probably experienced by such individuals were readily imaginable. But, for Orwell, meaningful revenge remained a psychological impossibility in that it could only ever be an imagined action intensely desired by the helpless but one rendered impotent and self-demeaning once that helplessness had been removed.

Christianity, Communism and *Animal Farm* (1945)

During his time in France as a foreign correspondent, Orwell was able to observe current responses to the legacy of institutionalized anti-clericalism under the Third Republic when education had been secularized, leading to the exile of the French Ursuline nuns who had run his Catholic school at Henley-on-Thames. In an article for *The Observer* (11 March 1945), 'Clerical Party May Re-emerge in France: Educational Controversy', he recorded the appearance throughout Paris of a yellow poster titled 'Secularism versus National Unity' which, he assumed, was being promulgated by the French Catholic press as a protest against anti-clerical intolerance. State subsidies to Catholic schools had been questioned by the Communist Party and, although some (mainly Catholic) religious schools had survived, post-war they were no longer eligible for state subsidies. During the wartime regime of the Pétain Government, religious instruction had again become compulsory and it was reported that private schools had received about £2.5 million in state subsidies. While Orwell understood why, like their co-religionists in England, French Catholic schools reasonably claimed that they and their children's parents paid taxes which supported the state sector, he feared that the growing strength of the Catholic Press would soon trigger the re-emergence of 'Clericalism as a political force'. Crucially, women had recently gained the vote in France and, as in England, devout female churchgoers were more numerous than their male counterparts. He also adopted an intriguing historical perspective on why sectarianism was a greater threat (particularly towards left-wing perspectives) than in England. This was, he proposed, because the Reformation had not been carried through in France. Not only had Protestantism failed there as a viable political entity but France also lacked the numerous gradations of non-conformist belief which thrived in England and, thereby, encouraged both toleration and the longevity of the established Catholic Church. In contrast, it seemed necessary to be Catholic in France simply to survive. However, even though the immediate post-war period in France had seen bishops uneasily collaborating with the military, communists and socialists, Orwell noted that they showed no genuine 'friendliness' to one another.

In France, Orwell explained, many of its citizens had chosen to exist outside any established religious framework, even to the point of being buried without religious rites. The Third Republic had been aggressively anti-clerical and a commitment to secularism was expected by all left-wing political parties, requiring an almost obligatory level of 'religious disbelief'. However, wartime conditions and the French Resistance had drawn together believers and secularists in a communal opposition to Fascist occupation, and Pétain's government had exploited the support of clerics to bolster its uncertain authority. While some church leaders seemed to act as apologists for the Germans, Orwell insisted that it was inaccurate to claim that French Catholics were generally either collaborators or Fascists. Indeed, Catholics formed a major presence in the Resistance and, of course, De Gaulle himself was a devout Catholic. Orwell was impressed to note that the French Communist Party seemed the least anti-clerical of all the left-wing political groupings for the very good reason that both sides had realized that they must be united to rid the country of Nazi oppression. In 1936 the leader of the Communist Party, Maurice Thorez, had first promulgated the phrase, 'We hold out our hand to our Catholic comrades', and the same phrase had begun to surface again in Communist newspapers, although to Orwell's eyes with a 'slightly menacing air' (XVII.86–8). Orwell reiterated these ideas in a report for the *Manchester Evening News* (16 April 1945) about the impending French General Election. Concerns were being expressed in the French Press over how the Church might seek to influence voting since there were signs that old hostilities between clerics and secularists were beginning to flare up again through arguments over the Provisional Government's continuation of state subsidies to Catholic schools. Orwell warned that the Church might issue pronouncements, as it had done before the war, against various political groupings, especially Communism. He felt that if this happened the now enfranchised female electorate might become a significant problem for left-wing political parties (XVII.127).

Comparisons between Catholicism and Communism continued to fascinate Orwell. In his essay, 'Notes on Nationalism', for *Polemic* (October 1945) he returned to one of his favourite topics – Chesterton-bashing. He argued that only ten or twenty years previously 'political Catholicism' resembled most closely the nationalism of modern-day Communism, with Chesterton as its most prominent exponent, even though he was at the extreme end of Catholic polemicists. Orwell accused him of suppressing his considerable intellect and literary talents in the service of unquestioning Roman Catholic propaganda. This resulted in most of his later writings being little more than an endless repetition of the same doctrinal axioms which sought to demonstrate the innate superiority of Catholicism over all other forms of religion including paganism. This approach might have been tolerable if Chesterton had limited his sense of superiority to mere intellectual or spiritual matters but, instead, he constantly interpreted his religious convictions in terms of 'national prestige and military power'. In particular, he fantasized over France as a country offering an ultra-idealized form of Christian socialism, with Catholic peasants joyfully singing the Marseillaise and quaffing glasses of red wine. This false religious utopia irritated Orwell, and in his opinion reduced Chesterton's works to the level of second-rate jingoistic polemics in which his blinkered Catholicism led him to admire Mussolini, imperialism and colonial suppressions, provided they were instituted by Catholic Italians or Frenchmen. Ultimately, Chesterton's fanatical Catholicism distorted not only the reality of his perceptions but also his literary tastes and 'moral sense' (XVII.144–5). Within these contexts, Orwell argued, there were unmistakeable similarities between Chesterton's political Catholicism and the views of militant modern Communists.

In contrast to his consistently derogatory views on Chesterton, Orwell held in much higher regard the French Catholic convert Jacques Maritain. Reviewing his *Christianity and Democracy* for *The Observer* (10 June 1945), he discussed Maritain's view that Christianity and Democracy were not necessary incompatible. Indeed, he argued, they should be mutually dependent since it was impossible to lead a fulfilling Christian life within an unjust society and, most importantly, purely secular democracies tended to metamorphose into emergent dictatorships. Christian Socialism was, to Maritain, compatible with material progress – a reasonable and constructive view in post-war Western Europe. But Orwell rightly pointed out that his book had been drafted in 1942 when the triumph of a godless Fascism under the Axis Powers still seemed likely from a French perspective. He commended Maritain's courage in expressing at such a period his firm adherence to Christian Socialism and also noted how he had been a lonely French Christian voice in refusing to support Fascism, despite 'lyrical praises' for it promulgated by some pre-war French Catholic clerics and apologists. Orwell commended Maritain's insistence that both social justice and democracy were intrinsic qualities of Christian Doctrine and approved, at least in theory, his concept of a Christian humanist. However, he personally felt that such an individual was as rare as an 'albino elephant' because, while Humanism placed man at the centre of the world, Christianity insists that this world is only a transitory state towards an eternal spiritual life. Such tensions may appear to have been resolved in philosophical tracts such as *Christianity and Democracy* but, Orwell argued, in practice democracy and Christianity will always approach social and political problems from starkly differing (and usually irreconcilable) perspectives. As he shifted into a more polemical tone, Maritain failed to acknowledge Orwell's personal sense that religious belief is sometimes merely a manifestation of a 'psychological' need to '*avoid* repentance'. Quite what he meant is not explained since the review concludes by firmly insisting that a 'religious attitude to life must be restored' (XVII.175–7), even though Orwell claimed that the central doctrines of Christianity seemed to mean less and less to ordinary people and the number of Christian believers in the world was constantly diminishing.

Orwell returned to his preoccupation with potential links between Catholicism and Communism in an essay, 'The Prevention of Literature', first published in *Polemic* (January 1946) and then reprinted in the American journal, *The Atlantic Monthly* (March 1947). It traced how their respective responses to opposition were usually comparable. Catholics and Communists, Orwell argued, were similar in assuming that their opponents could never be both 'honest and intelligent'. Each tended to assume that they exclusively possessed the one and only true creed and heretics to their views acted only out of either folly or self-interest. This unwavering doctrinal attack on intellectual liberty and freedom – in effect, forms of totalitarian authoritarianism – was usually hidden for Catholics behind a condemnation of behaviour deemed sinful and immoral while for Communists 'petty-bourgeois individualism' was to be repressed and eradicated at all costs. Orwell concluded this section of his analysis by emphasizing humanity's timeless ability to create organizational barriers to individual freedom. Fifteen years earlier the enemies of freedom of thought had seemed to be Conservatives, Catholics and Fascists, but now it was necessary to protect it against the mounting threat of Communism. His ultimate warning axiomatically gestured towards the dystopian worlds of *Animal Farm* and *Nineteen Eighty-Four*: 'Totalitarianism ... does not so much promise an age of faith as an age of schizophrenia' (XVII.372–3, 376).

Orwell noted in a long essay, 'The Freedom of the Press' (intended as a preface to *Animal Farm* but never published), that he had first thought of its central anthropomorphic idea as far back as 1937. However, it was not until November 1943 that he found time to begin writing, completing it with remarkable speed in February 1944. This preface detailed how difficult it had proved to find a publisher for the work, primarily because of its assumed anti-Stalinist perspective and a fear that the casting of pigs as the ruling elite would cause offence. These problems raised for Orwell the greatest obstacle facing any writer or journalist – 'intellectual cowardice' (XVII.254), a quality which his own fictions and journalism had always resolutely sought to avoid. While he readily appreciated the need for wartime state censorship, it seemed to him that the British Government had commendably avoided any totalitarian tendencies in its handling of news reports and the dissemination of personal opinions. In contrast, the centralized nature of the British press had for decades rendered it easy for powerful individuals or influential interest groups to suppress the circulation of information and opinions deemed unhelpful or contrary to their perspectives. Similarly, the English intelligentsia had, from 1941, readily accepted Soviet propaganda for the simple reason that Russian support was viewed as vital if the threat of Nazi Fascism was to be overcome. Perhaps surprisingly for a preface which otherwise occupied itself with various forms of political censorship and repression, Orwell also noted that the Catholic Church exerted significant influence over the national press and could even sometimes repress criticism of itself. Scandals involving Catholic priests were routinely kept out of newspapers while notorious members of other denominations (such as the Rector of Stiffkey) became headline news. Anti-Catholic sentiments were hardly ever expressed in either plays or films and, if they did appear, tended to attract derogatory comments in reviews or were even 'boycotted' (XVII.256) by the press, presumably through Catholic pressure.[6]

It is interesting that the authoritarian control of the Catholic Church was so prominently in Orwell's mind as he completed *Animal Farm* since its fictional narrative contains few religious or sectarian references. The only direct mention of God comes when the cynical donkey Benjamin remarks that if 'God had given him a tail to keep the flies off' he would prefer to have 'no tail and no flies' (VIII.2). The satiric character of Moses the raven perhaps parodies earnest Christian evangelists who promise the faithful a delightful heaven in the form of Sugarcandy Mountain where all animals supposedly go after they die. Like a saccharine version of the Christian heaven, it is imagined to be situated somewhere in the sky beyond the clouds where it is 'Sunday seven days a week', with clover, sugar and linseed cake

permanently available for all animals. Old Major's teachings are categorized into the secular creed of 'Animalism' (VIII.10) and the regular Sunday
meetings of the animals may be equated not only to hectoring Communist
assemblies but also to the coming together of a new Nonconformist sect.
The animals have imposed upon them 'The Seven Commandments', an
obvious Biblical travesty, which are tacitly emended and corrupted by the
devilish pigs. But other than these few superficial references, *Animal Farm*
seems to concentrate primarily upon political parody rather than offering
any religious, sectarian or spiritual commentary. On one level, this is understandable since Orwell himself had categorized this 30,000-word novella as
a 'fairy story, really a fable with a political meaning' (XVI.126). But there are
also moments in the narrative when Orwell's authorial persona seems more
of a satiric Jeremiah than a secular political commentator. The renowned
axiom 'All animals are equal but some are more equal than others' (VIII.90)
seems to echo the self-deceiving thoughts of Milton's Eve in *Paradise Lost*
when she wonders whether to tell Adam of her newly attained knowledge,
thinking that withholding it might 'render me more equal, and perhaps, / A
thing not undesirable, sometime / Superior' (IX.823–5).

Furthermore, when Orwell's journalism from mid-1944 until early 1945
(the period when he was planning and drafting *Animal Farm*) is considered
alongside this novella, a clearer sense emerges of how Orwell's creative
thinking and anti-totalitarian stance was formulated by not only his distaste
for Stalinist Russia but also his equally pungent dislike of the authoritarian
tones and rhetorical methodologies of Catholic apologists. In a letter of
11 April 1940 to the academic Humphrey House, Orwell had remarked
that all morally concerned people had been aware since about 1931 that
the 'Russian regime stinks' (XII.141). His emphasis here upon the need
to adopt a judgemental moral perspective towards Soviet Communism
is pertinent to his satiric methodology in *Animal Farm*. In his 'London
Letter' of 17 April 1944 for the *Partisan Review*, drafted soon after his
completion of the novella, he observed that British sympathy for Russia was
stronger than ever. Only Catholic publishers seemed willing to disseminate
anti-Soviet material from a 'religious or frankly reactionary angle' and the
ideas behind Trotskyism were even more rigorously repressed than during
the pre-war period (XVI.159). It would seem, then, that by denouncing
through allegorical mockery the banishing of Trotsky (Snowball) by the
emergent dictator Stalin (Napoleon), Orwell was aligning himself with the
Catholic polemicists, although he would have argued, of course, that his
perspective in *Animal Farm* was secular and 'morally sound' rather than
reactionary and sectarian in any religious sense. Nevertheless, *Animal Farm*
marked the culmination of Orwell's concerns in his earlier journalism over
how the loss of a belief in either a God or an afterlife inevitably facilitated the emerging dominance of the modern cult of power-worship. His
writings had become preoccupied with the dangers inherent in the rise of
a godless power-worship with the 1941 publication of *The Lion and the*

Unicorn (XII.393–5). He had developed these concerns in his 'As I Please' column for 3 March 1944 (XVI.111–13), his correspondence in April 1944 with Antonia White (XVI.169–71) and his booklet *The English People* (XVI.204–6), drafted in May 1944.

The two false gods of *Animal Farm*, Farmer Jones and Napoleon, are equally unsatisfactory replacements for an ordered Deo-centric society, with only the deceptive prophet Moses the raven offering brief nostalgic glimpses of the possibility of a trust in 'individual immortality' which provides, as Orwell argued in *The Lion and the Unicorn*, the basis of distinguishing between good and evil. In his review of Harold Laski's *Faith, Reason and Civilisation* (13 March 1944) Orwell emphasizes how Christianity had remained an essentially unchanging doctrine through the centuries, thereby providing a sense of continuity and clarity of conviction necessary to all flourishing societies. But, in contrast, the Communist doctrine (as evidenced in its most extreme form in Soviet Russia) was constantly evolving and intrinsically deceptive towards its own citizens. As he noted in this review, if a dictatorship is established, there is no way of guaranteeing that a dictator will act as he has 'promised to do'. Hence, in *Animal Farm*, The Seven Commandments are readily corruptible to suit the elite regime's personal preferences and comforts. Just as the rousing egalitarian anthem 'Beasts of England' (VIII.8) is suddenly replaced by an anodyne 'Animal Farm, Animal Farm, / Never through me shalt thou come to harm' (VIII.60), so the fourth commandment, 'No animal shall sleep in a bed' (VIII.15) can be surreptitiously emended by Squealer to 'sleep in a bed *with sheets*' (VIII.45). The replacement anthem, 'Animal Farm, Animal Farm', is composed by Minimus, the regime's poet-propagandist pig, who also writes a quasi-religious panegyric poem in praise of Napoleon which he orders to be inscribed on the wall of the barn at the opposite end to the Commandments, surmounted by a grandiose portrait of himself. The poem celebrates Napoleon as a pagan deity and venerates him as the 'giver of / All that thy creatures love' (VIII.63). The novella concludes with the animals gazing through the farmhouse windows as the pigs and neighbouring farmers play a drunken game of cards in a tragi-comic reworking of the pagan myth of Circe, since it is now impossible to differentiate between the greed and self-interest of the Stalinist pigs and the capitalist humans.

1946: Secular or Christian Socialism, anti-Semitism and pamphleteering

Although predominantly secular in tone, drafting *Animal Farm* in no way diminished Orwell's fascination with religious issues and the problems posed by a loss of belief in an afterlife. In late January and early February 1946 Orwell wrote four related articles for the *Manchester Evening News*, focusing on a familiar subject, the post-war demise of traditional *laissez-faire* capitalism. In the first article, 'The Intellectual Revolt', he identified various still-developing alternatives, including left-wing Socialists and reformist Christians who sought to blend their revolutionary socialist ambitions with a loyalty to Christian doctrines (XVIII.57). The third article (7 February 1946) was devoted entirely to this grouping and opened with the assertion that aspirations for earthly happiness were not necessarily incompatible with a Christian belief in life after death. But this perspective posed the problem that, if the eternity of the next world was the ultimate goal of humanity, then all the qualities which the social reformer wished to eradicate from daily life, such as poverty and unemployment, should be regarded as an expression of 'necessary spiritual discipline'. This situation created an irreconcilable paradox in that the concept of a traditionally devotional submission to the authority of God and a modern aspiration towards greater human control over the natural world were seen to be contradictory. This meant, Orwell argued, that most of the Christian churches, especially Catholic, orthodox Anglican and Lutheran, remained intrinsically opposed to all concepts of social progress and were specifically opposed to any political creed which might diminish the dominant social concept of 'private property' (XVIII.63). In contrast, Orwell argued that the origins of Socialism partly lay centuries earlier in the independent spirit of Nonconformist religious groupings. He suggested that, following the demise of Catholicism in England during the Reformation, close intellectual and spiritual links had developed between radical politics and Protestantism. More recently, revolutionary Socialism had been supported by those who also professed 'orthodox, other-worldly, Christian belief'. He noted with approval the development of Catholic Socialist parties in various parts of the world and how the Russian Orthodox Church had reached an understanding with the Soviet Government, with a comparable working relationship established in England between Atlee's Labour Government and the Anglican Church.

These new politico-religious working relationships were due, Orwell felt, to the increasing number of individual Christians, both clerics and laity, who had grown convinced during the last twenty years of the 'inherent wickedness' of capitalism. He sought to identify three distinct categories of reformers. The first grouping included the renowned Marxist Dean of Canterbury, Dr Hewlett Johnson, known as the 'Red Dean', who unquestioningly identified the spirits of Christianity and Communism as compatible and naïvely considered Soviet Russia as the nearest approximation to a 'truly Christian Society'. He added to this category Professor John MacMurray and Sidney Dark, whose books, *The Clue to History* and *I Sit and I Think and I Wonder*, he had previously reviewed.[7] He also drew an interesting distinction between the two major English Christian churches, noting that there seemed no signs of any working relationship developing between Russian Communism and the Catholic Church, while some of the Anglo-Catholics of the Church of England seemed much more sympathetically disposed to the Soviet regime.

The second grouping comprised individuals who viewed Socialism as a desirable and inevitable state of progress for humanity but who were equally concerned to Christianize their idealized new socialist societies so that spiritual links with past devotional traditions were not lost. Among the leading promulgators of these hopes was Jacques Maritain, whose *Christianity and Democracy* Orwell had reviewed in June 1945, admiring its reconciliation of concepts of social progress with 'strict Catholic orthodoxy' and its author's courageous opposition to the regimes of Pétain and Franco. He also included in this group George Bernanos (whose views he had discussed with Antonia White) and the Catholic historian Christopher Dawson whose *Medieval Religion* he had reviewed in 1934. His final example in this grouping was the Russian émigré writer and political philosopher Nicolai Berdyaev, who in later life had combined Christian belief with his Marxist Socialism and had denounced the Bolshevik regime for its grim totalitarianism and suppression of individual liberty. All of these writers, Orwell concluded, knew that the established Christian churches had lost the loyalty of the common people by their passive tolerance of extreme social injustice, and, therefore, they keenly supported a new form of Christian Socialism.

Some familiar figures from Orwell's earlier religious critiques provided the focus for his third grouping of writers and thinkers, who accepted the inequalities of modern society and hoped for radical change but, at the same time, vehemently rejected both Socialism and industrialism. He noted that Hilaire Belloc's *The Servile State* (1911) had prophesied how Western European capitalism would inevitably degenerate into the political frameworks which fostered the rise of Fascism. Belloc advocated the dividing up of large properties among a new 'peasant proprietorship', and his friend G. K. Chesterton, imbued with the spirit of nineteenth-century radicalism, rooted this concept in a political creed called Distributism. This cause died away after Chesterton's death in 1936 and, while some of his former adherents drifted into the British Union of Fascists, others supported T. S. Eliot's concept of a Christian society in which tight-knit and mutually supportive local communities would foster a broadly Christian ethos. But, Orwell insisted, this kind of agrarian utopianism or 'Mediævalism' could never enter mainstream politics since it was not a viable political solution to society's ills but was merely symptomatic of the unease which all clear-thinking individuals should experience when faced with the overwhelming nature of 'machine civilisation'. The key question for Orwell was a clear one: if a civilization cannot morally regenerate itself then it is likely to wither and fall into the hands of self-interested extremists. But if the solution lay in inculcating some form of moral framework based upon the centuries-old Christian tradition, then society faced a major problem in the generally undisputed decline (at least in Orwell's opinion) of a belief in personal immortality. Nor could this article offer any clear solutions to this dilemma since Orwell saw no way of reconciling the other-worldliness of Christianity with worldly Socialism. He concluded that virtually all contemporary religious debates focused on this problem without a reasonable answer ever having been found (XVIII.63–6).

In mid-April 1946 Orwell suspended his journalistic work for six months to focus on a new novel. Henceforth, he split the remaining time left to him between a bleak farmhouse, Barnhill, on the Isle of Jura, in Scotland, where he lived from 23 May until 13 October, and London, living at 27B Canonbury Square, Islington, from 15 October until 10 April 1947. He gradually resumed journalism and his first major essay was one on 'Politics vs. Literature: An Examination of *Gulliver's Travels*', for *Polemic* (September–October 1946). Swift's satiric fable was a natural choice for Orwell's critical attention after the publication of *Animal Farm* since both works exposed the foibles and corruptions of politicized societies. He also admired Swift's boldness in his pamphlet *A Tale of a Tub* (1704), a virulent satire on excesses in religious practices, which had earned him the disfavour of Queen Anne even though it attacked Dissenters and Catholics while respecting the 'Established Church' (XVIII.418). He favourably compared Swift, a life-long political outsider, to the Catholic apologists from the time of W. H. Mallock onwards, whose *New Republic* Orwell especially despised, since these Catholic polemicists specialized in 'cracking neat jokes' at whatever was the current religious or political status quo with their opinions becoming ever more extreme because they knew that they had little or no influence over actual events. After some passing digs at Knox and Wyndham Lewis (as 'Christopher Sly'), Orwell notes the ease with which the 'blasphemies' of *A Tale of a Tub* had been interpreted by generations of readers as conclusive evidence of the 'feebleness of religious sentiments' when compared with political debate (XVIII.419).

Focusing on Swift's sceptical mockery of empirical sciences, Orwell detects in his cynicism parallels to the attitude of current Catholic apologists who are stunned to find scientists or other non-experts expressing views on such issues as the 'existence of God or the immortality of the soul'. They seem to imply, Orwell argues, that theology is as specialized a science as chemistry, and that a priest or theologian must be regarded as an oracle of wisdom whose judgements should not be questioned (XVIII.421). Although Swift had been ordained a priest in the 1690s and was Dean of St Patrick's Cathedral in Dublin from 1713 until his death in 1745, Orwell failed to spot any conclusive evidence in his writings of conventional religious beliefs or even any serious adherence to the concept of everlasting life after death. Furthermore, his ideas about goodness seemed to blend republicanism with a love of liberty, human benevolence and a belief in the powers of reason. He concludes, therefore, that Swift's writings offer an important message for the 1940s in that his world retained an essential ethos of Christianity without allowing a need to believe in everlasting life to dominate. Or, as Orwell preferred, Swift adopted a generally Christian attitude to life, 'minus the bribe of the "next world"'. He concludes his essay with a characteristic emphasis upon the value of sincerity and conviction, noting that a propagandist – since most writers tend to gravitate towards elements of this role – should always have a genuine belief in the thoughts that he seeks to promulgate.

Orwell imagined how worthy books could be written by Catholics, Communists, Fascists, pacifists, anarchists and (tongue in cheek) even old-style Liberals and traditional Conservatives, but never by spiritualists, Oxford Buchmanites or adherents of the Ku Klux Klan. In other words, a writer's views may be starkly contrasting to those of the norm but they must always be sensibly sane and combined with a genuine talent which Orwell interprets as 'conviction'. Most significantly, he notes a distinctive quality of Swift's writings which corresponds closely to his own polemical style when considering religious (especially Roman Catholic) matters. Swift, Orwell argues, did not share conventional wisdom but, instead, possessed a 'terrible intensity of vision' which enabled him to select a 'single hidden truth' and then explore its significance by 'magnifying it and distorting it' (XVIII.430). This is a crucial and revealing statement when attempting to tease out the reasons for Orwell's apparently pathological and long-sustained dislike of Roman Catholicism. In this respect, it seems that Swift's satiric spirit lived on in Orwell's bitter writings about Catholicism. The question remains, however, with regard to Orwell's religious polemics whether a writer who deliberately seeks to magnify and distort what he views as an essential truth (such as Socialism) or a problem (such as Roman Catholicism) will be able either to convey the objective essence of that issue to his readers or even fully appreciate the essential qualities of such supposed truths or problems.

Orwell also continued to explore manifestations of anti-Semitism alongside his concerns with the role of Christianity and the decline of personal faith in modern society. For example, in his 6 December 1946 'As I Please' column for the *Tribune* he described his pleasurable re-reading of George du Maurier's engaging novel *Trilby* (1895), the story of three artists, an orphaned Irish girl called Trilby and the Jewish musician, hypnotist and rogue Svengali. It had been published at the height of anxieties over the waves of Jewish immigration from Eastern Europe instigated by the Tsarist pogroms, resulting in the notorious Aliens Act of 1905 which introduced for the first time in Britain immigration controls and registration.[8] He proposed, as a sentiment relevant to all right-minded individuals, that his first youthful reading of the novel and then his post-Hitler re-reading had provoked radically different responses in his own psyche. He now recognized that Svengali is depicted as vain, treacherous, selfish and deficient in personal hygiene, qualities constantly linked to his Jewishness. Du Maurier's own illustrations also sketched him as a typical Jewish caricature. But of most interest to Orwell is how two distinct racial types of Jew are presented in the novel. The 'good' Jew is represented by the character Glorioli who is of Spanish Sephardic extraction while Svengali is from German Poland and, in Du Maurier's words, is an 'Oriental Israelite Hebrew Jew'. It is also suggested that it can be positive to have some Jewish extraction since Jews are often so intelligent, dynamic and entrepreneurial. Du Maurier notes of another character, Little Billee, that he may have some Jewish blood, concluding that it is fortunate for world affairs and 'especially for ourselves' that 'most of us have in our veins at least a minim of that precious fluid'. Clearly, Orwell observes, this kind of response contrasts starkly with the more familiar type of Nazi anti-Semitism. Nevertheless, in Svengali's case, the Jew was seen as a calculating opportunist, parasitically living off the talents of another, richly endowed with intellect and cunning but lacking the essential qualities of a good character. Orwell supposes that Du Maurier was guilty in the 1890s of no more than expressing the 'normal attitude' of the time towards Jews and, therefore, content to confirm the unthinking racial stereotype that Jews were often more intelligent, sensitive and creative than Gentiles but still their 'natural inferiors'. While Englishmen were now less sure of their elevated position in world affairs and the prevailing form of anti-Semitism was very different from that of Du Maurier's generation, Orwell was clear that this, in something of an understatement, was 'not altogether for the better' (XVIII.511).

Another important element in Orwell's literary activities at this period relates to his substantial personal collection of pamphlets which he had been assembling from about 1935 onwards. By January 1946 he estimated its number as in the region of 1,200 items and in 1949 when he bequeathed them to the British Museum (now the British Library) he thought that the total was somewhere between 1,200 and 2,000 items.[9] The argumentative selectivity and calculated biases of pamphleteering had long been of central importance to Orwell's style as an essayist, just as he had admired in Swift's writings his tendency to magnify and distort for polemical purposes whatever he viewed as an essential truth. Subdivided into various political, historical, literary and religious categories, Orwell's collection of pamphlets contained about sixty-five items on religious and anti-clerical issues, forty-eight on Zionism and anti-Semitism and another forty on subjects mischievously labelled 'Lunatic', including works on Jehovah's Witnesses, Nostradamus, astrological prophecies and British Israelites (XX.259–61, 264). Browsing through the subject matter and titles of these pamphlets serves to confirm how often when writing about certain subjects Orwell regarded himself a pamphleteer in the guise of an essayist and novelist, a perspective confirmed by V. S. Pritchett in his review of *Nineteen Eighty-Four* in which he commended his new novel as the work of a 'great pamphleteer'.[10]

This kind of perspective helps to clarify how and why Orwell so often adopted such a partisan and distorting attitude towards Roman Catholicism – or at least to the writings of its most vociferous apologists, led by Belloc and Chesterton. He had been applying the literary strategies of pamphlet-eering to his writings about Christianity and Roman Catholicism since the mid-1930s and, in this respect, he had tended to write not as an impartial journalist, essayist or reviewer but as a highly partisan polemicist. In his introduction to *British Pamphleteers, Volume 1*, co-edited with Reginald Reynolds, written probably in the spring and published in November 1948, Orwell described the pamphlet as a distinctive literary genre which had formed a staple part of literary publication for centuries and, no less importantly, that the first half of the twentieth century had become a 'pamphleteering age', with the Catholic Church especially prone to their promulgation. Usually cast between 5,000 and 10,000 words in length (Orwell's own ideal word count for personal commentary), a pamphlet might be written 'for' or 'against' someone or something but is essentially 'always a protest'. For Orwell, 'Violence and scurrility' were integral aspects of pamphleteering and of crucial significance for his ongoing composition of *Nineteen Eighty-Four*, since pamphlets were strictly forbidden forms of publication within a 'modern totalitarian state'. Orwell proposed that a pamphleteer must always feel that he possessed a central truth which was not available to the general public who would support him if given his version of the full facts. Reginald Reynolds had made the selection of sixteenth- to eighteenth-century pamphlets included in *British Pamphleteers* and Orwell was struck by how much of their subject matter focused upon two issues central to his own discussion of contemporary religion, politics and society: the struggle between Feudalism and Capitalism and the unending 'battle of Catholic against Protestant'. He noted with pleasure how the last item in the series, dealing with the Catholic–Protestant struggle, was Swift's *A Modest Proposal* in which Swift (although not a Catholic) supported the suppressed Irish. Most relevantly to his own polemical style when writing about Christianity, Orwell explained how a pamphlet – which he felt should always be 'topical, polemical and short' – allowed a writer a satiric flexibility possible in 'no other medium'. It permitted him, if necessary, even to be 'scurrilous, abusive and seditious', all three qualities being much in evidence in Orwell's writings about Roman Catholicism which frequently encompassed a shift from 'earnest argument through satire and rhetoric to sheer abuse' (XIX.106–15).

The section of Orwell's pamphlet collection on 'Religion and Politics', as it is headed in his handwritten list (XX.277–8), illustrates the partisan nature of these items. Although Orwell's heading implies a range of approaches to religion and politics, most of the items had been written from a pacifist point of view. Although no pacifist himself, he respected the right to dissem-inate such views and, in summer 1945, agreed to serve as Vice-Chairman of the Freedom Defence Committee which sought to preserve the liberty of Britain's citizens and freedom of speech. It had been formed in response to governmental wartime measures to restrict freedom of expression, with Herbert Read as its Chairman and Bertrand Russell and E. M. Forster as members.[11] When five individuals were arrested outside Hyde Park for selling pacifist and anarchist pamphlets, including *Peace News*, Orwell was prompted to write an essay, 'Freedom in the Park' (*Tribune*, 7 December 1945) in their support. Orwell asked whether the police would have also arrested anyone selling the Catholic *Tablet* or Anglican *Church Times* and argued that no seller of newspapers or pamphlets should be arrested by the police, regardless of whether they were Communists, pacifists, anarchists or even Jehovah's Witnesses and the 'Legion of Christian Reformers who recently declared Hitler to be Jesus Christ' (XVII.417).

Five of the items in Orwell's pamphlet collection were published by the Fellowship of Reconciliation, an international peace movement founded in August 1914 at the outbreak of the First World War by two Christians, Henry Hodgkin (an English Quaker) and Friedrich Siegmund-Schultze (a German Lutheran), who met while participating in a Christian pacifist conference in Konstanz in southern Germany. At Cologne railway station they had pledged to each other: 'We are one in Christ and can never be at war.' Two of Orwell's other pamphlets, *Christ and Our Enemies* (1941) and *Retribution and the Christian* (1942) were the work of the Quaker pacifist, Stephen Hobhouse. His cousin Emily Hobhouse had been prominent in bringing international attention to British concentration camps in South Africa during the Second Boer War – an issue of special interest to Orwell when news of the German concentration camps began to be disseminated during the early 1940s. He also possessed a copy of *Towards a Christian Economic* (1940) – mistitled in his list as *Economics and the Christian* – by the United Reform minister, Leslie Artingstall, the Secretary of the Fellowship of Reconciliation.[12] The publications of another major pacifist organization, the Peace Pledge Union (founded in 1934 to renounce all forms of warfare), were represented in Orwell's collection by four items. *Religion and the Quest for Peace* (1942) by the MP and President of the Welsh Pacifist Society, George M. Lloyd Davies, who also worked for the Fellowship of Reconciliation; *Christian Pacifism and Rearmament* (1943) by the Cambridge scientist Alexander Wood; *Conscripting Christianity* (1937) by Canon Stuart Morris, the General Secretary of the Peace Pledge Union; and *God or the Nation* (1937?) by John Middleton Murry, whom Orwell knew well as the founder of *The Adelphi* magazine.[13] The Union's magazine, *Peace News*, also published *Big Powers and Little Powers* (1944) by the playwright and author Laurence Housman, the brother of the poet A. E. Housman.

Other pacifist organizations represented in Orwell's pamphlet collection included the Peace Committee of the Quaker Society of Friends with five separate publications.[14] Items issued by the Anglican Pacifist Fellowship included the work of two famous names: the writer Vera Brittain, whose brother and fiancé had been killed in the First World War and whose pamphlet asked, *How Shall the Christian Church Prepare for the New World Order?* (194?); and the Anglican actress Dame Sybil Thorndike who *Writes an*

Open Letter on Why She, as a Pacifist, Believes that it is Right to Remain in the Church of England (1940).[15] Orwell also owned copies of Archdeacon P. Hartill's *The Archbishop of Canterbury and Pacifism* and *Anglicans & War* (1941). The former focused on the work of the social reformer William Temple, Archbishop of York and Canterbury. He published *Christianity and Social Order* (1942), attempting to marry faith and socialism, and jointly founded with Chief Rabbi Joseph Hertz the Council of Christians and Jews to combat anti-Semitism and other forms of prejudice in Britain. In another section of his pamphlets catalogue, 'Germany: Internal Affairs', Orwell listed Victor Gollancz's *What Buchenwald Really Means* (1945) and, under 'Zionism & Antisemitism', *Nowhere to Lay Their Heads: the Jewish Tragedy in Europe and its Solution* (1945).

Predictably, Orwell also collected materials on Catholicism, including *The Roman Catholic Church & the Modern Age* (1940) by the secular Marxist Francis A. Ridley, who was a stalwart of Speaker's Corner from 1925 until 1964; and two works on the Spanish Civil War: Oliveira A. Ramos, *Catholics and the Civil War in Spain* (1936); and Jose Maria de Semprun Gurrea, *A Catholic Looks at Spain* (1937). Unusually for Orwell, Scottish religious affairs were also represented by *Whited Sepulchres: a Political Record of the Church of Scotland* (1942) by the Scottish schoolmaster and pacifist Oliver Brown; and *The Foundation of Economic Reconstruction* (1942) by John MacMurray, a Professor of Philosophy at the University of London whom Orwell described in a letter to Dwight Macdonald of 2 May 1948 as a fellow traveller of an especially 'slimy religious brand' (XIX.328). In his review of *Animal Farm* for *Horizon*, Orwell's fellow student at Eton, Cyril Connolly, stated that his novella had restored 'the allegorical pamphlet to its rightful place as a literary force'.[16] This comment would have presumably pleased Orwell since he had noted in his introduction to *British Pamphleteers* that, although the number of modern pamphlets was considerable, their quality was generally very poor and rarely merited close scrutiny. This was because they were not usually penned by individuals who were 'primarily writers', and he struggled to name a single notable English writer who had published a pamphlet of any literary quality during the preceding fifteen years. Given Connolly's and Pritchett's praise of *Animal Farm* and *Nineteen Eighty-Four*, coupled with Orwell's own polemical writings on religion (especially Roman Catholicism), Orwell may be regarded as systematically reworking during the preceding fifteen years the arts of pamphleteering so that they could be powerfully revivified in the concluding two works of his literary career as a novelist.

7

1947–9 and
Nineteen Eighty-Four

1947–9

In his 'As I Please' column for 24 January 1947 Orwell focused on how hostility towards post-war Polish immigrants in Scotland could be compared to anti-Semitism. By then even the most xenophobic British citizens recognized the discreditable status of overt hostility towards Jews. Scapegoats were sought elsewhere with attention focusing on other recently arriving ethnic groupings. The central problem of contemporary racial hatred, Orwell felt, was one of casual ignorance, and he considered it essential for journalists to highlight how such shallow enmities could foster dangerous 'mass delusions' (XIX.24) within British and other Western European societies still traumatized by six years of warfare.

Soon after the publication of this article he began drafting one of his most interesting essays on the morality of Christianity, published in *Polemic* (March 1947) as 'Lear, Tolstoy and the Fool'. Shakespeare's later tragedies, Orwell argued, showed little interest in either a Christian or a more general religious ethos. Only two of these plays, *Hamlet* and *Othello*, seem set within the Christian era but neither (apart from the stage-antics of the ghost of Hamlet's father) reveals any concern for an afterlife in which the wrongs of this world would be righted. In contrast, Orwell's Tolstoy was a writer who felt that if only the petty vicissitudes of life could be conquered, this painful earthly existence could be transcended and the 'Kingdom of Heaven would arrive'. The flaw in this perspective, Orwell felt, was that most ordinary humans simply wished for a happy and productive earthly existence. These sentiments did not necessarily mean that they were weak, sinful or self-indulgent but rather that the Christian perspective was intrinsically self-focused, or even (in Orwell's deliberately provocative choice of word) 'hedonistic', since its primary aspiration was to escape from the tribulations of this world into some a form of 'Heaven or Nirvana'.

For Orwell the 'great humanist', as Christopher Hitchens describes him, it was crucial to realize that earthly existence would always require a testing struggle and that the ultimate price of life is death.[1] Shakespeare's famed sentiment in *King Lear*, 'Men must endure / Their going hence, even as their coming hither; / Ripeness is all' (V.ii.10–12), may ultimately be viewed from conflicting spiritual perspectives. It can be taken either as a committed Christian concept (i.e. God will decide when you die) or as a secular or pantheistic one (nature will ultimately take its course), confirming for Orwell that there can never be a final reconciliation between humanist and religious beliefs since it is unavoidable that a choice must ultimately be made between 'this world and the next'. Given the persecutions of post-Reformation England, Orwell argued, little could be deduced about Shakespeare's personal religious beliefs and his plays provide only the scantiest of evidence that he had ever held any. But in view of the playwright's posthumous semi-sanctification by his many admirers, Orwell's conclusions seem as much about himself as Shakespeare and they offer a prophetic warning to his own posthumous venerators. He counselled that Shakespeare was no 'saint or a would-be saint' but merely an ordinary human and probably not a 'very good one' (XIX.63–4).

Having rented Barnhill on Jura from 23 May until 13 October 1946, Orwell returned there from 11 April until 20 December 1947 with a view to completing *Nineteen Eighty-Four* (originally titled 'The Last Man in Europe') by hiding away from his other metropolitan writing commitments. He was often ill and his journalistic output was significantly reduced since he now realized that his own remaining time as a writer was probably limited – a sentiment implicit in his semi-elegiac views of Shakespeare's and Tolstoy's differing perspectives on the human condition. Henceforth, his writings were dominated by a sense that the so-called civilized world was a manmade construct in which individuals had to make the best of often testing and grim conditions. Indeed, the established churches seemed to Orwell to have offered only impediments and outright hostility towards secular aspirations aimed at social progress and global peace. In an essay for the *Partisan Review* (July–August 1947), 'Towards European Unity', he suggested that the growing post-war tensions between the East and the West might well drive both reactionaries and democratic socialists into combining to form a kind of 'Popular Front'. The danger, Orwell speculated, was that the Christian Church would opportunistically step in to offer the most convenient bridge between them but only because, thereby, it could seek to control and 'sterilize' any attempts to facilitate genuine European unity. For Orwell, the mid-twentieth-century Church was as threatening an institution as other recently experienced totalitarian organizations in that, while it did not appear overtly reactionary in any familiar sense, its long-established tendencies towards systematic subversion remained insidious. Since it was directly associated with neither laissez-faire capitalism nor the existing class system, it would be unthreatened if political forces swept away either of these current staples of Western democracies. Indeed, its essentially authoritarian character, Orwell argued, tempted it into the extremes of non-toleration of individual liberties. While the Church might pragmatically be willing to live alongside Socialism if its own position remained unthreatened, its presence as a still powerful organization would render impossible the promulgation of true socialism. The Church invariably opposed concepts of equality, free speech and even 'freedom of thought' and would tacitly subvert any attempt to promote earthly contentment over the promise of a glorious heavenly eternity (XIX.165–6).

Although this *Partisan Review* article commented only in generalized terms about Roman Catholicism, the Church's supposed threat continued to preoccupy Orwell during the last two years of his life. On 17 July 1948, *The New Yorker* published his review of Graham Greene's *The Heart of the Matter*, a novel which did not impress him. He acknowledged that the conflicts between goodness and sanctity, as well as those between this world and the next, provided fruitful fictional contexts from which a novelist who was a believer – even such a sceptical and paradoxical Christian as Greene – could derive challenging plots and intriguing moral dilemmas. Indeed, he felt that Greene had put these tensions to good imaginative use in *The Power and the Glory* and, to a lesser extent, *Brighton Rock*. But, in contrast, *The Heart of the Matter* seemed to present its spiritual conflicts in a formulaic manner and lacked that sense of psychological conviction essential to engage and sustain the reader's interest. Above all, Greene's attempt to depict the fictional inner turmoil of Scobie as a disillusioned colonial officer deeply irritated Orwell's responses as an experienced colonial officer. His adultery and planned suicide seemed petty self-indulgences to Orwell and the novel promulgated the dubious idea that it was more spiritually elevated to be an 'erring Catholic than a virtuous pagan'. He winced at the book's epigraph from the French philosopher and poet Charles Péguy, which implied that the sinner stands at the very heart of Christianity and knows more about his faith than anyone except a saint. Such an idea implied that basic human decency had little value when compared with the grandeur of the sinner's self-absorption. Orwell sensed a kind of spiritual 'snobbishness' in Greene's perspectives, in both this novel and some of his other ones written from a Catholic perspective. He also mocked his apparent fascination with the Baudelaire-like idea that there was something 'rather distingué in being damned' and teasingly cast Greene's concept of Hell as a 'sort of high-class night club' with a strict entry policy, allowing in only Catholic devotees.

Warming to his denunciation, and genuinely irritated by the novel, Orwell noted how it seemed to have become fashionable in both modern French and English Catholic novels to depict flawed or inadequate priests, a trend which at least provided a welcome contrast to G. K. Chesterton's incorruptible sleuth Father Brown whom, Orwell felt, had been exploited by his creator as a crude 'instrument of religious propaganda' (XV.315). Indeed, most young Catholic English writers, he assumed, were keen to avoid any resemblance to Chesterton's extremist and now dated depiction of the Church in his writings. Nevertheless, no matter how criminal, drunken or 'damned outright' a Catholic might appear in one of these novels, the character still seemed to retain an unjustifiable and tedious sense of superiority since both he and his initiated (i.e. Catholic) readers retained an unshakeable sense that they alone knew the true meaning of good and evil. Orwell's most potent complaint over the moral framework of Greene's novel was provocatively cast and presented a clear dilemma for the modern prose moralist. He deemed Greene's 'cult of the sanctified sinner' as ridiculous and probably expressive of its author's own wavering sense of faith, since those who really believed in Hell, Orwell jibed, tended not to strike 'graceful attitudes' on its edge. No less significantly, by attempting to express complex theological speculations through the paltry actions of flawed and tedious human beings, Greene had managed only to produce in Scobie a psychologically absurd character.

Greene's *The Power and the Glory* afforded an interesting point of comparison with *The Heart of the Matter* because in it, Orwell proposed, the clash between the earthly and heavenly worlds had been more persuasively presented through Greene not attempting to position his theological tensions within the mind of a single character. Instead, this novel's bedraggled and despairing Whiskey Priest was a pathetic individual but one made somehow heroic through his dogged belief in his 'thauma-turgic' (miracle-working) powers as a priest. Similarly, the arch-secularist Lieutenant viewed himself as an incorruptible exponent of civic justice and social progress and, thereby, remained an understandable, almost heroic figure. Both men could respect and sympathize with each other even though neither could comprehend the other's belief systems. In contrast, *Brighton Rock* seemed to Orwell a far less sophisticated novel in that it required its readers to accept that a 'brutishly stupid' individual like the petty gangster and proto-Satanist Pinkie could aspire to theological subtleties merely by having been brought up as a Roman Catholic. Similarly, it stretched credibility that his dim girlfriend Rose became the central vehicle, along with the blowsy goodtime girl Ida, for the fiction's differentiation between the key Christian categories of good and evil, and right and wrong.

Broadening his literary discussion, Orwell draws a comparison with François Mauriac's *Thérèse Desqueyroux*, arguing that her spiritual dilemma does not offend probability because her creator does not seek to present her as an ordinary or normal person. Instead, she becomes a 'chosen spirit' who seeks salvation through a long series of difficult but credible experiences. Similarly, although Orwell found improbabilities in Evelyn Waugh's *Brideshead Revisited*, he recognized that the characters were encountering real-life problems and, therefore, did not seem to move into a rarefied and unbelievable intellectual framework whenever the focus shifted to their religious beliefs. But Scobie's supposed tragedy in *The Heart of the Matter* did not fit with either of these persuasive narrative patterns. Instead, his two halves were incompatible and it stretched credibility to imagine that such a hopeless character would not have created domestic chaos around him much earlier in life. Anyone who considers adultery to be a mortal sin – an alien concept to Orwell's own moral framework since he readily admitted his own infidelities to Eileen – should either stop committing it or realize that, if they carried on, their sense of it being a sin would probably diminish. Similarly, if Scobie had really believed in Hell, surely he would not have risked going there simply to protect the sensitivities of a couple of two-dimensional neurotic women, neither of whom he really seemed to love. Most tellingly for Orwell, he confirmed Scobie's total lack of verisimilitude by cynically noting that if he were really so sensitive towards causing pain in others, then he would never have succeeded as a colonial police officer. Instead, Greene seemed to have cast him as a 'highbrow ... theologian' and, in a damning conclusion, Orwell remarked that, while an awareness of the 'vanity of earthly things' (XIX.404–6) may assist entry into Heaven, it is not generally helpful for the process of writing a novel.

In a letter of 15 April 1949 to Tosco Fyvel he sustained his discussion of Greene's problematic Catholicism. He took issue with Fyvel's view that Greene was an 'extreme Conservative' and a typical 'Catholic reactionary type'. Instead, Orwell viewed him as a Catholic who sometimes supported the political views of his church but, more frequently, preferred a mildly Left standpoint with even occasional 'faint C[ommunist] P[arty] learnings'. He noted the familiar left-wing scenarios in such novels as *A Gun for Sale*, *England Made Me* and *The Confidential Agent*, with their corrupt millionaires and armaments manufacturers, and how their positive characters often reveal communist leanings. He recalled how Rayner Heppenstall had once claimed that Greene had been a reluctant supporter of Franco but noted that *The Confidential Agent* had been written from a contrasting point of view. Orwell's perspective on Greene's allegiances during the Spanish Civil War was the correct one since Greene had supported the Basques whose priests fought alongside them and, unusually for Catholics, were staunch opponents of Franco. He concluded with a striking observation about Greene by wondering whether he might eventually become 'our first Catholic fellow-traveller' (XX.85–6).

Orwell's interest in the impact of Catholicism on English prose fiction dated back at least to the mid-1940s. In his essay, 'The Prevention of Literature' (*Polemic*, January 1946), he argued that orthodox Catholicism seemed to have had a claustrophobic effect upon the novel. Looking back over the previous 300 years of literary history, he asked whether it had ever been possible to be both a good novelist and a good Catholic. He implied that this was unlikely because the virtues of ecclesiastical 'tyranny' cannot be celebrated in mere words and, consequently, no author had ever succeeded in writing a good or morally sound book in 'praise of the Inquisition'. This characteristic leap of logic assumed that his readers accepted unquestioningly that tyranny was a prerequisite of the Catholic Church. More persuasively, he argued that modern English prose literature, especially the novel, was ultimately a by-product of the rise of Protestantism with its emphasis upon rationality and the independent individual, adding that the eradication of intellectual freedom inevitably handicaps the 'journalist, the sociological writer, the historian, the novelist, the critic, and the poet, in that order' (XVII.377–8).

While Greene – whose works Orwell genuinely admired (apart from *The Heart of the Matter*) – may be described as being far from either a 'good' or orthodox Catholic, Evelyn Waugh was the one English Catholic novelist whom Orwell readily placed in a distinctly higher category of achievement. In a review (*The Times Literary Supplement*, 7 August 1948) of *The Novelist as Thinker*, edited by the Cambridge academic Balachandra Rajan, he criticized an essay by the poet Derek S. Savage, 'The Innocence of Evelyn Waugh', for its omission of any mention of Waugh's conversion to Catholicism which, Orwell argued, should never be disregarded when studying his works. He dismissed Savage's view that the central concern of *Brideshead Revisited* was a nostalgic retrospective upon adolescence, instead insisting that its essential theme was the tensions between 'ordinary decent behaviour' and Catholic doctrinal concepts of 'good and evil' (XIX.416–17). It should be noted, however, that Orwell's intentions in this review were finely balanced between his insistence upon the importance of Waugh's Catholicism to his fiction and his long-standing hostility towards Savage, who was a noted pacifist, conscientious objector and General Secretary of the Anglican Pacifist Fellowship. In 1942 Savage had been in correspondence with Orwell, insisting that Hitler required 'not condemnation but understanding' since he was '"realler" than Chamberlain' and, far more than Churchill, 'the vehicle of raw historical forces' (XIII.393–4). Despite Orwell's probable wish to demean Savage in this review, his considerable respect for Waugh's literary skills was to form the focus of his last, unfinished literary work as he lay dying in University College Hospital.

In his other journalism during 1948 and 1949 Orwell remained preoccupied with the interaction of politics and religion in both Western Europe and the Middle East. In his essay 'The Labour Government After Three Years' (*Commentary*, October 1948) he argued that tensions had developed between various socialist factions because the Labour Party had an 'ethical, quasi-religious tradition', drawn from 'evangelical Protestantism' which was not generally approved of by liberal middle-class intellectuals. Similarly, while he felt that the left-wing English elite were aggressively opposed to Ernest Bevin's policies on the Mandate of Palestine and the State of Israel, ordinary people were far less hostile towards his attempts to establish some sort of peaceful resolution to this destructive civil conflict. Indeed, Orwell felt that few ordinary British citizens understood the government's policy towards Palestine and were far more moved by reports and images of terrorists attacking and blowing up British soldiers (XIX.443).

Such concerns inevitably brought Orwell back to the subject of anti-Semitism, which he reconsidered from a post-war perspective in an acerbic review (*The Observer*, 7 November 1948) of Jean-Paul Sartre's essay 'The Portrait of the Anti-Semite', translated by the journalist and Catholic convert Erik de Mauny. He begins by insisting that, for as long as anti-Semitism remains categorized merely as a 'disgraceful aberration', anyone with enough knowledge to understand the term will automatically assume that they are personally immune from it and that it is a problem generated by others. He also notes that books on anti-Semitism written by those who had not suffered directly from its persecutions tended to degenerate into the well-intentioned process, in Orwell's Biblical phraseology, of 'casting motes out of other people's eyes' (Matthew 7.3-5). Sartre's study, he proposes, falls into this category and is further diluted by having been written in 1944 during the quisling-hunting months immediately following the Liberation. Sartre, of course, insisted that anti-Semitism was anti-rationalist and could not exist in a truly classless society, arguing that education and propaganda might well mitigate its most extreme aspects. Orwell dismisses out of hand such trite assumptions and wonders at Sartre's naïve assertion that anti-Semitism was virtually unknown within working-class environments since, true to his own philosophical convictions, Sartre viewed it as a weakness of his preferred sociological scapegoat, the petty bourgeois. Orwell engages more positively with the hypothesis that anti-Semitism was rarer among scientists and engineers and instead categorizes it (no doubt with Palestine in mind) as a characteristic of those who tended to define nationality through concepts of a traditional culture and property through land ownership. He also dismisses the easy assumption that anti-Semitism had originated from a supposed Christian hatred of the Jews for being responsible for the Crucifixion and, instead, emphasizes the usefulness of linking it within modern contexts with other clearly related social bigotries such as colour prejudice.

Sartre fails in Orwell's eyes to realize that there is no such thing as a unified concept of anti-Semitism since for centuries it had cut across all classes and backgrounds and tended to appear intermittently and unpredictably in most societies. He is also sceptical over Sartre's division of Jews into 'Authentic Jews' and 'Inauthentic Jews', the latter wishing to be totally assimilated into all societies. This differentiation, Orwell argues, is simply wrong headed and perhaps another implicit form of anti-Semitism. Instead, he proposes that racial prejudice of any kind is a form of social neurosis which remains impervious to mere intellectual debate and unintentionally renders books like Sartre's as a potential catalyst for further racial segregation and hostility. The only viable solution, Orwell proposes, is for studies of anti-Semitism to cease endowing it with the term 'crime' since such a nomenclature tends to stall constructive attempts to understand its origins and diminish its inherent malevolence. Above all, neither the Jew nor the anti-Semite should be regarded as a 'species of animal different from ourselves' (XIX.464–5).

Orwell's hostility towards Sartre's diffuse perspectives on anti-Semitism was matched by his personal distaste for the pacifist teachings of Mahatma Gandhi. In an essay for the *Partisan Review* (January 1949), 'Reflections on Gandhi', Orwell argued that it was impossible to reconcile Gandhi's ascetic religious disciplines with the idea that humankind should not be demeaned since life should be made worthwhile on the 'only earth we have'. Instead, his self-mortifying views could be logically justified only by the assumption that there is a God and that the earthly world is one from which each individual must ultimately aspire to escape to a better place. In particular, Orwell was uneasy over Gandhi's abstemious demands for self-purification, including the avoidance of alcohol, tobacco and meat and other animal products, along with no close friendships and the avoidance of sexual activity except for procreation. This seemed to Orwell to diminish the value of humanity's earthly existence and hint at aspirations not only to human purity but also to an ethereal sanctity and he warned that idealized aspirations to sainthood should always be avoided by human beings. Just as problematically, he was appalled by Gandhi's views on how to deal with the rise of Fascist totalitarianism and anti-Semitism. When as a pacifist he was faced in 1938 with the question of how the Jews should respond to the oppressions of Nazi Fascism Gandhi proposed that German Jews should commit collective suicide so that their actions would arouse international indignation and horror at 'Hitler's violence'. After the war, according to Orwell, Gandhi justified this ludicrous view by claiming that since the Jews had been killed anyway, they 'might as well have died significantly' (XX.7–8). Orwell was no less disturbed by the Fascist sympathies of the poet Ezra Pound, and his receipt in February 1949 of the Bollingen Prize for poetry prompted angry comment from Orwell in the *Partisan Review* (May 1949). Pound had supported Mussolini during the 1930s and lived in Italy during the Second World War. From 1941 he had broadcast propaganda in support of the Fascist powers, according to Orwell, motivated by his intense dislike of the British, Americans and Jews. He was disgusted by Pound's radio broadcasts, recalling one in which he appeared to commend the massacre of East European Jews and to warn American Jews that 'their turn was coming presently' (XX.101). Sartre, Gandhi and Pound represented for Orwell a trinity of self-deluding but dangerous individuals who conspicuously failed to support their rarified intellectualism with compassionate humanitarianism.

Nineteen Eighty-Four (1949) and its precursors

Within the context of Orwell's anxieties over the loss of a sense of the religious in modern society, it is important to note that several earlier works exerted a significant influence over his creation of a distinctively godless dystopia in *Nineteen Eighty-Four* where all institutionalized religion has been eradicated. Wells's *A Modern Utopia* has already been considered in relation to Orwell's youthful reading but several other fictions directly contributed to Orwell's preoccupation during the 1940s with the destructive effects of secular totalitarianism insidiously filling the void left by the decline of established religion and personal spirituality. Jack London's *The Iron Heel* (1908) imagines the rise of a totalitarian oligarchy of capitalist robber-barons in America between 1912 and 1932, supported by a proto-SS called the mercenaries, and also depicts a political movement which comes to power in 1984.[2] This novel, supposedly based upon a manuscript written by Avis Everhard found many centuries after her death, is laced with a range of characteristically Orwellian anti-clerical sentiments.

In the novel's opening scene, a group of churchmen discuss metaphysics and science with a revolutionary socialist, Ernest Everhard (Avis's future husband), who mocks their earnest intellectualism in terms reminiscent of Orwell's castigation of the quasi-feudalism of the Roman Catholic Church:

> You reminded me for all the world of the scholastics of the Middle Ages who gravely and learnedly debated the absorbing question of how many angels could dance on the point of a needle. Why, my dear sirs, you are as remote from the intellectual life of the twentieth century as an Indian medicine-man making incantation in the primeval forest ten thousand years ago. (9)

Everhard's views on the role of the established churches in society largely coincide with Orwell's as he condemns how the established 'Church condones the frightful brutality and savagery with which the capitalist class treats the working class', thereby alienating the loyalty of the 'proletariat'. He adds bitterly, 'While a slaughter-house was made of the nation by the capitalists, the Church was dumb' (30–1). As Avis falls in love with Ernest, she imagines him 'transfigured' as a socialist 'apostle of truth, with shining brows and the fearlessness of one of God's own angels, battling for truth and the right' (53) alongside the figure of Christ himself. He condemns in American capitalist society its well-intentioned but naïve churchmen who preach 'without real morality', rich tradesmen who contribute generously to foreign missions but pay their shop girls 'a starvation wage and thereby directly encouraged prostitution' and wealthy merchants who erect 'magnificent chapels' but readily perjure themselves 'in courts of law over dollars and cents' (70–1). A 'saintly' local clergyman, Bishop Morehouse, is persuaded by Ernest's radical socialism and begins to preach that the 'Church had wandered away from the Master's teaching, and that Mammon had been instated in the place of Christ', tragically resulting in his incarceration in a 'private sanitarium for mental disease' (162).

Aldous Huxley's *Brave New World* (1932), set in AD 2540, is also often compared with *Nineteen Eighty-Four*, and it offers a range of representations of religious matters which may have influenced Orwell's own perspectives. The important point, however, is not to attempt to trace the minutiae of specific links between the two novels but rather to recall how Huxley's work offers a potent contemporary questioning and parodying of the power of religious organizations and their manipulation of the faithful. His novel's mock-religious ceremonies or Solidarity Services, focusing on the quasi-devotional 'loving cup' and Solidarity Hymns, promise a climactic transcendental unification with the great god-like being, Ford. The Second Solidarity Hymn offers a secular echo of the Christian afterlife:

> Come, Greater Being, Social Friend,
>   Annihilating Twelve-in-One!
> We long to die, for when we end,
>   Our larger life has but begun ...

The 'sense of the Coming's imminence' pervades the brainwashed worshippers 'like an electric tension in the air', and a Third Solidarity Hymn culminates with a stark parody of religious faith in the final heavenly unification of all into one greater unity which, perversely, then climaxes in an orgy of sensual and sexual gratification: 'Feel how the Greater Being comes! ... For I am you and you are I' (81–2). Within the World State's hyper-controlled environment, unhappiness has been eradicated and only the 'Savages' are prone to religious tendencies, such as when 'John the Savage' bitterly laments the death of his mother Linda with the archaic but still powerfully despairing chant: 'Oh, God, God, God' (184). Later, the Resident World Controller of Western Europe, Mustapha Mond, discusses with John how there 'used to be something called God' before the Nine Years' War and shows him copies of long-neglected ancient books, such as 'The Holy Bible, containing the Old and New Testament', 'The Imitation of Christ' and 'The Varieties of Religious Experience, by William James' (203). These volumes are now suppressed because, although God remains constant, man continually evolves and ancient gods are no longer deemed compatible with a progressive totalitarian civilization. The Controller also reads to the 'Savage' from the works of Cardinal Newman, dismissed as 'a kind of Arch-Community-Songster', and the French philosopher and mystic theosophist Maine de Biran. Although Mustapha Mond is willing to accept that there still may be a God, any such Deity is deemed redundant because of the supposed perfection of this 'brave new world'. Ultimately, a belief in the potency of God is no longer viewed as 'compatible with machinery and scientific medicine and universal happiness' (206). The citizens now regularly take the ritualistic drink 'soma', a powerful hallucinogen, because it provides a sense of spiritual communion and a soothing kind of escapist morality 'in a bottle. Christianity without tears – that's what soma is' (209). But this world without commonplace human experience and suffering horrifies the 'Savage' whose lament concludes the chapter, echoing Orwell's concerns over the void created by the loss of organized religion and personal spirituality in Western European societies: 'But I don't want comfort. I want God, I want poetry, I want real danger, I want freedom, I want goodness, I want sin' (211).

Another possible influence on the religious elements in Orwell's *Nineteen Eighty-Four* is the fantasy novel *Swastika Night* (1937) by the pacifist feminist writer Katharine Burdekin, who published under the male pseudonym Murray Constantine. Both novels depict brutal totalitarian regimes under which individuality has been repressed, the cultures of the past destroyed and history rewritten. Although there is no certainty that Orwell had read this novel, like *Brave New World* it usefully illustrates the European (and especially German) pervasiveness of Orwell's concerns over the eradication of personal spirituality by totalitarian regimes and, specifically, the dangers faced by Jews from twentieth-century Fascist xenophobia. Set 700 years after the rise of Nazism, Burdekin's dystopian vision presents a world divided between German and Japanese Empires and a Germanic society in which the dominant males are Fascist homosexual misogynists, all Jews have been eliminated, Christians are regarded as disgusting untouchables and women are despised and treated like the proles in *Nineteen Eighty-Four*. *Swastika Night* was published by Victor Gollancz, who had been Orwell's first publisher, and *The Road to Wigan Pier* had been the Left Book Club's choice in 1937 just as *Swastika Night* was in 1940 when its prophetic visions of Nazi fascism were rapidly coming true. Its first chapter opens with a high-status Germanic Knight entering a temple with its 'Holy Hitler Chapel' set in the western arm of a Swastika architectural design and its Goebbels side-chapel in the northern arm. A beautiful boy soloist is singing the 'Creed' to the Orwellian 'Big Brother' of this totalitarian empire:

I believe in God the Thunderer, who made this physical earth on which men march in their mortal bodies, and in His Heaven where all heroes are, and in His Son our Holy Adolf Hitler, the Only Man. Who was, not begotten, not born of a woman, but Exploded! (5)

In the same service the 'fundamental immutable laws of Hitler Society' are loyally recited by a military dignitary in 'his aged knightly German':

As a woman is above a worm,
So is a man above a woman.
As a woman is above a worm,
So is a worm above a Christian.

The meanest, filthiest thing
That crawls on the face of the earth
Is a Christian woman.
To touch her is the uttermost defilement
For a German man. (7)

Although written during the mid-1930s, Burdekin's *Swastika Night* anticipated the Holocaust with disturbing accuracy. It records how the Christians had 'persecuted and humiliated the Jews for nearly two thousand years, and then the Germans took on the persecution' and, as Orwell would have agreed, 'made it racial, and after a time killed all the Jews off' (72). Alfred, a young Englishman undertaking a pilgrimage and, therefore, hated by the Nazi regime since his country was the last to fall to their tyranny, possesses the only true history of the world and meets the aged Joseph Black, the head 'Christian of the Amesbury community' (172). Joseph teaches Alfred that before the dominance of the Germans there were 'Jews and Christians. But first there were only Jews. The whole world of men descended from the blessed race of Jesus' (177). He promises that if Alfred can accept the existence of sin and believe in the 'Lord Jesus Christ, the Son of God' he might then be received into the Christian community and would be saved on the 'Last Day' (178). However, Alfred advises his son Fred to be wary: 'You can't really trust any man who is religious. If your interests conflict with the religion the man breaks his word and betrays you and thinks he's right to do it' (186). At the end of the novel, in a scene of high gothic drama at Stonehenge, Alfred is beaten up by Nazi SS soldiers and dies but just before doing so manages to pass on the truth about Nazi history to his son.

Most significantly for Orwell's dystopian inspiration in *Nineteen Eighty-Four*, Yevgeny (Evgenii) Zamyatin's fantasy novel *We* (written in 1921 but banned in Russia; translated and published in the West, 1924) is of central importance in terms of the ways in which its schematic totalitarian regime seeks to replace society's traditional religious frameworks and suppress individual spirituality. Over dinner with Rayner Heppenstall and Michael Sayers, Orwell once mentioned that he was planning to take *We* as the model for his next novel.[3] Zamyatin, the son of an Orthodox priest and admirer of the 'heretic Christ', became a noted political satirist and science fiction writer who from 1931 lived in exile in Paris.[4] He first attracted Orwell's attention when he enthusiastically reviewed *We* for *Tribune* (4 January 1946) under the title 'Freedom and Happiness'. He was intrigued by Zamyatin's depiction of the 'rebellion of the primitive human spirit against a rationalised, mechanised, painless world', in which the concept of a beneficent God had been replaced by a personage known as 'Him whom we call the Benefactor' (42) and the 'new Jehovah' (123). This figure was clearly a precursor to both Aldous Huxley's World Controller and Orwell's Big Brother: 'In the Garden of Eden man was happy, but in his folly he demanded freedom and was driven out into the wilderness. Now the Single State has restored his happiness by removing his freedom.' Recognizing that Zamyatin had drawn ideas for his One City from H. G. Wells (whose works he had edited in Russian translation), Orwell commended his 'intuitive grasp of the irrational side of totalitarianism' and the folly of the compulsory worship of a 'Leader who is credited with divine attributes' (XVIII.13–17).[5]

We is set in the far future of the thirtieth century when individuals have only code numbers and live in the soulless One State where urban buildings are constructed almost entirely of glass-enclosed structures so that the secret police can spy upon the repressed population. Humans are rigorously standardized so that males are known only by odd numbers prefixed by a consonant and females by even numbers prefixed by a vowel.[6] D-503 is a chief engineer (Zamyatin had trained as a naval architect and had worked in naval dockyards at Newcastle-on-Tyne during the First World War) constructing a state-of-the-art spaceship, the *Integral*, which is being designed to conquer other extra-terrestrial planets. Although D-503 has an allocated official lover, the gently mindless O-90, he meets another more vibrant female, I-330, who first addresses him as though he is 'some mythical god on the seventh day of creation' and, like Eve to Adam, insists that 'I was created by you, and by no one else' (7). I-330 rejects state conformity by wearing old-style clothes, smoking, drinking alcohol and flirtatiously seeking illegal sex with him. Her official lover, R-13, is a black state poet who recites his verses at public executions and is D-503's closest friend. D-503 discovers that I-330 is involved with MEPHI, a secret opposition to One State which aims to destroy the Green Wall separating its citizens from other animalistic humans in the outside world whose bodies are covered with thick fur (precursors to Orwell's lowly proles in *Nineteen Eighty-Four*). Against regulations, D-503 impregnates O-90 and with I-330's assistance seeks to smuggle her and her baby outside the Green Wall. However, his plans are exposed and he is diagnosed with a serious illness – he 'has developed a soul' (79) – which is viewed as an incurable condition. He is neutralized by being subjected to the 'Great Operation', which utilizes x-rays to destroy the parts of the brain responsible for imagination and the emotions. D-503 then readily informs on the activities of MEPHI but is shocked that even under brutal torture I-330 refuses to betray her comrades. Nevertheless, a rebellion gathers pace and sections of the Green Wall are toppled, leading to civil disobedience and birds repopulating the city state with even the great 'Benefactor' himself under threat.

The Christian and Biblical elements of *We* are especially interesting in terms of Orwell's preoccupation in *Nineteen Eighty-Four* with society's loss of inner spirituality and external religious frameworks. Zamyatin's fantasy is set after a Two Hundred Years' War over an unnamed valuable substance (perhaps petroleum) during which all but 0.2 per cent of the world's population has been eliminated by weapons of mass destruction. In the post-apocalyptic world of 'One State', recollections of this war are cast almost entirely in biblical metaphors with the precious substance denoted as 'bread' and dim memories recalled of how the peasants fought over it prompted by 'religious prejudice' (21). The novel's chapter headings are rich in religious terminologies, including 'Liturgy' (41), 'An Angel' (58), 'I Am to Burn Eternally' (71), 'Incurable Soul' (76), 'Easter' (119), 'Descent from Heaven' (123) and the culminating phrase 'I Do Not Believe'

(163). Dim recollections of the uplifting value of Christian spirituality still occasionally permeate D-503's mind since pre-One State history cannot be entirely obliterated even by the most ruthless totalitarian state:

> We walked – a single million-headed body, and within each of us – that humble joy which probably fills the lives of molecules, atoms, phago-cytes. In the ancient world this was understood by the Christians, our only predecessors (however imperfect): humility is a virtue, and pride a vice; 'We' is from God, and 'I' from the devil. (112)

Similarly, the great holiday of 'Unanimity Day', intended to draw together all citizens in absolute conformity, recalls for D-503 the value of Easter 'to the ancients' (120) and he unintentionally but persistently lapses into archaic spiritual language: 'we are a single, mighty, million-celled organism, that – in the words of the ancients – we are the Church, one and indivisible' (121).

Echoes of Genesis, Chapters 1 to 4, resonate throughout *We*, with the One State described as 'Paradise' and D-503 and I-330 resembling Adam and Eve. The treacherous double agent S-4711 is 'bent like an S' (15) and 'double-curved' (31) with a 'double-edged smile' (32), equating to Satan's serpentine form. 'Religious Law' and 'God's Law' have been entirely replaced by the 'law of the One State' (38) and references abound to ancient religious mythologies, such as when R-13 recalls the folly of Adam and Eve:

> Those two, in paradise, were given a choice: happiness without freedom, or freedom without happiness. There was no third alternative. Those idiots chose freedom ... We have helped God ultimate to conquer the devil – for it was he who had tempted men to break the ban and get a taste of ruinous freedom, he, the evil serpent. And we, we've brought down our boot over his little head, and – cr-runch! Now everything is fine – we have paradise again. And we are as innocent and simple-hearted as Adam and Eve. No more of that confusion about good and evil. Everything is simple – heavenly, childishly simple. (55).

The rebellious MEPHI recalls Mephistopheles and alludes to Satan's rebellion against God's Heaven as described in Ezekiel 28.11-19, Isaiah 14.12-15 and Milton's *Paradise Lost*. Ultimately, the dangers of the imaginative responses of Eve (and, implicitly, I-330 who influences D-503 and, in turn, prefigures Julia's relationship with Winston in *Nineteen Eighty-Four*) to the Divine gift of free will to humans lie behind the social and political tribulations of *We*, leading inexorably to the repressions of a secular totalitarian state bent upon the elimination of both organized religion and personal spirituality. The novel concludes with the totalitarian regime's rabid denunciation of the old Christian God as D-503 is made to recall:

A blue hill, a cross, a crowd. Some – above, splashed with blood, are nailing a body to a cross; others – below, splashed with tears – are looking on. Does it not seem to you that the role of those above is the most difficult, the most important? If not for them, would this entire majestic tragedy have taken place? They were reviled by the ignorant crowd: but for that the author of the tragedy – God – should have rewarded them all the more generously. And what about the most merciful Christian God, slowly roasting in the fires of hell all those who would not submit? Was He not an executioner? And was the number of those burned by the Christians on bonfires less than the number of burned Christians? Yet – you understand – this God was glorified for ages as the God of love. Absurd? (187)

It is important to reiterate that none of these works acted as a singular dominant source for *Nineteen Eighty-Four*. Orwell's compositional methodology was essentially eclectic and while he drew significant ideas from Wells, London, Huxley, Burdekin and Zamyatin, his blending of these sources was strikingly original and, it may be surmised, also influenced by an increasing awareness of his own mortality. There is some uncertainty over exactly when Orwell first conceived of the central idea behind his novel's dystopian world. On 22 October 1948 he told Frederic Warburg that he had first thought of the novel in 1943 and it is possible that he had begun early plans or drafts by late September.[7] But in a letter to Roger Senhouse, written on 26 December 1948, he was more specific and explained that he was intent upon exploring the 'intellectual implications of totalitarianism' by depicting a world divided up into 'Zones of influence'. This concept had been derived from his observation of the Tehran Conference, a strategy meeting between Churchill, Stalin and Franklin D. Roosevelt to discuss post-war Europe, which was held from 28 November until 1 December 1943 (XIX.487). Hence, early 1944 seems the most likely date for Orwell's initiation of the central concepts of his novel. However, progress was slow since, by 25 June 1945, Frederic Warburg noted (XVII.177–8) that Orwell had only completed the first twelve pages.

Fortunately, the chronology of Orwell's progress with the novel is much clearer from 1946 onwards. His review of Zamyatin's *We* was published in *Tribune* on 4 January 1946 and it immediately exerted a potent influence over his imagination as he focused exclusively (at least in terms of his creative fiction) on *Nineteen Eighty-Four* from early July.[8] By 26 September 1946 he had completed about fifty pages but, with his health in serious decline, the first draft was not finished until 7 November 1947. He began the second draft in May 1948 but had only concluded the laborious and exhausting task of typing a fair copy by 4 December 1948.[9] Frederic Warburg was astonished when he received this typescript, writing in his formal report of 13 December 1948 that '"1984" is "Animal Farm" writ large and in purely anthropomorphic terms'. Noting Orwell's latent 'sadism and its attendant masochism', he found it 'almost intolerable to read Part III which, more even than the rest of the book, smells of death, decay, dirt, diabolism and despair' (XIX.479–81).

These compositional dates are of interest because they coincide with a period when Orwell was still repeatedly confirming his unwavering distaste for the Catholic Church. In a letter of 26 August 1947 to Richard Usborne, the editor of *The Strand*, he explained how throughout the war he had been horrified by the threat of political totalitarianism, an anxiety initially instigated by his longstanding 'hostility towards the Catholic Church'.[10] In the same letter he noted that there was little to choose between Fascism and Communism but if he had to make a decision then he would definitely choose Communism, thereby implicitly suggesting similarities between Catholicism and these two political extremes. Similarly, in an unpublished article written probably in August or September 1947, about the left-wing Labour MP Konni Zilliacus, Orwell confirmed how closely he tended to link the extremes of Catholicism with those of Communism. He recalled that the British intelligentsia had once regarded Catholicism as almost as fashionable as Communism and how anyone criticizing the Church as a 'sinister organization' opposed to democracy was sternly dismissed as a mindless adherent of the 'No-Popery organizations'. Nowadays, Orwell felt, such opinionated and elitist perspectives had withered away and he was convinced that the Roman Catholic Church had become far less fashionable (XIX.183). In his November 1948 review of T. S. Eliot's *Notes Towards the Definition of Culture*, Orwell argued that it was impossible to imagine or understand how any other global organization could have lasted as long as the Catholic Church without major changes over the centuries to its structures and aims. Again drawing links between Catholicism and Communism, he wondered whether the Russian Communist Party might be able to learn some lessons from the Catholic Church to ensure its own longevity. As an 'adoptive and authoritarian organization', the Russian hardline Communists might formulate their social beliefs into a stratified class system which would inevitably change and develop organically, just as class systems always do. But if, like the Catholic Church, it continued to draw its membership from all levels of society and, at the same time, ruthlessly inculcated a conformist mentality, then it might possibly retain its identity virtually unaltered for generations (XIX.474).

The narrative of *Nineteen Eighty-Four* is rich in implicit religious references and associations. V. S. Pritchett remarked in his *New Statesman* review (18 June 1949) that Orwell wrote 'like some dour Protestant or Jansenist who sees his faith corrupted by the "doublethink" of the Roman Catholic Church and who fiercely rejects the corrupt civilizations that appear to be able to flourish even under this dispensation'. The Christian concept of the Fall of Man leading to the loss of a heavenly eternity, drawn from Orwell's youthful reading of both the Bible and classic English authors such as John Milton, remains of central importance to the novel. The Miltonic structuring of *Paradise Lost* and *Paradise Regained* is reversed in *Nineteen Eighty-Four* with Winston stranded in the hellish world of Airstrip One (as England has been rechristened in the agglomeration of international territories known as Oceania) but still aspiring to a lost paradise. Julia becomes his potential route to regaining the paradise of individuality and independence from the all-seeing eyes of Big Brother but the relationships of Milton's Adam and Eve and Orwell's Winston and Julia are tragically inverted. The desiccated, 39-year-old Winston (the same age as Orwell's father Richard when he married his mother Ida) wishes for his Eve to be irrevocably fallen since he hates 'purity' and 'goodness' and wants to see virtue entirely eradicated: 'I want everyone to be corrupt to the bones' (IX.132). In contrast, when Milton's Adam learns of Eve's transgression in eating the forbidden fruit his response is first to celebrate the inherent perfection of Eve's pre-fall state:

> O Fairest of creation, last and best
> Of all God's works, creature in whom excelled
> Whatever can to sight or thought be formed,
> Holy, divine, good, amiable, or sweet! (IX.896–9)

In a loving gesture, paradoxically guaranteeing his own ejection from Paradise but also confirming his act of Christ-like self-sacrifice and potential for salvation, Milton's Adam willingly embraces mortality and death for the sake of his Eve:

> Certain my resolution is to die.
> How can I live without thee, how forego
> Thy sweet converse, and love so dearly joined,
> To live again in these wild woods forlorn? (IX.907–10)

In contrast, as Winston gazes upon mortality and death as represented by the metal cage containing rats which O'Brien threatens to fit over his head, his terrified horror is transformed by the realization that he would willing pass over his punishment to Julia. In an absolute betrayal of his own humanity, he cries out for the torture to be applied to her, insisting that he no longer cares what happens to her: 'Tear her face off, strip her to the bones. Not me! Julia! Not me!' (IX.299–300). Only by denying his former love can Winston save himself in such an irrevocably fallen world where O'Brien – an *agent provocateur* and perverse inversion of the Archangel Raphael (traditionally associated with healing in Christianity, Judaism and Islam) who is sent to teach, advise and guide Milton's Adam – consistently acts not as a moral mentor but as his malign, controlling torturer.

Sir Richard Rees identified a potent subtext of religious meaning in *Nineteen Eighty-Four*, viewing the momentous act of Winston's forced betrayal of Julia as a key philosophical moment in the novel that confirmed humanity's essential egotism and irrevocably fallen nature. In this sense, the novel offers a sombre religious meditation on the fallen state of humankind, alongside its more readily recognizable pessimistic political philosophy. In a letter of 8 March 1955 to Malcolm Muggeridge, Rees explained that he was drafting a study of Orwell's writings and was concerned to demonstrate that 'his value consists in his having taken more seriously than most people the fundamental problem of religion'. He regarded Winston's offering up of Julia instead of himself for torture as proving that the totalitarian state can only be regarded as complete when it 'has been demonstrated to the last resister that in the last resort he would sacrifice the person he loves best in order to save his own skin'. Although Rees acknowledged that the grim morbidity of the novel must have owed something to Orwell's suffering and discomfort during his final illness, he believed that *Nineteen Eighty-Four* revealed 'his true and permanent preoccupation; and that is why I always think of him as a religious or "pious atheist"'. Muggeridge confirmed this perspective by emphasizing Orwell's moral commitment to common decency without necessarily having to dress it up in a cloak of transcendental belief:

> He was allergic to institutional and devotional Christianity, and considered himself – in a way, justly – as being temperamentally irreligious. Yet there was in him this passionate dedication to truth, and refusal to countenance enlightened expediency masquerading as it.

More speculatively, Muggeridge insisted that only 'someone who was naturally religious – even if unconsciously so – could possibly have made a friend of Rees, whose own view of life was essentially a mystical one'.[11]

From this perspective, *Nineteen Eighty-Four* offered a significant contribution to a vigorous English tradition of politicized religious writing with its author cast, in Gordon Bowker's phrase, as the '"happy vicar" turned secular socialist'. Since the 1930s, Orwell had sought to depict the rise of Fascist totalitarianism as a form of repression and brutality comparable to that of the Spanish Inquisition and probably worse, 'thanks to the radio and the secret police' (XII.126). In contrast, his journalism consistently identified Protestantism with individuality and freedom of thought and he considered the novel as one of its most significant cultural achievements. Some of the names of characters in *Nineteen Eighty-Four* implicitly recall persecuted religious dissenters. Rutherford – one of the original leaders of the revolution whom Winston (born in 1945) remembers before his execution in the mid-1960s – recalls the Scottish Presbyterian dissenter Samuel Rutherford (c. 1600–61) whose anti-royalist *Lex Rex, or, the Law of the Prince* (1644) was publicly burnt at Edinburgh and St Andrews after the restoration of King Charles II, with Rutherford facing a charge of treason and possible execution. Tillotson, a fellow worker with Winston in the Records Department, echoes the name of John Tillotson (1630–94), Archbishop of Canterbury, who was a virulent opponent of Catholicism and who had continued to denounce papists even during the reign of the Catholic King James II. Another of Winston's former colleagues, Withers, who had been suspected of 'heretical tendencies', recalls the name of the non-conformist Protestant minister George Withers (c. 1540–1605). The poet Ampleforth, who is imprisoned with Winston because he was revising Kipling's poems but had left the word 'God' in one of them because he could not find another feasible rhyme with 'rod' (IX.242), recalls the Benedictine Ampleforth Abbey and College in North Yorkshire. Even the apparently innocuous appearance in *Nineteen Eighty-Four* of the old nursery rhyme, 'Oranges and Lemons', seems to evoke distant memories of cruel religious persecutions. As Gordon Bowker concludes, these elements of the novel ensured that it became 'more than just a warning based on the rundown England of 1948; it also offers a comparison with a barbaric past, underlining the disconnection between scientific advance and moral progress'.[12]

The mid-twentieth century's most ignominious and genocidal period of religious and racial persecution also provides a key element of the totalitarian repression in the first half of *Nineteen Eighty-Four*. At the beginning of the novel, Winston notes in his diary for 4 April 1984 his recollections of a barbarous film in which a middle-aged woman, possibly a 'jewess' (IX.10), sits in the bow of lifeboat clutching a small child after their ship has been sunk by bombing. The party members in the audience are delighted when the lifeboat is blown up by a helicopter and the camera gruesomely follows one of the child's arms spinning up into the air. Only one prole woman verbally protests against such barbaric violence but she is rapidly ejected from the theatre by the state police. Even the date of this entry in Winston's diary is significant in that the Schutzstaffel (SS) had been founded in Germany on 4 April 1925 and twenty years later on the same date in 1945 the Ohrdurf forced labour and concentration camp (part of the Buchenwald network) was the first with prisoners still resident to be entered by advancing American troops from the US Third Army. This liberation exposed for the first time the full magnitude of the horrors of the Holocaust and the Supreme Commander of Allied Forces in Europe, General Dwight D. Eisenhower, visited the camp so that he could personally testify to the extent of these atrocities. Hence, the 4 April (both in 1925 and 1945) possessed a special resonance in the history of Nazi totalitarianism.

Emmanuel Goldstein, the supposed arch-traitor and 'Enemy of the People' (IX.13) and head of the mysterious 'Brotherhood', becomes a convenient scapegoat for the totalitarian regime in *Nineteen Eighty-Four* and his negative reputation is utilized to justify the State's surveillance and eradication of civil liberties. 'He is a composite scapegoat', David Walton explains, 'deriving from Christianity's Devil, Stalinism's Trotsky, and Animalism's Snowball'.[13] He is sketched as a typical anti-Semitic caricature, possessing a 'lean Jewish face', capped with white hair and a small goatee beard. He possesses an intelligent expression and yet, somehow, it is 'inherently despicable' (IX.14). However, Goldstein is only ever heard and seen on the telescreen and might well be no more than a convenient fabrication promulgated by the Ministry of Truth. Certainly, he becomes a central and necessary aspect of the Party's manipulative propagandist repertoire. Ultimately, in *Nineteen Eighty-Four* the opposing duality of Goldstein and Big Brother becomes a Bad Father/Good Father opposition in terms of the psychological manipulation of Oceania's citizens by the Party. As David Walton explains:

> The Jew is apt for the Bad Father figure because, briefly, Judaism has a 'father-son' relationship to Christianity; the popular conception of Judaism is a God-the-Father dominated religion (Orwell's 'tribal deity of the worst sort'), as opposed to the Christian Trinity; the Jews have perhaps the longest record of monotheism.[14]

It is claimed that Goldstein had formerly been a leading member of the Party and an early and trusted associate of Big Brother, the leader of the privileged 'Inner Party' elite. But he had written an anti-state tract, The Theory and Practice of Oligarchical Collectivism, and proved disloyal by founding the Brotherhood. In his appearance, personal history and political thought Goldstein bears obvious comparison to Leon Trotsky, who was once a close associate of Lenin and later a major rival of Stalin. He had been exiled from Russia in 1927 and wrote *The Revolution Betrayed*, exposing the totalitarianism and corruptions of Stalin's brutal regime, probably parodied in Goldstein's Oligarchical Collectivism. During the Stalinist purges of the 1930s, Trotsky was repeatedly accused of being the instigator or inspiration for dissident plots against Stalin's authority. He was eventually murdered in exile in Mexico City by a Spanish communist and Stalinist agent, Ramón Mercader, who was awarded the Order of Lenin while serving a twenty-year prison sentence in Mexico and made a Hero of the Soviet Union after his release in 1961.

Mercader possesses an intriguing link with Orwell through an English communist and Soviet agent, David Crook, who had volunteered for the International Brigade during the Spanish Civil War. Crook was seriously wounded in the Battle of the Jarama Valley in February 1937 and, while recuperating, he transferred to Albacete, supposedly for officer training. At this period he also received Spanish language and surveillance tuition from Mercader. Then, following orders from the Russian NKVD (Secret Police), Crook took up a post as a war reporter for the *News Chronicle*, which enabled him to spy on Orwell and his Independent Labour Party associates in the POUM militia.[15] The image of Goldstein's Jewish face staring out from the telescreen in *Nineteen Eighty-Four* perhaps also recalls Crook who was the son of Jewish immigrants to the East End of London. During the 'Two Minute Hate', which occurs every day at 11 a.m., an image of Goldstein appears on the telescreen and the viewers are expected to subject him to extreme contempt. As the 'Hate' rises to a communal climax, Goldstein's face and voice changes into that of a mindlessly bleating sheep. In contrast, the thought of a manichean blending of a satanic and Christ-like Big Brother inspires the haters with a quasi-religious, evangelical zeal. A. J. West explains how psychologically the 'underlying totalitarian principle in *Nineteen Eighty-Four*' is the 'worship of Big Brother replacing that of Christ'.[16] One woman flings herself towards the screen with her arms outstretched and cries out, 'My Saviour,' as she sinks into a prayer-like posture. A group chant arises of 'B-B! ... 'B-B!', a refrain often heard in times of overwhelming emotion as a 'hymn to the wisdom and majesty of Big Brother' and as a means of mindless self-hypnosis through repetitious sounds (IX.18–19). Party loyalists talk of the final and absolute 'elimination of Goldsteinism' (IX.57) – recalling the Nazi's anti-Semitic 'Final Solution' – and during a Eurasian bombardment an effigy of Goldstein is burnt. Finally, in order to ingratiate himself with Winston, the sinister O'Brien at first pretends to be a secret Goldstein loyalist and when they share a drink he offers the toast to Emmanuel Goldstein as 'our Leader' (IX.178).

In Orwell's mind all forms of totalitarianism, including Fascism, Communism, Capitalism, anti-Semitism and traditional Roman Catholicism, require an acceptance of an imposed orthodoxy defined in *Nineteen Eighty-Four* as an entire absence of thought or blissful 'unconsciousness'. Children's history books under Big Brother record the numerous inequities of the old capitalist regime and bizarre Catholic religious superstitions such as 'kissing the Pope's toe' to demonstrate absolute subservience (IX.56). When Winston meets an old man who can still vaguely recall the days before the Revolution he asks him about those times when a minority of wealthy capitalists, along with a few privileged lawyers and priests, were effectively the 'lords of the earth'. The Old Man fondly recalls listening to speeches in Hyde Park made by the 'Salvation Army, Roman Catholics, Jews, Indians' (IX.93–4) but it becomes impossible for Winston to gauge from him whether life before or after the Revolution was better for the average citizen. Instead, he realizes that under the new totalitarian regime of the Party – as with authoritarian religions – current practices and customs simply have to be accepted because there no longer survive any tangible comparative memories of what had preceded them. The whole world is now divided into conflicting philosophies: Ingsoc (English Socialism) in Oceania, Neo-Bolshevism in Eurasia and the cult of 'Death-Worship' or 'Obliteration of the Self' in Eastasia (IX.205). But, as Winston now realizes, 'hereditary aristocracies' such as these modern secular creeds tend to be short-lived while 'adoptive organisations', represented by the Catholic Church, can last for thousands of years (IX.218). It becomes essential, therefore, for the religious spirit of humankind to be totally suppressed and ultimately eradicated within the totalitarian state.

The culminating onslaught against religion in *Nineteen Eighty-Four* comes with O'Brien's authoritarian denunciations in which political and religious orthodoxy are woven together. Orwell sensed and feared that power-worship – pre-war with the rise of German and Spanish Fascism, throughout the Second World War, and now post-war with the dominance of Stalinism in Russia and the beginnings of the Cold War – had become in itself a malevolent intellectual fad. It was typified by sympathy, especially among intellectuals and the social elite, for both Hitler and now Stalin. His longstanding hostility towards Catholicism was ever more strongly linked with these fears since he envisaged the age-old traditions and doctrinal authority of the Roman Catholic Church as directly comparable to the quasi-religious power-worship which had surrounded Hitler. Its devices for controlling the populace and eliminating enemies had now been embraced by Stalin and his ruthless henchmen, led by the psychotically brutal and depraved Lavrentiy Beria, Marshal of the Soviet Union and head of state security, who effortlessly blended charm and torture in his treatment of his numerous victims. Big Brother's Beria-like enforcer, O'Brien, seeks to create in his destruction of Winston's individuality and free will a cruelly dialectical tension between the concept of a 'safe haven' (in a kind of mindless Heaven) and the threat of grotesque and unending suffering in a highly personalized, bespoke Hell in which the 'thing that is in Room 101 is [for each individual] the worst thing in the world' (IX.296). Winston readily confesses – in a grim parody of the Catholic Sacrament of Confession – that he has been a religious believer, a sexual pervert and at heart an old-style capitalist. But, like a deranged cross between a medical doctor – reminiscent of those who treated Orwell in his Gloucestershire sanitarium for his last illness and University College Hospital where he died – and an apparently benign sacerdotal confessor and educator, O'Brien takes over every aspect of Winston's physical and mental existence. Supposedly as a means of repossessing his soul, O'Brien becomes his protector and tormenter, his 'inquisitor' and 'friend' (IX.256). The traditional Catholic Profession of Faith requires the believer to state:

> With firm faith, I also believe everything contained in the word of God, whether written or handed down in Tradition, which the Church, either by a solemn judgment or by the ordinary and universal Magisterium, sets forth to be believed as divinely revealed. I also firmly accept and hold each and everything definitively proposed by the Church.

Similarly, O'Brien instructs Winston in similar fashion during the extremities of his torture, insisting that 'Whatever the Party holds to be truth, *is* truth', and that perceptions of reality are impossible 'except by looking through the eyes of the Party' (IX.261).

Recalling the Jesuit motto, 'Give me a child until he is seven and I will give you the man', based upon an axiom of Saint Francis Xavier, O'Brien tells Winston that he has been watching over him for 'seven years' but promises that the moment has now come for O'Brien to save him by making him 'perfect' (IX.256). As the electric shock tortures begin to inflict exquisite pains on Winston, O'Brien momentarily relents, adopting a less severe manner, speaking gently and patiently like a doctor, teacher or 'even a priest' (IX.267) who seeks to explain his actions rather than merely punish Winston. At this point O'Brien seems to become 'Father O'Brien', Orwell's fantasy figure of a malignantly manipulative Irish Catholic priest who, in turn, cajoles and torments Winston.

O'Brien adopts an increasingly evangelical tone, insisting that reality can never be found in the individual mind but only in that of the Party, which, like a church or religious sect, is 'collective and immortal'. He categorically asserts that whatever the Party regards as truth is the absolute truth. Winston's torture continues relentlessly, like a purgatory driving him to the edge of madness. His mind is forced to conform via O'Brien's testing over whether two plus two make four or five, parodying the Soviet Communist Party slogan which encouraged the completion of its second five-year economic plan (1933–7) in four years. Ultimately, O'Brien becomes his only trusted 'protector' (IX.263), an implacable religious dictator whom, like an Old Testament patriarch, Winston must please by his absolute submission and obedience. At this point in the concluding phase of the novel, religious and secular totalitarianism blend seamlessly as O'Brien ultimately seeks to convince Winston that he and his associates are the new 'priests of power. God is power' (IX.276).

As O'Brien leans over Winston, his face infused with a sort of lunatic revelation, he completes his transformation into an obsessive evangelical preacher. He advises Winston that he must first understand that there are no longer any 'martyrdoms' in Oceania, reminding him of past 'religious persecutions' and the Inquisition of the Middle Ages. O'Brien is triumphant in his insistence that the Inquisition failed because, although it sought to eliminate heresies, it ended up by perpetuating them. By burning heretics and martyrs at the stake, it merely ensured that thousands of others would take their place. This was because, O'Brien carefully explains, the Inquisition made the error of killing its opponents while they were still proudly unrepentant. Their victims died because heroically they would not 'abandon' their faith or beliefs. This meant that ultimately their victims were triumphant and the persecutors were defeated by their fortitude and self-sacrifice (IX.265–6). He then links this phase of religious totalitarianism directly to the twentieth century with the 'German Nazis and the Russian Communists'. O'Brien recounts how the Russians under Beria's supervision persecuted heresy even more savagely than the Inquisition, but to no avail. They at least had realized that they should not allow their victims to become martyrs and so, before setting them up in show trials, they attempted to obliterate their dignity. As with Winston's own treatment at the hands of O'Brien, the Russians oppressed their political victims with such brutal tortures that, pleading for mercy, they were willing to confess to any crime. But, like the Inquisition, such mindless measures entirely failed since after only a few years those who had been tortured, tried and executed came to be regarded as heroic 'martyrs'. The key to avoiding such a dilemma, according to O'Brien, is to control the concept of truth itself – an attitude which, Orwell proposes, religious organizations especially Roman Catholicism had pursued for centuries. He admits that the confessions of the Russian dissidents had been patently untrue and extorted by threats and torture. But in the world of Oceania such errors are no longer made and all confessions are true because 'We make them true.' In this way the dead can no longer come back to haunt the presiding political regime and he assures Winston that the future will know nothing about him since the purpose of his current re-education is to lift him entirely out of historical memory. As Winston himself had done in his work for the Ministry of Truth (or Minitrue), the state agency responsible for historical revisionism and propaganda, he will be effectively eradicated from time and truth itself as if he had never existed.

Speaking in the inspired tones of a religious proselytizer, O'Brien explains how Winston's eventual submission to Big Brother must be given in the Miltonic spirit of his own free will. He insists that it is never wise simply to destroy the heretic and, thereby, create a martyr. Instead, he must be converted so that his 'inner mind' can be captured and entirely reshaped. Like religious missionaries, the authorities seek to 'burn all evil and all illusion out of him' so that he can be brought back within the obedient and unquestioning flock of loyal adherents. Although the dissident must still usually die, the regime's pursuit of the uniformity of the soul rather than merely the body or other external affiliations lies as the heart of Orwell's linkage of religious and political totalitarianism in the final phase of *Nineteen Eighty-Four*. The authority of Big Brother is enshrined within a set of counter-Biblical commandments promulgated by the Ministry of Love (or Minilove) which oversees social conformity through brainwashing and torture. The authority of the old despotisms, O'Brien explains, was mistakenly imposed by the imperative 'Thou shalt not', while his brand of totalitarianism seeks to cleanse and purge all opposition by the control of the minds and souls of individuals to ensure that they accept the counter-imperative of 'Thou shalt' (IX.265–7).

O'Brien ultimately promises Winston that his re-education will comprise three key stages, equating to a quasi-spiritual journey or pilgrimage of 'learning', 'understanding' and 'acceptance' (IX.273). Inevitably, Winston readily capitulates once he realizes that his torture has ended and, like an enthused recent convert, he keenly embraces the task of re-educating himself. He realizes that for seven years – this timescale is a key period in Winston's personal history – the Thought Police (based on the Russian NKVD) had kept him under surveillance and that he must now accept without question the authority of the 'immortal, collective brain' of the Party. He scrawls clumsily in a pencil three key axioms of belief which will enable him to be absorbed into the great whole of society and to avoid further pain, suffering and mental anguish. He now accepts without question that freedom equates to slavery and, crucially, that two plus two make not four but five. Most significantly, he concludes in a darkly inverted parody of religious faith that 'GOD IS POWER' (IX.290). With relief, he realizes that he has now accepted his new faith and he can rejoin Oceania's loyal and unquestioning flock.

These sensations of spiritual release trigger in Winston's mind a soothing dream of an almost heavenly state in which all doubts, arguments, pains and fears have been purged. This dream sequence was perhaps inspired by a similar dream passage in Graham Greene's *Heart of the Matter* when his disconsolate hero Scobie dreams of walking through cool, green fields with his boy Ali. Although Orwell's review of Greene's novel had been critical of his unconvincing depiction of a colonial officer, it seems likely that Orwell – increasingly aware of the mortality of his own ravaged body – appreciated the reassuring sense of momentary spiritual transcendence encapsulated in Scobie's soothing dream. Winston imagines in his own dream that his body is once more strong and vigorous as he walks 'with a joy of movement' down an enormous sunlit passage over a kilometre wide. He happily enters the 'Golden Country', strolling down a pathway across gentle pasture. As he luxuriates in the soft green turf under his feet and the gently warming sunshine on his face, he seems to re-enter the Edenic world of Eric Blair's rural childhood around Henley-on-Thames and he gazes across a field edged by elm trees and a stream where shallow pools have formed beneath the graceful willow trees (IX.292–3).

There is a Miltonic flaw, however, in Winston's cathartic sense of spiritual release because he suddenly awakes to the realization that he is still, like Adam, obsessed with the potential loss of Julia as his Eve. He experiences a potent hallucination of her physical presence in which she seems not only to come alongside him but to enter the flesh beneath his skin. The realization that comes with these sensations is tragic in the extreme since he now knows that his love for her is undiminished and that she was still alive somewhere and 'needed his help' (IX.293). At this point, Winston experiences exactly the same emotions as Adam in *Paradise Lost* when he realizes that Eve has eaten of the forbidden fruit and betrayed him: 'Certain my resolution is to die. / How can I live without thee.' But Winston immediately realizes that the Thought Police will detect, through this gesture of lingering earthly passion, that he still possesses dangerous traces of his former identity as a dissident who once belonged to a world in which its God was the embodiment of Christian Love rather than godless Power. As O'Brien enters the room, Winston admits that he still hates Big Brother, and the hellish consequence of his mortal sin of non-conformity is Room 101 with its threatened torture of the head-cage and rats. Only his absolute betrayal of Julia – a final renunciation of both earthly and Divine Love – ultimately saves him: 'Not me! Julia! Not me!' (IX.299–300).

The concluding pages of *Nineteen Eighty-Four* confirm how the traditional phraseologies of religious love have been absorbed as a tool of mind-control by the malevolent Ministry of Love. Sedated with gin, Winston sits quietly in the Chestnut Tree Café with rays of yellow sunlight playing on the table tops. He browses through *The Times* and with a 'cloudy mysticism' studies endless chess problems in which the white pieces always triumph over the black ones, symbolizing the 'eternal, unvarying triumph of Good over Evil' (IX.302). Winston and Julia now meet whenever they wish, their destabilizing love neutralized by their shared indifference and the curse of Adam and Eve's love for one another finally eradicated. Instead, the telescreen plays a corrupted rendition of Longfellow's charming pastoral verse, 'Under the spreading chestnut tree', in which the second line, 'I loved him and he loved me', is revised to commemorate Winston's and Julia's betrayal of one another to 'I sold you and you sold me' (IX.307). Traditionally, the chestnut tree represented Justice, Honesty and Chastity, qualities which have been ruthlessly eradicated in the totalitarian world of Big Brother to ensure that blind obedience to the presiding regime replaces Christian love and devotion. The word 'spreading' also encapsulates the insidious permeation of the State's malevolence into the deepest recesses of the human mind and soul. Big Brother is now a 'colossus that bestrode the world' (IX.310), echoing Cassius's denunciation of Caesar's imperialistic ambitions in Shakespeare's *Julius Caesar* (I.ii.136–7). As he listens to the telescreen broadcasting news of Oceania's glorious victory over Eurasia by conquering all of Africa, Winston feels as though he is in a 'blissful dream' and that he has been forgiven all of his earlier non-conformity, re-purifying 'his soul white as snow'. He realizes, in the concluding four words of the novel, that finally 'He loved Big Brother' (IX.311), a confession evoking a cruel parody of the remote, immortal authority of the Judeo-Christian God since this final triumph of totalitarianism confirms the eradication of all that was once nourishing and admirable in the human spirit.

POSTSCRIPT

One of Orwell's last intended essays was on the devout Catholic convert Evelyn Waugh for the *Partisan Review*. Although it was never completed or published, both its surviving preliminary notes and a typescript draft confirm how religious issues remained dominant in Orwell's mind up to the very end of his literary productivity. In handwritten notes in his final Literary Notebook, probably made in the spring of 1949, he copied out a brief passage from *Brideshead Revisited* (about Sebastian's drunkenness and 'Moral obligation') and two passages from *Robbery Under Law*. The second (much shorter) passage recorded Waugh's statement that 'There is no more agreeable position than that of dissident from a stable society', while the longer focused on Waugh's assertion of his confirmed Conservatism. It contained a mixture of radical and reactionary thoughts, some of which were obviously the antithesis of Orwell's own views while others would have rung true with his socialist perspectives. Orwell noted down Waugh's specific words:

> I believe that man is, by nature, an exile & will never be self-sufficient or complete on this earth; that his chances of happiness & virtue, here, remain more or less constant through the centuries &, generally speaking, are not much affected by the political & economic conditions in which he lives, that the balance of good & ill tends to revert to a norm ... that the intellectual communists of today have personal, irrelevant grounds for their antagonism to society ... there is no form of government ordained from God as being better than any other.

Waugh goes on to insist that anarchic elements are a natural part of all societies and that inequalities in wealth and social position are always inevitable, so much so that it is 'meaningless to discuss the advantages of their elimination' since humans 'naturally arrange themselves in a system of classes' (XX.78).

Orwell's notes following this quotation described Waugh's motivating forces as either 'Snobby Catholicism' or 'Snobbery' and 'Catholicism' (his writing is indistinct). He had recently been re-reading various works by Waugh, including *Robbery Under Law*, *When the Going Was Good*, *Rossetti: His Life and Works*, and *Work Suspended* (XX.219–20), and he concluded that not even Waugh's earliest books were either anti-religious or explicitly immoral. Following an underlined heading, 'Catholicism', he made a note that not all Catholic writers necessarily had to be politically Conservative and that in his essay he should carefully differentiate Waugh's traditional brand of Catholicism from the more idiosyncratic and sceptical devotions of Graham Greene. The distinct advantage of a novelist being a Catholic, in Orwell's opinion, was that he could exploit a narrative collision between two contrasting forms of 'good'. He was unimpressed by the first person narrator of *Brideshead Revisited* but admitted that the novel was not 'puritanical' nor were its priests depicted as unrealistically 'super-human'. However, the scene in which Lord Marchmain makes a deathbed Sign of the Cross struck Orwell as deeply melodramatic and he noted that the novel's surface veneer of cohesion was bound to crack sometime since it was impossible to be both a true Catholic and fully 'grown up'. His concluding note commended Waugh's skills as a novelist while condemning his religious affiliation, concluding that he was as good a novelist as it is possible to be 'while holding untenable beliefs' (XX.78–9).

In an incomplete typescript draft of this essay, probably written in about April 1949 at Cranham Sanatorium in the Cotswolds, where Waugh later visited him, Orwell felt that he had sought, with varying levels of success, to conform rigorously to the traditional tenets of the Roman Catholic Church. While he considered that it was now unremarkable to claim that one was an anarchist or an atheist, he admired the courage of Waugh's religious convictions, noting how daring and unfashionable it had become to affirm a belief in God or to admire capitalism. Although he regarded some of Waugh's perspectives on life to be 'false' and even 'perverse', he merited respect for having the courage publicly to adopt such views when, in Orwell's opinion, they were likely to hinder his literary career. While most of his generation was politically left wing with sporadic Communist leanings, Waugh remained, as stated in the extract which Orwell had copied out from *Robbery Under Law*, a true Conservative in spirit and social outlook. Even his first book, his life of Dante Gabriel Rossetti (published in 1928, not 1927 as Orwell's typescript states), promulgated a kind of 'defiant Conservatism' expressed in 'aesthetic rather than political terms'. For Orwell, of course, Waugh's Conservatism remained of paramount importance because it was so closely linked to his adopted Catholicism, even though his early novels, especially *Decline and Fall* and *Vile Bodies*, were constructed around an amoral love of sheer anarchy. Orwell especially enjoyed one of the most amusing episodes in *Decline and Fall* when a clergyman is decapitated by a lunatic, and he felt that these early novels were essentially comic sermons 'kept in farcical shape by avoidance of comment' (XX.75–8).

In a letter to Orwell of 17 July 1949, Waugh begins by explaining that he had not written to thank him for a copy of *Nineteen Eighty-Four* because his publisher had not sent one to him (perhaps indicating an earlier unrecorded contact between the two men about this work). Waugh goes on to explain that he had bought a copy and read it with great admiration.

However, the letter makes clear that he held some important reservations over Orwell's treatment of Winston's soul and, specifically, Waugh felt that its 'metaphysics are wrong'. He took Orwell to task for having Winston deny the existence of the human soul and felt that the novel was spurious because of its eradication of the Church. While a critic might mock the Church's 'supernatural implications', it was impossible to disregard its 'unique character as a social & historical institution'. Waugh considered the Roman Catholic Church to be 'inextinguishable', even though tyranny could repress it in certain places for certain periods of time. But even then, total suppression was always very difficult to achieve and he cited the example of the Japanese descendants of those first inspired by St Francis Xavier's mission who had secretly retained their faith for three centuries and were 'found saying "Ave Marias" & "Pater Nosters" when the country was opened in the last century'. In a statement of particular relevance to O'Brien's brutal treatment of Winston Smith in *Nineteen Eighty-Four*, Waugh concluded that 'men who love a crucified God need never think of torture as all-powerful'.[1] Given the clear interest of Waugh and Orwell in debating religious issues, it is to be regretted that no record of their personal meeting (or meetings) at the Cotswold sanatorium has survived. Malcolm Muggeridge noted:

> Waugh did go and see Orwell several times, and afterwards corresponded with him in a very delightful way. Despite all Waugh's efforts to appear to be an irascible, deaf old curmudgeon, a sort of innate saintliness kept breaking through. I should have loved to see them together; complementary figures, his country gentleman's outfit and Orwell's proletarian one both straight out of back numbers of Punch.[2]

The trajectory of Orwell's comments, during his short literary career, on anti-Semitism and Roman Catholicism have been intriguing to map alongside one another. While he indulged in *Down and Out in Paris and London* in the casual verbal hostilities towards Jews which were prevalent within much of European society during the 1920s and early 1930s, his attitudes towards them radically changed once he acquired knowledge of the racial suppression of Nazi Fascism and the horrors of their concentration camps. By the end of the war, Orwell was recognized as a stern voice against the dangers and barbarism of anti-Semitism and his careful analyses of the reasons for such racial hostilities and genocidal tendencies in supposedly civilized societies remain of importance today. But, in contrast, his responses to Roman Catholicism barely changed during his lifetime and he sustained an incorruptible pessimism over the motives and actions of the Catholic Church. Although his first school was run by exiled Catholic French Ursuline nuns – themselves victims of vicious religious persecutions – he tended always to denigrate and dismiss the doctrinal, spiritual and social tenets of Catholicism. Unlike Greene and Waugh he displayed no knowledge of, or interest in debating, theological issues and, instead, doggedly insisted that the Roman Catholic Church, especially through its ancient processes of Inquisition, was a direct precursor to Nazi and Spanish Fascism and, ultimately, Stalinist authoritarianism. In an essay for *Tribune* in 1944, for example, he categorically stated that beyond its own adherents, the 'Catholic Church' was virtually 'universally regarded as pro-Fascist, both objectively and subjectively' (XVI.132).

It is interesting to note, however, that such a devout Catholic convert as his friend Christopher Hollis was not entirely negative in assessing Orwell's responses to mid-twentieth-century Catholicism. He knew that Orwell possessed very little relevant knowledge about Catholic theology and confirmed that his views of the Church were based upon highly selective and anecdotal 'personal experience', drawn from his time in Spain and the ultra-loyal 'Catholicism of certain Catholic journalists'. However, echoing Orwell, Hollis suggested that the ardent promulgation of the Roman Catholic Church by its most vociferous adherents during the twentieth century had in some ways proved problematic:

> Indeed the most obedient of Catholics must agree that there has grown up in modern times in certain Catholic circles a contention that it is a failure in loyalty not to champion wholly the side in every passing controversy of any one who takes the Catholic name and that no word of criticism of authority must at any time be permitted. This disease within is certainly an obstacle to the health of Catholicism as potent as any of the attacks on it from without, and Orwell was only one of many in the modern world who was prevented from a proper examination of Catholicism's claims by the conduct of Catholics.[3]

Nevertheless, as a documentary journalist Orwell was at fault in entirely ignoring the steadily growing statistical importance of the Roman Catholic Church within the British Isles during his lifetime. In 1900 its estimated Catholic population stood at just over two million, rising to over two and a half million by 1920, three million by 1930 and three and a half million by 1950. Furthermore, as Callum Brown explains, 'by 1900 Catholics in Britain had significantly higher levels of church practice than Protestants – with between a third and two thirds of Catholics attending mass weekly ... Of all the major denominations in Edwardian Britain, Catholics achieved the most significant growth in numbers as a proportion of the British people.'[4] But this huge increase of 175 per cent in the number of British Catholics between Orwell's birth and death seemed irrelevant to him. Some of the reasons behind this strangely unshifting vision may lie rooted in a psychological response to experiences in his childhood, family life and early manhood. But exactly what these issues were remains uncertain since he never considered it necessary to compile an objective self-analysis of his virulent hostility towards Roman Catholicism.

However, on a literary level, at least one major stylistic reason may be offered for Orwell conveying a constant and intense enmity towards a long-established religious institution about which he seemed to have known little of substance. His literary papers suggest that he never evinced any curiosity over acquiring either the specifics of Catholic doctrinal knowledge or informed personal Catholic contacts who might have been able to ground his polemics in fact or first-hand observation. Orwell has long been acclaimed for his two major novels, *Animal Farm* and *Nineteen Eighty-Four*, but most of his other works, especially *Down and Out in Paris and London* and *A Clergyman's Daughter*, are far more episodic and fragmentary in their structure, depending heavily upon disparate elements of journalistic observation and a style of writing more akin to the skills of an essayist and polemicist. Indeed, Orwell is rightly acclaimed as one of the most important essayists of the twentieth century, combining a fluently eloquent style with the potency of powerfully focused arguments. And in these admirable characteristics lies a clue to his strangely intense and long-expressed hostility towards Roman Catholicism. As previously noted, Orwell was a compulsive collector of pamphlets during the late 1930s and 1940s. The numerous examples of his deep personal hostility towards Catholicism cited in this study – characterized by single-track arguments habitually utilized to convey deductions about the typical from the extreme – suggest that whenever he considered Catholicism he automatically adopted an intrinsically polemical mode of both thinking and writing comparable to the styles of pamphleteering found in his large personal collection of such documents.

The job of the writer of a successful pamphlet is rarely to provide a balanced and objective assessment of both sides of an argument or to tease out the complexities of political, social or religious issues. Instead, the most potent style of pamphleteering requires the writer to fixate upon a single-track argument and adopt an unwaveringly monochrome perspective on the chosen topic. An ardent left-wing pamphleteer does not waste time and argumentative energy by carefully assessing the potentially positive attributes of policies adopted by an opposing government, even though, as Orwell himself would have readily admitted, no political structure – unless it aspires to the dreaded state of a totalitarian regime – can ever hope to be totally right and its opponents totally wrong. Similarly, Orwell consistently wrote about Roman Catholicism from the perspective of an unbending pamphleteer whose brief was to confirm it as an authoritarian, elitist, retrogressive and ultimately totalitarian religious organization. He saw it as committed only to its own survival and continuity, complacently basing its moralities upon centuries-old traditions rather than self-interrogating reassessments of its relevance to twentieth-century communities. Furthermore, the Catholic Church seemed to be represented in Orwell's writings exclusively by an elite, self-interested cadre of intellectuals, literary figures, high-ranking clerics and, to a lesser extent, professionals and businessmen who were firmly ensconced within the upper reaches of British society. In this respect, Orwell's close friend and literary executor Sir Richard Rees was right to describe his hostility as specifically directed towards 'political Catholicism'.[5]

Strangely, Orwell chose almost entirely to ignore the vast majority of Catholics in Britain who not only included his often-mentioned immigrant Irish labourers but also second- and third-generation Catholic families who by the 1930s and 1940s occupied positions in many professions and a wide range of businesses. But, of course, when viewed from the stance of a rhetorically charged pamphleteer, it was to be expected that Orwell would always write about Roman Catholicism from a polemical and intrinsically biased perspective. Likewise, Orwell's second wife of fourteen weeks, the convent school educated Sonia Brownell, also firmly rejected her childhood Catholicism and regular church attendance. She had so hated her schooldays at the Sacred Heart Convent in Roehampton (the school depicted by Antonia White in *Frost in May*) that she reputedly spat if she passed a nun in the street. It seems ironic, therefore, that after her death on 17 December 1980 she received a traditional Requiem Mass at the Roman Catholic Church of St Mary's, Cadogan Street, during which the same passage was read from Ecclesiastes (12.6: '[Remember your Creator before] the silver cord be loosed, or the golden bowl be broken') which she had requested Anthony Powell to read at Orwell's funeral thirty years earlier. She was also buried according to the full Catholic rites just as her husband who had been baptized seventy-seven years earlier at Motihari's Protestant mission, the 'Regions Beyond Missionary Union', had insisted upon an Anglican burial service and interment in an Anglican country churchyard.[6]

Ultimately, it was the institutionalized Catholic Church, along with its most privileged members, that most deeply irritated Orwell. He said little about the silent private devotions of the millions of ordinary British Catholics and the commendable labours of hardworking parish priests and Catholic charities. Such matters were clearly not the business of an anti-Catholic polemicist. Nevertheless, Orwell undoubtedly recognized – and frequently assessed in the latter part of his literary career – the individual's personal need for a sense of spirituality and even a firm and guiding personal faith. Totalitarian states sought systematically to eradicate elements of individuality, imagination and private spirituality from their citizens and, predictably, Orwell viewed such suppressions as archly destructive acts against the very core of humanity's creativity, vigour and potential happiness. But it remained pointless for Orwell to acknowledge the potency of Christian principles when he personally and so firmly disbelieved in the possibility of an afterlife or eternity. Also, he was convinced that the majority of British citizens quietly shared this view or at least sympathized with such a sceptical perspective on the ultimate point of all forms of Christianity – a final escape through mortality and death into an everlasting afterlife and reunification with the host of other true believers and God Himself.

Orwell was willing to accept that numerous forms of religious belief were necessary components of the daily lives of individuals but, at the same time, he found them utterly unbelievable. Key aspects of Christianity became for him influential elements in a kind of self-deluding fairy tale which flourished simply because it was one of the means by which individuals felt they could make their lives more profitable, rewarding and even tolerable. Yet, as Robert Gray has noted: 'In spite of himself, the shadow of Christianity lay deep in Orwell. Very few Christian writers have associated themselves with the cause of the exploited to the extent that he did; and very few have shown such disdain for the comforts of this world.' Seven months before his death in January 1950, Orwell sent to to his childhood friend Jacintha Buddicom a now lost letter. Her diary recorded a 'Letter from Eric about "Nothing Ever Dies"', and she recalled that it 'defined his faith in some sort of after-life. Not necessarily, or even probably, a conventional Heaven-or-Hell, but the firm belief that '"nothing every dies", that we must go on *somewhere*'.[7] It is also interesting to note that during his last weeks of life Orwell reputedly chose to read Dante's *Divine Comedy*.[8] Sir Richard Rees, himself a committed Christian, recalled that for Orwell to 'accept death as final was for him a test of intellectual honesty' but 'to care passionately about the fate of mankind after your death was an ethical imperative'.[9]

In conclusion, this study has proposed that Eric Blair's knowledge of, and responses to, religious and spiritual issues impacted both implicitly and directly upon his stridently secular writings as George Orwell. A strongly humanitarian instinct and ethos, common to both Christianity and Marxist socialism, became a central formulating element in his private and published writings. It is, therefore, misleading to disengage entirely the secular George Orwell from the personal ethics of Eric Blair, not least because the identities of both Blair and Orwell sometimes tended to merge in his writings into an undifferentiated unity of thought. The poet Paul Potts, who knew Orwell well and visited him on the Isle of Jura, stated that he had 'hated Catholicism, Communism and the whole caboodle of "filthy little doctrines striving for our souls"'. In this respect, Orwell's sheer intensity of thought and clarity of opinion against all forms of authoritarianism and totalitarianism remain one of the most attractive qualities of his writings for readers of today.[10]

Finally, it is intriguing to note how the posthumous Orwell was rapidly appropriated by Catholic writers of the 1950s who viewed him as a potent ally and kindred spirit through his ascetic style of life and the moral integrity of his writings. Catholics respected his uncompromising and independent argumentative literary style and, as John Rodden observes, accepted 'his criticism as the fire of a man passionately committed to the truth'. Orwell and Catholicism were united in their deep scepticism over the views and motives of left-wing Russophiles, and some of the inherently conservative elements of Orwell's social perspectives (and personal life) appealed strongly to like-minded Catholics. In this sense, the intensely secular Orwell could and did seem to 'Catholic intellectuals a man who, after all, was really in their camp'.[11] Orwell frequently wrote with subtlety and intellectual rigour about the complexities of national and international politics, colonialism, racism, anti-Semitism, and, above all, the profundity of the loss of the spiritual in the modern world. However, throughout his literary career his comments on Roman Catholicism remained – as befits a deeply partisan pamphleteer – essentially unchanging, polemical, incendiary and often ill informed. As Leroy Spiller remarks, Orwell 'lived and died as an enemy of the Catholic Church' and was never 'able to see Catholicism as anything other than a delusion and a fetter on mankind's struggle for liberty'.[12] At the conclusion of this comprehensive study of Orwell's writings on religion, it is difficult to disagree with such a judgement.

NOTES

Preface

1   All references to Orwell's works are to *The Complete Works of George Orwell*, ed. Peter Davison, 20 vols, London: Secker & Warburg, 1986–98; and *The Lost Orwell. Being a Supplement to The Complete Works of George Orwell*, ed. Peter Davison, London: Timewell Press, 2006.

2   The name 'George Orwell' was first adopted in January 1933 for the publication of *Down and Out in Paris and London* but was not consistently used for reviews and articles until December 1936. See X.243, 274, Stansky and Williams, xix–xx, Bowker, 40 and Taylor, 126 for Blair's choice of this penname.

3   Bowker, 123, 421. See also Bowker, *The Spectator*, 2003; revised 2011.

4   Taylor, 8, citing Muggeridge's unpublished typescript journals (26 January 1950).

5   Bowker, 21.

6   In this review (*Observer*, 12 November 1944), Orwell commended Hopkins's unique poetic blending of his Catholic convert's devotions with an 'almost pantheistic' passion for Nature. XVI.460. On 14 May 1941 he gave a BBC radio talk on Hopkins, praising his distinctive 'Christian vision' and compassion for the sorrows of human mortality in his poem 'Felix Randall', XII.498.

7   [Obituary], *New Statesman*, 28 January 1950. *New Statesman and Nation*, 15 August 1953, 183.

8   Hollis, 20, 23. Powell quoted in Hitchens, 88.

9   Atkins, 110. Brendon, *The Guardian*, 7 June 2003.

10   Taylor, 2; Conquest, 'George Orwell' (1969), quoted in Hitchens, 1.

11   Williams BBC report on Orwell, 1943, quoted in Brendon, *The Guardian*, 7 June 2003. Gray, *The Spectator*, 11 June 2011.

12   Rees, *Scots Chronicle*, (1951), 7–14; quoted in Rodden, 1989, 325–6. Rees, the baronet son of a Liberal MP and former Indian administrator, had driven ambulances in Catalonia during the Spanish Civil War.

13   Rees (1961), 117. Lucas, 133–9.

14   Hitchens, 150.

15   Hoggart, 59. Trilling, 69.

16   Ingle, 17.

17   Hollis, 40.

18   Rodden, 1989, x–xi. Lucas, 117–32.

19   Rodden, 1989, 322–4, illustrates this metonymic process by citing how
     'Orwell's poorly rolled shag cigarettes recall The Common Man; the "pure"
     prose suggests The Saint'.

20   Rodden, 1984, 45.

21   Calder, 429.

22   Muggeridge, 172.

23   Bowker, 22.

24   Buddicom, 14.

25   X.xviii. Hitchens, 4.

26   'George Orwell: An Accident of History' [review of Collected Essays],
     Anarchy: A Journal of Anarchist Ideas, 8, October 1961, 246–55.

27   Rodden, 1984, 46.

28   Patai, 71.

29   Hitchens, 101.

30   Newsinger, x.

31   Robert Harris, The Sunday Times, 10 May 2015, 1, writing about Ed
     Miliband's role in Labour's defeat in the 2015 General Election.

32   Orwell, an enthusiastic collector of pamphlet publications, formed a
     collection important enough to be donated to the British Museum (now
     British Library).

33   Wain, 89.

34   Muggeridge, 170–1.

35   Patai, 9–10.

36   Hitchens, 6, 87.

37   Taylor, 2.

Chapter 1

1   [interview] Stansky and Abrahams, xii.

2   International Genealogical Index (IGI) https://familysearch.org/search/
     collection/igi (accessed 20 December 2015).

3   Hollis, 42, quoted in Spiller, 151.

4   BBC radio talk, 1945; quoted in Bowker, 1.

5   The name was also sometimes spelled 'Lemoizin' or 'Limonzin' in parish
     records.

6   Frank's father was John Eugene Limouzin (d. 1863). He had a brother Joseph
     Edmund who married in Rangoon on 27 June 1879. Theresa Halliley's father

was William Halliley, possibly the individual (1820–86) who was a senior civil servant in the Customs Department at Trincomalee, Ceylon, and died in Bedford, England. Other members of the Halliley family held positions in the armed and civil services. See McCann, Chapter 1.

7   Emma Larkin, 160–2, visited the ruined Anglican church at Moulmein and found stored there the black marble headstone, salvaged from the old cemetery, of Eliza Limouzin and her two children, Emily and Arthur.

8   The IGI misspells her name as 'Limoulin' and gives the place of Ida's birth as Dungemarsh (Denge Marsh), Kent. She may have been baptized at All Saints Church (known as 'The Cathedral in the Marsh'), Lydd.

9   These three children probably returned to Burma after their secondary education. They were accompanied at Parkfields by Elizabeth Austin Halliley, aged thirteen and born in Ceylon.

10   *Catholic Encyclopedia*, Burma.

11   Bowker, 7.

12   Nellie is listed in the 1901 National Census as a 'visitor' and is described as an 'actress'. She is also listed in the London electoral registers during the 1920s.

13   The twelve-year-old Margaret Roseabel Blair, also resident at this address, was a daughter of Horatio Douglas Blair (b. 1854), an elder brother of Richard Walmesley Blair (Eric's father). Frances Blair, then living at 31 The Paragon, Bath, died on 1 January 1908.

14   Bowker, 5. This Charles Blair died in 1802, not 1820 as stated in Crick, 46. He was the grandfather of Thomas Blair (1802–67), not father as stated in Bowker, 4.

15   In 1982, this Bible was seen by T. R. Fyvel and was then in the possession of Humphrey Dakin, widower of Orwell's sister Marjorie. See Fyvel, 13.

16   Stansky, 8–10. See also Eileen Blair's account of the Blair genealogy in her letter to Nora Myles (3 or 10 November 1936), *The Lost Orwell*, 64–5.

17   Brendon, 3.

18   Coppard and Crick, *Orwell Remembered*, 254.

19   Quoted in Taylor, 281.

20   Shelden, 19.

21   Cf. *Coming Up for Air*, in which the protagonist's wife, Hilda, comes from an 'Anglo-Indian colony in Ealing'. VII.138.

22   Ida Orwell's diary for 1905 records her regular Sunday attendance at church.

23   Charles William Limouzin is listed as living in Paddington in the London Electoral Registers for the 1930s. He died at Plymouth in 1947.

24   Bowker, 16. Leech.

25   Buddicom, 21. Stansky and Abrahams, 34. Crick, 50. Shelden, 24. Taylor, 21, also refers to this school as Sunnydale rather than Sunnylands. Davison, xviii, 5.

26   Peter Davison's *The Orwell Diaries* (2010), 1, states that he was 'educated first by Anglican nuns'. However, his *George Orwell: A Life in Letters* (2010)

emends this error by noting: 'From 1908-11, Orwell attended a Roman Catholic day-school run by Ursuline nuns' (x, 493).

27 Bowker, 21–2, 436, n.22.

28 See Mullett, 108–9, for details of their education regime.

29 The Ursuline College at Westgate is still a Roman Catholic Diocesan School based at 225 Canterbury Road.

30 They also rented some outbuildings from the nearby Royal Hotel. Hazeldine, n.p. *Kelly's Directory* for Henley (1907) lists: 'Covent des Ursulines, private boarding school for girls, 23 Station Road'.

31 Catholic Diocesan Archives, 31 bis Quai du roi de Pologne, 49100, Angers. Information supplied by Marie Andrée Jégou. See Charles Whittaker, *Sacred Heart Parish: A Pugin Legacy* (Henley-on-Thames: St Mark's Publishing, 2012).

32 Blair estimated Elsie's age at about fifteen but this conflicts with an advertisement for the school in the local newspaper, stating that they accepted children from 'five to eleven years old'. Crick, 51. Buddicom, 129, tentatively identifies her as Elsie Gorell-Barnes, whose parents may have recommended the Ursuline convent school at Henley to the Buddicoms.

33 Buddicom, 2–12.

34 Bowker, 21–2, 39.

35 Crick, 59, notes that 'Marjorie and Avril were both sent away at a later stage, at the age of 11, to a girls' boarding school at Oxford, a decent enough place but by no means famous or front rank'. This school may have been the small school run by the Ursulines at 38 St Giles from 1890 until 1922 rather than Oxford High School, attended by Jacintha Buddicom.

36 Taylor, 25.

37 Quoted in Gray, 3–4.

38 She wrote: 'My parents were agnostics … [and] had recounted to me the legends of almost every possible mythology: with the result that I was a natural Pantheist, believing implicitly and impartially in all the Gods'. For Christmas 1919, Eric Blair gave her a copy of *Dracula* and an antique crucifix. Buddicom, 74, 97.

39 Buddicom, 39.

40 Wells, xxxiv.

41 'The Scientific Aspects of Positivism', quoted in James, 129.

42 Cyril Connolly also transferred from St Cyprian's to Eton but since they were in different years they had little contact with one another.

43 Orwell used the word 'antinomian', which he also attributed to A. E. Housman (XII.95), to define his cynically blasphemous desire at Eton to repudiate the official beliefs and devotional conventions of the school.

44 Bowker, 64.

45 Hopkinson, 453.

46 Buddicom, 122.

47 Bowker, 62.

48 Hollis, 16.

49 Spiller, 150–1.

50 See X.45 for possible attributions.

51 It may have been written when Blair was at St Cyprian's, Wellington, Eton or even Henley during a vacation period. The last scene (IV.i) ends abruptly with 'FINIS'.

52 Gray, 3–4. Hollis, 16, 18.

53 Ibid., 15. Crick, 115. Stansky and Abrahams, 105–6.

54 Ibid., 90.

55 Orwell commented in *Homage to Catalonia* that he had been old enough to recall the Great War but 'not old enough' to have fought in it. VI.17–18.

56 Rees (1961), 154. Bowker, 59. Crick, 107, 118. Gray, 3–4.

57 Orwell noted in March 1946 that his grandmother had lived for forty years in Burma but still knew no Burmese, typifying the 'ordinary Englishwoman's attitude' (XVIII.128).

58 Bowker, 10–11. See Orwell's biting comments on the British in Burma in February/March 1946. XVIII.124–8. Another family member, George Limouzin (b. 1860), was the son of Eugene Limouzin (possibly Ida's uncle) and Ma Soe, probably a Burmese Buddhist woman. Larkin, 163–4.

59 5 December 1969 BBC interview; quoted in Crick, 148. Bowker, 81. *The Observer*, 18 September 1942. XIV. 34–5.

60 Hollis, 27–8. Crick, 152–3, 159. Bowker, 84–5. Taylor, 65.

61 On 16 May 1942, Orwell advised E. Rowan-Davies, a transcription assistant in the BBC's Eastern Service, on native Christians in Burma, especially Karens. XIII.328. See also his review of *Burma Surgeon* by Gordon S. Seagrave, *The Observer*, 11 June 1944, for his sustained interest in Christian Karens. XVI.253–5.

62 Bowker, 10.

63 Probate was granted to 'Peter McNeill esquire'.

64 Taylor, 72–3, 88–9. His resignation was deemed by the authorities as effective from 1 July, thereby losing him about £140 in holiday pay.

65 Larkin, 2–3.

Chapter 2

1 *Kelly's Directory* for Henley (1907). Bowker, 31.

2 Bowker, 105. Orwell tried to assist Nellie in publishing her fiction by sending two samples to Leonard Moore in January 1935. X.367.

3 See the 1935 French edition of *Down and Out in Paris and London* (*La Vache Enragée*). X.114, 355.

4   Hollis, 41–2.

5   Rodden, 1984, 48.

6   Adam's book had been lent to him by Mrs Carr, a Roman Catholic friend of his parents in Southwold. Taylor, 122.

7   Orwell retained a lifelong pleasure in mocking Anglo-Catholicism, for example noting in a *Tribune* essay (12 April 1946) that after hibernation the common toad seemed to have a deeply 'spiritual look' resembling an 'Anglo-Catholic towards the end of Lent'. XVIII.238.

8   'P. S. Burton' was probably borrowed from an athletic boy, Cliffy Burton, whom Blair had disliked at St Cyprian's. X.274.

9   Walton, 21.

10 I.133.

11 See Brennan, 52–4.

12 See Orwell's comments on the Mormons' polygamy in his film review of *Brigham Young, Time and Tide*, 18 January 1941. XII.369–70.

13 Bowker, 124.

14 XVI.509.

15 Bowker, 110. Taylor, 122.

Chapter 3

1   Hollis, 64.

2   X.361–2, 368, 371.

3   Hollis, 59.

4   O'Casey, quoted in Crick, 258.

5   Crick, 256. Taylor, 137.

6   Hollis, 71.

7   See also 'Bookshop Memories', *Fortnightly*, November 1936. X.510–13.

8   Wadhams, 55.

9   Villis, 77.

10 Hollis, 76.

11 Bowker, 388.

12 It is sometimes assumed that this book was commissioned by Gollancz for the Left Book Club. However, the Club had not been formed when Orwell left for the north and his work was only accepted for publication in January 1937 after he had submitted the typescript to his agent Leonard Moore on 15 December 1936.

13 Bowker, 196. Hoggart, 40.

14 Hitchens, 26.

15 Orwell, *Letters and Documents* [microfilm edition], 8, should be consulted

for the full range of his *Wigan Pier* notes (University College, London, Orwell Archive, A/2: 1935–6) since only a selection are printed in volume X of Peter Davison's edition.

16 See Lucas, 38, 144 n.106, for Orwell's political bias in his comments on the Liverpool Corporation.

17 Bowker, 215.

18 Chesterton did write: 'Tea, although an Oriental, / Is a gentleman at least' (*The Flying Inn*); and two of his fictional characters say: 'sunrise is a better beginning of the day than tea or coffee ... but not better than beer or rum' (*The Man Who Knew Too Much*).

19 Neal, 224–49.

20 Smith, 110–24. The National Archives, MEPO 38/69 (Special Branch) and KV 2/2699 (MI5).

Chapter 4

1 Bowker, 189.

2 Taylor, 201.

3 Hollis, 42, 90–2, 94.

4 Bowker, 234–5.

5 Schwartz communicated these views to Bowker, 235, in July 2001.

6 The Spanish Secret Police (SIM) seized all of Orwell's diaries, press cuttings and notes made at the front and so much of the factual detail in *Homage to Catalonia* was reconstructed from memory.

7 Coppard and Crick, *Orwell Remembered*, 152.

8 In 'Caesarian Section on Spain' (*The Highway*, March 1939) Orwell again condemned the powers of the Church and privileged landowners as the real reason for anti-clericalism in Spain.

9 See Villis, 42–57, for an assessment of political views, especially about Spain, Germany and appeasement, expressed in the *Catholic Herald*.

10 Wain, 79.

11 Taylor, 253.

12 Orwell's 'Domestic Diary' notes how, on the sea-voyage out, Roman Catholic Mass and Anglican Holy Communion were held daily aboard the *Stratheden*. XI.268.

13 Orwell reused the same sensory description in a 1946 essay on Jonathan Swift, recalling the words of the burial service and the 'sweetish smell of corpses' in the churchyard. XVIII.430.

14 See also Orwell's lyrical praise of the beauty of St John's Church, near Lord's Cricket Ground, which he could never pass 'without a pang'. XVI.46.

15 'War-time Diary', 8 June 1940, states that Orwell realized in 1931 that the 'future must be catastrophic'. XII.182.

16 Probate (£505 16s 1d) was granted on 28 July to his wife Ida.

17 Villis, 1.

18 Orwell reviewed Muggeridge's book in *New English Weekly*, 25 April 1940, noting that it concluded on a tone of 'extreme defeatism'. XII.151.

19 The *Oxford English Dictionary*'s earliest citation of 'concentration camp' in the British media is a *Manchester Guardian* article of 31 January 1941.

Chapter 5

1 Broadcast 21 May 1941, delivered at the Oxford Democratic Socialist Club on 23 May; published in *The Listener*, 19 June 1941.

2 Zwerdling, 45.

3 XIII, 431. XIV.5.

4 See Orwell's review of *Letters on India* by Mulk Raj Anand, *Tribune*, 19 March 1943, claiming that virtually all English left-wingers were 'pro-Jew' over the Palestine question, XV.34; and Tosco Fyvel's analysis of Orwell's views on anti-Semitism, Zionism and Palestine in his *George Orwell*, 176–82.

5 See XVI.152 for Dark's later denunciation of Orwell's view that belief in personal immortality was decaying.

6 Bowker, 315. Lucas, 90–2.

7 Orwell's denunciations of Morton were compromised by his insistence in another 'As I Please' column (16 February 1945) that he had detected marked changes in tone in the 'Beachcomber' columns, indicating that this contributor unlike Morton was 'not a Catholic'. XVII.51. Morton, however, was still the column's author.

Chapter 6

1 Shelden, 433. Probate (£1,042 0s 11d) was granted to her husband on 5 December 1945.

2 Orwell returned home for Eileen's funeral and to make arrangements for their adopted son Richard.

3 Tosco Fyvel (140) records that at a *Tribune* editorial meeting its editor, the left-wing Labour MP Aneurin Bevan, gave a pro-Zionist speech, prompting Orwell to remark that Zionists were a 'bunch of Wardour Street Jews who had a controlling interest over the British press'.

4 See Orwell's comments to Fyvel in a letter of 31 December 1947, suggesting that there was no point in worrying about the Palestine issue because they both pessimistically suspected that an Atomic War would break out during the coming decades. XIX.240.

5 Walton, 30.

6 The Reverend Harold Davidson, the Rector of Stiffkey, was defrocked for immoral practices and his disgrace was covered in the British press. He then earned a living entertaining audiences at cinemas, pleasure beaches and circuses. He was killed in 1937 while being exhibited in a cage of lions.

7 Orwell included in his personal collection of pamphlets one by Dark, *Letter to a Country Clergyman* (1942), and another by MacMurray, *The Foundation of Economic Reconstruction* (1942). XX.278.

8 Walton, 19.

9 There are about 1,340 items in the collection since not all items (e.g. single-sheet 1945 election leaflets) are, strictly speaking, pamphlets. XX.263.

10 *New Statesman*, 18 June 1949, 645–8.

11 Shelden, 435.

12 The two other Fellowship of Reconciliation tracts in Orwell's collection were *Social Control and Personal Freedom* (1940) by Leyton Richard and *Christianity and the State* (1942) by Glyn Lloyd Phelps. Anna Ruth Fry, an editorial board member of the Fellowship's journal *Reconciliation*, self-published two other items: *Religion and Science & Co. Unlimited* (1942) and *The Quakers. Who Are They?* (1942).

13 Orwell also owned a copy of *For Christ's Sake* (1936) by Laurence Murfitt, a self-published member of the Peace Pledge Union.

14 W. E. Wilson, *Retribution or …?* (n.d.); Theodore C. Hume, *Justice & Love* (n.d.); Karlin C. Capper-Johnson, *Christian Responsibility in the Present War Situation* (n.d.); Stanley C. Farrar, *Our Peace Testimony in Total War* (1942); and Thomas Corder Catchpool, *Peace Aims & War Methods* (1940).

15 Orwell's Anglican Pacifist Fellowship items also included Evelyn Underhill, *The Church and the War* (n.d.); and Fr. Henry. E. H. Andrew, *The Logic of Faith* (1939), published by the Fellowship of Reconciliation although its author was a member of the APF.

16 Crick, 489.

Chapter 7

1 Hitchens, 7.

2 G. K. Chesterton's futuristic fantasy *The Napoleon of Notting Hill* also opens at London in 1984. See XIII.332, 361, 369 and Bowker, 382, for other possible sources for this title.

3 Bowker, 340. See Deutscher, 120–6, for Orwell's debt to Zamyatin.

4 Zamyatin's essay, 'Tomorrow', advised contemporary writers to follow the example of 'the heretic Christ, the heretic Copernicus, the heretic Tolstoy. Our symbol of faith is heresy', *We*, Introduction, ix.

5 In a letter to *Tribune* (25 January 1946), Gleb Struve noted that Zamyatin had also written a satirical play, *The Fires of St. Dominic*, set in Spain during the Inquisition. XVIII.17.

6   Jerome K. Jerome's 'The New Utopia' (1891) also uses this device for numbering its male and female characters and Zamyatin may have lifted the idea from this essay.

7   *The Lost Orwell*, 128. XIX.457

8   Orwell had first read *We* in the French edition (*Nous Autres*) in 1944. Orwell, *Letters and Documents* [microfilm edition], 16.

9   XVIII.xxi, xxxv, 408. XIX.xxxiii.

10 *A Life in Letters*, xi.

11 Muggeridge, 167–8.

12 Bowker, 386.

13 Walton, 32.

14 Ibid., 33.

15 Bowker, 213.

16 West, 27.

Postscript

1   Waugh, 302. Orwell had sent to Waugh a copy of *Animal Farm* in August 1945 and on 21 June 1948 Waugh had written to Orwell (then in hospital in Scotland) about P. G. Wodehouse. In January 1950, Waugh wrote to Nancy Mitford: 'G. Orwell is dead and Mrs Orwell presumably a rich widow. Will Cyril [Connolly] marry her?', ibid., 211, 279, 320.

2   Muggeridge, 173. Taylor, 408, states that Waugh visited Orwell for 'at least two face-to-face meetings' and reported that the TB-ravaged Orwell was 'very near to God', according to Cyril Connolly's *Sunday Times* review of *The Collected Essays, Journalism and Letters*, reprinted in Connolly's *The Evening Colonnade* (1973), 343–9. Crick, 556, states that Waugh visited Orwell 'several times'.

3   Hollis, 174–5.

4   Brown, 25, 45–6.

5   Rees (1961), 120.

6   Taylor, 423.

7   Buddicom, 157.

8   Gray, 1–5.

9   'George Orwell', *Scots Chronicle*, 1951, 11; quoted in Crick, 576.

10 Coppard and Crick, *Orwell Remembered*, 211.

11 Rodden, 1984, 50–1.

12 Spiller, 151, 161.

BIBLIOGRAPHY

The National Archives

MEPO 38/69 (Special Branch, Orwell files, 1936–42) and KV 2/2699 (MI5, Orwell files, 1936–51).

University College, London

The Orwell Archive, A/1–A/9, B–O and L.

Atkins, John, *George Orwell: A Literary and Biographical Study*, London: Ungar, 1954.

Barbusse, Henri, *Under Fire*, London and New York: Dent, [1916] 1926.

Bowker, Gordon, *Inside George Orwell: A Biography*, London: Palgrave Macmillan, 2003.

Bowker, Gordon, 'George Orwell and the Church of England', *The Spectator*, [2003] revised 2011.

Brendon, Piers, 'The Saint of Common Decency', *The Guardian*, 7 June 2003.

Brennan, Michael G., *Graham Greene: Political Writer*, London: Palgrave Macmillan, 2016.

Brown, Callum G., *Religion and Society in Twentieth-Century Britain*, Harlow: Pearson, 2006.

Buddicom, Jacintha, *Eric & Us. A Remembrance of George Orwell*, London: Leslie Frewin, 1974.

Burdekin, Katherine (Murray Constantine), *Swastika Night,* 1937, New York: The Feminist Press, 1985.

Calder, Angus, 'Orwell: the Rarer Animal', *New Statesman*, 4 October 1968, 429.

The Catholic Encyclopedia, 15 vols, New York: Robert Appleton Company, 1907–12.

Coppard, Audrey, and Bernard Crick, *Orwell Remembered*, London: BBC, 1984.

Crick, Bernard, *George Orwell. A Life*, 1980, Harmondsworth: Penguin, 1982.

Deutscher, Isaac, '1984 – The Mysticism of Cruelty', in *George Orwell*, ed. Raymond Williams, 119–32.

Fyvel, Tosco R., *George Orwell a Personal Memoir*, 1982, rpt London: Hutchison, 1983.

Gray, Robert, 'Orwell vs God A Very Christian Atheist', *Spectator*, 11 June 2011, 3–4.

Gross, Miriam (ed.), *The World of George Orwell*, London: Weidenfeld and Nicholson, 1971; rpt. 1972.

Hazeldine, Elizabeth, *Henley-on-Thames Through Time*, Amberley Publishing: Stroud, 2014.

Hitchens, Christopher, *Orwell's Victory*, London: Penguin Books, 2002.

Hoggart, Richard, 'Introduction to *The Road to Wigan Pier*', in *George Orwell*, 1965, ed. Raymond Williams, 34–51.

Hollis, Christopher, *A Study of George Orwell: The Man and His Works*, London: Hollis and Carter, 1956.

Hopkinson, Tom, 'George Orwell – Dark Side Out', *Cornhill Magazine* 166 (1953), 453.

Huxley, Aldous, *Brave New World and Brave New World Revisited*, London: Chatto & Windus, 1984.

Ingle, Stephen, *The Social and Political Thought of George Orwell: A Reassessment*, London: Routledge, 2006.

James, Simon, *Maps of Utopia. H. G. Wells, Modernity, and the End of Culture*, Oxford: Oxford University Press, 2012.

Kershaw, Tom, 'The religion and political views of George Orwell', *The Hollowverse*, 18 November 2012 http://hollowverse.com/george-orwell/

Larkin, Emma, *Finding George Orwell in Burma*, London: Granta, 2004; rpt 2011.

Leech, Kenneth, 'Conrad Le Despenser Roden Noel (1869–1942)', in *Oxford Dictionary of National Biography*, ed. H. C. G. Matthew and B. Harrison, 60 vols, Oxford: Oxford University Press, 2004.

London, Jack, *The Iron Heel* [1908], New York: Sagamore Press, 1957.

Lucas, Scott, *Orwell*, London: Haus Publishing, 2003.

McCann, Graham, *Do You Think That's Wise? The Life of John Le Mesurier*, London: Aurum Press, 2010.

Muggeridge, Malcolm, 'A Knight of the Woeful Countenance', in *The World of George Orwell*, ed. Miriam Gross, New York: Simon and Schuster, 1971, 165–75.

Mullett, Michael, *The Catholic Reformation*, London and New York: Routledge, 1999.

Neal, Frank, *Sectarian Violence – The Liverpool Experience 1819–1914*, Manchester: Manchester University Press, 1988.

Newsinger, John, *Orwell's Politics*, Basingstoke: Macmillan, 1999.

Orwell, George, *A Life in Letters*, ed. Peter Davison, 2010; rpt London: Penguin, 2011.

Orwell, George, *Letters and Documents to be Found in Libraries and Archives in the United Kingdom* [microfilm edition], ed. Peter Davison, Wakefield: Microfilm Academic Publishers, 2004.

Orwell, George, *The Collected Essays, Journalism, and Letters*, ed. Sonia Orwell and Ian Angus, 4 vols, New York, 1968.

Orwell, George, *The Complete Works of George Orwell*, ed. Peter Davison, 20 vols, London: Secker & Warburg, 1986–98.

Orwell, George, *The Lost Orwell. Being a Supplement to The Complete Works of George Orwell*, ed. Peter Davison, London: Timewell Press, 2006.

Orwell, George, *The Orwell Diaries*, ed. Peter Davison, London: Penguin Modern Classics, 2010.

Patai, Daphne, *The Orwell Mystique: A Study in Male Ideology*, Amherst: University of Massachusetts Press, 1984.

Pritchett, V. S., [Obituary], *New Statesman*, 28 January 1950.

Pritchett, V. S., 'George Orwell', *New Statesman and Nation*, 15 August 1953, 183.

Rees, Richard, 'George Orwell', *Scots Chronicle*, 26 (1951), 7–14.

Rees, Richard, *George Orwell. Fugitive from the Camp of Victory*, London: Secker & Warburg, 1961.

Rodden, John, 'Orwell on Religion: The Catholic and Jewish Questions', *College Literature*, 11 (1984), 44–58.

Rodden, John, *The Politics of Literary Reputation. The Making and Claiming of 'St George' Orwell*, New York and Oxford: Oxford University Press, 1989.

Shelden, Michael, *Orwell. The Authorised Biography*, London: Heinemann, 1991.

Smith, James, *British Writers and MI5 Surveillance, 1930–1960*, Cambridge: Cambridge University Press, 2013.

Spiller, Leroy, 'George Orwell's Anti-Catholicism', *LOGOS* 6, 2003, 150–63.

Stansky, Peter, and William Abrahams, *The Unknown Orwell*, St Albans: Granada Publishing, 1974.

Stricherz, Mark, 'Why George Orwell was Pro-Life', InsideCatholic.com, 24 August 2010 http:www.catholicity.com/commentary/stricherz/08545.html (accessed 20 December 2015).

Taylor, D. J., *Orwell. The Life*, 2003; rpt London: Vintage, 2004.

Thiemann, Ronald F., 'The Public Intellectual as Connected Critic: George Orwell and Religion', in *George Orwell into the Twenty-First Century*, ed. Thomas Cushman and John Rodden, Boulder and London: Paradigm Books, 2004, 96–110.

Trilling, Lionel, 'George Orwell and the Politics of Truth', in *George Orwell*, ed. Raymond Williams, 62–79.

Villis, Tom, *British Catholics and Fascism. Religious Identity and Political Extremism Between the Wars*, London: Palgrave Macmillan, 2013.

Wadhams, Stephen (ed.), *Remembering Orwell*, Harmondsworth: Penguin, 1984.

Wain, John, 'In the Thirties', in *The World of George Orwell*, ed. Miriam Gross, 75–90.

Wain, John, 'George Orwell as a Writer of Polemic', in *George Orwell*, ed. Raymond Williams, 89–102.

Walton, David, 'George Orwell and Antisemitism', *Patterns of Prejudice* 16, 1982, 19–34.

Waugh, Evelyn, *The Letters of Evelyn Waugh*, ed. Mark Amory, London: Weidenfeld & Nicolson, 1980.

Wells, H. G., *A Modern Utopia*, ed. Krishan Kumar, Everyman, London: J. M. Dent, 1994.

West, A. J., *The Larger Evils. Nineteen Eighty-Four. The Truth Behind the Satire*, Edinburgh: Canongate Press, 1992.

Williams, Raymond (ed.), *George Orwell. A Collection of Critical Views*, Englewood Cliffs, NJ: Prentice-Hall, 1974.

Zamyatin, Yevgeny, *We*, translated Mirra Ginsberg, New York: Viking Press, 1972.

Zwerdling, Alex, *Orwell and the Left*, New Haven and London: Yale University Press, 1974.

INDEX